M000206205

Telling Rhythm

Telling Rhythm
Body and Meaning in Poetry

Amittai F. Aviram

Ann Arbor

THE UNIVERSITY OF MICHIGAN PRESS

Copyright © by the University of Michigan 1994
All rights reserved
Published in the United States of America by
The University of Michigan Press
Manufactured in the United States of America
∞ Printed on acid-free paper

1997   1996   1995   1994   4   3   2   1

A CIP catalogue record for this book is available from the British Library.

Library of Congress Cataloging-in-Publication Data

Aviram, Amittai F., 1957–
      Telling rhythm : body and meaning in poetry / Amittai F. Aviram.
         p.   cm.
      Includes bibliographical references and index.
      ISBN 0-472-10513-2 (alk. paper)
         1. Poetry—History and criticism. 2. Rhythm   I. Title.
   PN1059.R53A95   1994
   809.1—dc20   94-2920
                                                                        CIP

For my son Blake

One of the few fundamental things we know about our universe is that everything in it is vibrating, is in motion, has a rhythm. Every molecule, every atom is dancing its own unique dance, singing its signature song. What we call sight is just the limited spectrum of vibrations that our eyes can perceive; what we call sound is just the limited spectrum of pulsations that our ears can hear. *And this noise begat rhythm and rhythm begat everything else.*

—Mickey Hart and Fredric Lieberman with D. S. Sonneborn,
Planet Drum

Acknowledgments

There are more people who have contributed to this book than I can possibly name. I shall try to thank a few.

Some of the earliest thinking toward this book was done while I was on a Mellon postdoctoral fellowship at Cornell University in 1986–87. I was also given a research leave grant from the University of South Carolina English Department in the summer of 1989, when I just began piecing my ideas together.

Eve Tavor Bannet contributed ideas, suggestions, and moral support as this project took shape. I also benefited much from the conversations, support, and encouragement of my friends Clement Hawes, Gregory S. Jay, Ann Kibbey, Kevin R. Kopelson, Robert K. Martin, Cary Nelson, and Kathryn Bond Stockton. I wish to thank the members of Scholars of Fortune, the informal theory-reading and ruckus-raising group at the University of South Carolina, including Alan Asnen, Scott Davidson, Stan Dubinsky, Martin Donougho, Larry Glickman, Kenneth Gouwens, Thavolia Glymph, Hayes Hampton, Romy Heylen, Nancy Lane, Nina Levine, Jeff Persels, and Brian Roots. Discussions with Jill Frank (also a Scholar of Fortune) on Heidegger and other topics were extremely helpful. Peter Harley, Meili Steele, and Jerry Wallulis gave me valuable input when this book was a mere draft essay. Ellen Wiley Todd helped choose a title and cover design. Thanks also go to the students in my graduate poetry theory classes. Finally, I am very grateful to my editor at the University of Michigan Press, LeAnn Fields, for her endless patience and her fine intellect, and to the other excellent professional staff at the press. My family—according to my definition—deserves much credit for unceasing support, encouragement, and interest: my mother Rachel, sister Mariva, brother Ari, and son Blake, and my friends Russell Anderson, Pedro Alejandro Rodríguez, Walter Grandberry, and Eric Schell.

It is very risky to say something relatively new in print. Without the help of these and other people, I could not have done it. I am only too aware of the flaws in this book. If there is anything in it that provokes fruitful thought in the service of poetry, then they must share in the credit.

I should like to thank these publishers for their kind permission to reprint the following poems:

"The Funky Cold Medina," written by M. Young, M. Ross, and M. Dike, from Tone Lōc's *Lōc'ed After Dark*, copyright © 1989. Reprinted with permission of Varry White Music, Inc.

Wallace Stevens's "Blanche McCarthy," from *The Palm at the End of the Mind*, ed. Holly Stevens, Copyright © 1971. Reprinted with permission of Peter R. Hanchak.

Contents

Introduction

Poetry is not very popular these days. This is an obvious, if lamented, fact for poets, teachers of poetry, and poetry-lovers in the United States—indeed, in the industrial West generally. A recent essay in *Atlantic Monthly*, aptly titled "Can Poetry Matter," observes that "poetry has vanished as a cultural force in America," that it is "no longer a part of the mainstream *of artistic and intellectual life*[;] it has become the specialized occupation of a relatively small and isolated group" (Gioia 1991, 94; emphasis added). This writer principally blames the decline of poetry on its professionalization in creative writing programs, specialized poetry magazines, and the like. While I agree that overprofessionalization is an important factor, this book begins with a different assumption: that at least part of the problem is *theoretical*, that *our very definition of poetry*, our sense of how to read and how to teach the reading of poetry and, consequently, some of our current methods and styles of making poetry are substantial causes of poetry's loss of importance.

I hope that this book will be of interest to anyone for whom poetry matters: teachers and students of poetry, readers of poetry (few though they may be), and poets. I also hope that it will be interesting to readers of literary theory. For them, issues surrounding poetry in this book may be viewed as instances of some more general theoretical questions. I shall raise some of these points briefly in this introduction, and I discuss them further in chapter 13, the summary of my theory, and elsewhere throughout the book. In addition, chapters 8 through 12 are each devoted to a major theorist or theoretical contribution, exploring the implications of each theory to the reading of poetry and to the theory developed here. These chapters include discussions of some very difficult theoretical texts, and some (Abraham, Lacoue-Labarthe) that are quite new to the English-speaking public. Hence, I hope that those interested in literary theory may be able to use this book as an explanatory aid on those theorists and on the modern history of theorizing about poetry and related matters—rhythm, the body, language, and interpretation.

But the initial impetus for this book was, and still is, an attempt to respond to and to resist the decline of poetry. Let us be more precise about the problem. What I have been calling the decline of poetry should more properly be called the decline of *literary* poetry, or of poetry meant to last or to be reread and studied or to be memorized and recalled long after composition. A different kind of poetry is very much alive today in the forms of popular music lyrics and raps, and in jingles both for advertisement and for political purposes. In these subliterary categories, one common factor in the most vital practices is their observance of traditional *metrical organization*, their audible and palpable *rhythmicity*. Indeed, their subordination of sense to rhythm seems to be one of the factors keeping rock lyrics and rap out of the purview of classroom and critic (which may be a good thing, for now—for the sake of the lyrics' and the raps' survival). But meanwhile, these forms are also subject to the commercial pressures that keep most lyrics and raps in listeners' memories only for a short while, until they are replaced by near-identical but newer products. Furthermore, many of these artifacts clearly depend on music, or on the interaction of words and music, or on the additional qualities of performance, in order to succeed; the written texts alone may be relatively uninteresting and may miss the special points made by the interaction of music and words in performance. Indeed, especially in the case of rap, the rhythm itself may be unintelligible in the written text alone, outside of performance—barring the possible invention of new graphic methods.

Meanwhile, in literary poetry, since the beginning of the twentieth century, practice has shifted away from audible rhythms and toward free verse.[1] For a few decades, while the traditions of rhythm

---

1. Here and throughout this book, I follow Steele (1990) in using the term *free verse* to refer primarily to unmetrical poetry, as a modernist translation of the French *vers libre*. In English, there are many poems which have recognizable metrical patterns

were still active in the minds of readers, the free verse of Eliot, Pound, Williams, and H.D. and the syllabic verse of Marianne Moore could be received as experiments in new sorts of rhythm, reactions toward or against conventions of meter, defamiliarizing the real rhythms of spoken words.[2] But in the ensuing decades, as the very notion of meter in written poetry has vanished from the public memory, so, too, has any interest in written poetry for the general readership.[3]

I believe that this shift is part of a larger trend in the history of Western poetry toward the effacement of the bodily pleasure experienced in the regular, musical rhythm of meter—away from the *nonsensical* aspect of poetry, and toward the *meaningful*—toward poetry as an act of communication or self-expression rather than as an experience of pleasure and rhythmicity confronting the world of sense. Using only slightly different terms, Anthony Easthope (1983) has described the history of this trend within the framework of the ascendancy of bourgeois culture and of individual (capitalist) subjectivity. Easthope's argument is deep and compelling, and I hope that this book can be seen as having something of a complementary relation

---

but freely change meters from line to line—for example, Matthew Arnold's "Dover Beach" and T. S. Eliot's "The Love Song of J. Alfred Prufrock." My arguments in this book can accommodate this type of poetry as well, insofar as it stands on a spectrum between metered and free verse.

2. Significantly, the leaders of the African-American Harlem Renaissance tended to conserve traditional (and folk) metrical forms, although Langston Hughes wrote many (not the majority) of his poems in a playful graphic and metrical collage that would drift in and out of traditional rhythms to imitate jazz. In the sixties, Black Arts movement poets, following Amiri Baraka's lead, embraced a more obvious modernism in form; but of these poets, the one with the longest-lasting and greatest popularity, Maya Angelou, shows the strongest continuity with folk-traditional metrical rhythms, especially the four-beat paradigm of ballads. Likewise, Gwendolyn Brooks has written most of her work in recognizable rhythmic patterns; even her poems in less traditional forms have clear signals of rhythmicity and metricality.

3. Graham Hough rightly points out that several of these modernists turned back to traditional meters, or at least signaled the necessity of these meters for many sorts of poetic practice. But a glance at poetry magazines today, or at the winners of poetry prizes, or at the products of poetry workshops, will generally reveal—among occasional instances of metricality—a practice that is closer to prose than to verse, although it is printed with line breaks—what Hough shows to be operative in the first half of D. H. Lawrence's poem, "The Snake" (1960, 94–97). That poetry still has some traces of rhythm is not disputed; but on a spectrum from prose to verse, general practice has shifted considerably toward prose.

with it (and, to a lesser extent, with Easthope's use of psychoanalysis to review that history of subjectivity in poetry [Easthope 1989]). But whereas Easthope emphasizes the revolutionary aspect of modernism in poetry, and thus sees poets like Pound as reversing or breaking the trend toward bourgeois subjectivity, I see Pound's abandonment of traditional form in the *Cantos*, his insistence on the *rhythm of each line representing or echoing the sense*, as only a continuation of that very trend. In short, it is a trend away from poetry and toward prose narrative or exposition; away from the rhythmic pleasures of the body and toward its repression in social discourse; away from the trans-subjective effect of rhythm and toward the expression of the individual, socially constructed self—even if, as in Pound (as Easthope shows), that self begins to reach the limits of its own undoing.[4]

The trend from poetry toward prose, which in our time has seen the waning of interest in poetry altogether, should be seen within the context of a *theory of poetry* that has prevailed since at least the seventeenth century, but has become especially prominent in modern times as society has shifted, not only toward the centrality of individual subjectivity that Easthope notes, but toward the importance of *information* in its material life. Things are not valuable for the physical adventures they offer so much as for what they mean in the most reductive sense—for example, how much they cost, what they are worth on the market. Now, the critical practice of the early twentieth century, called either the New Criticism or (with Easthope) "conventional criticism," clearly avows an aim against this reductionist tendency—as can be seen in the moralism of F. R. Leavis, Yvor Winters, W. K. Wimsatt, and Cleanth Brooks. But on the whole, the *method* followed by these critics was to approach, and to judge, poetry on the basis of *what it says*. The model of poetry here is a communicative one: poetry is a way of getting a message across (however ambiguous that message may be), in which the verse rhythm

---

4. I wish to emphasize, here, however, that Pound, Eliot, and other modernists were experimenting in ways that often still enabled the reader/listener to perceive a strong sense of audible, palpable rhythm—so long as the reader or listener was still conditioned to be sensitive to the presence of rhythm. The problem today is largely the result of the loss of this ability on the part of the audience—but contemporary poets do not always help the situation by freeing themselves of metrical fetters that no longer exist, if they ever did.

is either a mere decoration (or convention) or a device to contribute to the effectiveness of the presentation of the message. As mere convention or ornament, verse rhythm is not worthy of comment, or at least cannot be integrated easily into a discourse on content. As rhetorical device, rhythm can only be the object of a local focus—that is, how it dramatizes *this* particular meaning at this moment. Such local uses of expressive or dramatic rhythm for mimetic purposes can be found plentifully in literary prose. It does not distinguish or characterize poetry.

The more successful conventional criticism became, the more poetry was evaluated according to its effectiveness as prose. And accordingly, readers' expectations of poetry are increasingly informed by the desire for a compelling message—in other words, a desire precisely for reducibility. But in these terms, poetry can never succeed. Prose will usually be better at the transmission of information, at reducibility, indeed, sometimes even at local mimetic expressiveness, than verse. So the theories guiding conventional criticism may have succeeded only too well in (*a*) effacing the difference between poetry and prose, and (*b*) removing from the reader's awareness any reason why one should even bother with poetry, when prose accomplishes the same communicative and expressive goals with less trouble for the reader.

The challenge to theory will then be to find a way to bring rhythm into consideration without demoting it to the position of a rhetorical aid to the communication of meaning. This is indeed a challenge because, as noted earlier, rhythm and meaning as aspects of poetry are quite different in nature. Although certain social meanings can be associated with a particular rhythm, rhythm also has physical effects that go beyond these semiotic properties. So it cannot be a question of bringing meaning and rhythm under one general category so as to render them homogeneous or equally meaningful in discourse—to do so will always result, I believe, precisely in the reduction or subordination of rhythm to meaning. As an alternative solution, I propose to maintain the independence of rhythm, and to view meaning in poetry as representing, allegorically, aspects of the power of the poem's own rhythm to bring about a physical response—to engage the reader's or listener's body, and thus to disrupt the orderly process of meaning. In this way, meaningful content in poetry paradoxically represents something that itself is outside of meaning; it is an attempt to represent the unrepresentable, and it often tells not only of this unrepresentable experience but of the impossibility fully to put it into words and symbols. Hence the title of this book, *Telling Rhythm*, for poetry attempts through its allegory to tell its rhythm— a paradox, since rhythm cannot be told, it can only be made. The result is "telling" in the other, ironic sense—it reveals the limits of the social construction of reality through language.

This view of the relation between poetic meaning and rhythm is developed in chapter 2, and then again more fully in chapter 13. The intervening chapters show that the idea of poetic meaning as an allegory for the sublime power of rhythm comes out of a modern tradition in philosophy and psychology beginning with Nietzsche, although it probably has mystical roots before him. My purpose is to place the theory presented here as a postmodern development of this tradition. The theory of poetry as telling rhythm is not an analysis of postmodern poetry (or rather poetries—that would be material for another book), but rather a postmodern theory of defining and reading poetry in general. It is thus not a theory of the evolving history of poetry as such (although the above comments suggest a view of the interactions of theory and practice in the history of poetry), but rather, I hope, a general framework that will make room for historicized readings of individual poems—as demonstrated in the sample readings in chapter 14.[5] At the same time, I hope, my historical review of modern theories within the Nietzschean tradition demonstrates an awareness of the historicity of my own model of poetry and thus its appropriateness to the current conditions of reading poetry.

The word *mystical* used in connection with the roots of the Nietzschean tradition may trouble some readers, as may the use of phrases such as "the sublime power of rhythm." By *mysticism,* I simply mean discourse about matters that are defined as inaccessible to language. Mystical discourse is thus inherently paradoxical and often acknowledges itself as such. The object of mysticism, being inaccessible to language, is typically characterized in religious terms—God, the

---

5. For a brief but perceptive historical insight into the development of modern free verse, see Hough 1960. A more recent and much more detailed treatment is given by Steele 1990. Easthope 1983 and 1989 provide a very powerful theory of the development of verse in English (and other Western languages) from the four-beat folk form (such as ballads) to the iambic pentameter to free verse.

transcendent truth, and so forth. These very terms, however, may be considered as representations for their unrepresentable object. In this book, the unrepresentable is associated with the *real* as it would be, hypothetically, without socially-mediated construction. But although the real is by definition not a representation, it can make itself felt in a physical way that involves sensation but not, immediately, meaning or representation. This is the case with rhythm. The phrase "sublime power of rhythm" conceives rhythm as having a distinctive property of "catchiness"—of inviting or urging or seducing the listener into participation. A regular rhythm urges one to move with it—often whether one consciously wishes to do so or not. An example from everyday life: I once witnessed a woman at the laundromat, in a moment of abstraction, dancing to the rhythm produced by the regular rolling and banging of a washing machine in the spin cycle. I was barely able to suppress the urge myself. We feel a *liberation* at the moments we give in to these rhythms, precisely when we are abandoning the activities we have chosen with our wills—even though individual conscious choice is usually thought of as the very heart of what we call freedom. Furthermore, everyone who has tried to engage in a conversation while playing an instrument or dancing has noticed how rhythm distracts us from the thoughts that we can express within the exchange of language that defines ordinary discourse. I conceive of this catchy, sometimes liberatory power of rhythm to disrupt the commerce of meanings and to impose its own transindividual order as *sublime* precisely because it is an experience that exceeds the sphere of ordinary language, much as do the thought of God or the view of the Milky Way. In speaking of the sublime power of rhythm in connection with the body, I conceive of the body's relation to language as an unknowable source of endless surprise and momentary subversion of the known—that is, of language.[6] I shall venture a few more comments on the term *sublime* in chapter 2.

Despite these explanations, my terms may sound fuzzy, unscientific, and irrational. But that is the case only if we see mysticism

---

6. This notion of the body bears a strong kinship to some current trends in French and French-influenced American feminist thought, especially Luce Irigaray. See Kathryn Stockton's two forthcoming essays (n.d.). I thank Professor Stockton for showing me her brilliant analyses of this feminist trend in the late revision stage of this book.

and rationality as having absolutely no meeting point. Such a binary opposition is akin to that between the mind and the body, and that can be replaced with a more complex and dynamic continuum. The present theory argues for a particular relation between the known and the unknown—between what can be placed under the heading *rational theory* and what might better be termed mysticism. Rather than conceive the unknown as a kind of wilderness, whose conquest by knowledge we must encourage and celebrate in imperialist fashion, we can understand the known and the unknowable as elements necessary to the process of knowledge itself. In the particular case of poetry, this process of knowledge is called reading. The rhythm of poetry is addressed by the images and ideas expressed in its words; but the effect of rhythm is always in excess of the capabilities of the cultural mediation manifested in those words, and the words, somehow, represent their very inadequacy. These points are developed more fully in chapter 13, and the reader may feel free to skip ahead if the present comments are understandably . . . mystifying.

It is my hope, then, that the theory of poetry as allegory of the sublime power of rhythm and its context in the Nietzschean tradition will meet needs within the present context of the troubled reception and appreciation—and to some degree even the practice—of poetry. But this very hope leads me to a larger question: What should a theory of poetry do? What do we look for in a theory? A brief exploration of these questions will help to place my theory of poetry, not only in the context of poetry, but also in the context of theory in general.

Theories of literary practice or of texts inform the ways in which we approach texts. They give us an idea of what to look for and what to do once we find it. But what, to begin with, do we need out of reading, whose fulfillment theory enables?

A theory, in reading as in the sciences, is a set of concepts that explains and predicts complex phenomena. Explanation is always (since Ockham) a reduction, a revelation of the complex phenomena as issuing from simpler, predictive rules. This revelation of the simple in the complex is what moves us from a state of unknowing to one of knowing. We may call the reading process just such a movement from unknowing to knowing. In the act of reading, every interpretive hypothesis (drawn up tentatively, as Peirce [1955] would say, by abduction) is a sort of low-level theory whose aim is to explain the signs in the text by finding in them a meaningful larger pattern, and to predict that signs to be read in the rest of the text or to be discovered upon rereading will conform to that pattern. If this local hypothesis succeeds, we shall have read the text and moved to a state of knowing. But this low-level theory is only made up within the framework of a higher-order theory that provides a model of the text, a sense of what a valid reading would look like, what sorts of elements in the text should be considered meaningful signs to be explained and what elements are merely accidental, and so forth.

We approach the text without knowing something that the text has to offer; we read the text, building and testing interpretive hypotheses, according to a particular higher-order theory; we now know something. This something is not at all the one thing to be found in the text, but one of a perhaps infinite set of somethings, each of which is made out of the text by means of the theory that we bring to bear. That process, of passage from unknowing to knowing through reading, we must own to be pleasurable. As Aristotle points out at the beginning of the *Poetics*, the acquisition of knowledge is a basic pleasure.

But is that the end of it? A theory that successfully renders a text entirely, transparently readable has done its job well—sometimes too well. For the *pleasure* of reading is precisely in the process of moving from unknowing to knowing, not the state of having arrived. For this reason, powerful theories in areas such as literature always run the risk of quickly outliving their viability. What may at first appear powerful in explaining a riddling text adequately may soon appear reductive in making the text no longer interesting. And whereas in the sciences, the reductiveness of theories is plainly desirable, in reading texts reductiveness eventually raises suspicions that the very mystery of the text that had provoked the reader's desire to know was excluded in order to create an appearance of transparency.

Explanation to exhaustion seems to have been a goal, if by no means an achievement, of conventional criticism. And precisely because of its success, it is often liable to the charge that it leaves out many elements of the text that might otherwise be considered important. More recent critical theories have helped to bring into the purview of knowledge such elements as the nature and operation of signs themselves (semiotics) and with them of basic concepts held without question or even consciousness but also without an unshakable justification (deconstruction); changes through history in modes of thought and even of the constitution of the subject of thought, as connected with either changes in material production or in the production of texts or both (cultural studies); and the function of textual signs to constitute or reinforce particular modes of subjectivity within the context of a culture's structures of gender, race, class, and so on (psychoanalysis, culture studies, feminism, etc.). These theories are at present rendering texts newly readable and restoring the process of movement from unknowing to knowing, while at the same time broadening the importance of the pleasure of reading itself, by connecting its knowing to other, clearly important sorts of knowing.

The present theory of poetry as telling rhythm derives much benefit from these theoretical trends. I have made an effort, however, to take a somewhat different strategy within the theory itself. By proposing to view a poem as a structured relation between the knowable— images, ideas, the meaningful aspect of the poem—and the unknowable—the effect of rhythm in relation to the reader's body, I have attempted to maintain a sort of preserve of the unknown side by side with the known. For poetry itself is, as I argue in chapter 2 and again in chapter 13, simultaneously transparent and opaque; it offers knowledge about something that that very knowledge acknowledges cannot be known—not, that is, in the mode of knowing that language has to offer. The energy of rhythm exceeds the limits of the limited moment in cultural knowledge reflected in the poem's images and ideas.[7]

In reviewing the Nietzschean tradition, through psychoanalysis and through recent writers who bring psychoanalysis and deconstruction together, I try to show how this peculiar relation of the known and the unknown within theory has developed in modern times, a trend that has tended to pass unnoticed. Chapter 13 proposes ways in which the conscious development of this theoretical structure, exemplified but by no means limited to my conception of poetry, may be brought in to address certain problems in the postmodern era, both in theory and in life. The aim is hardly to show how poetry can change the world—mine is not a Shelleyan apology. Rather, poetry,

---

7. This is not to say that such a "preserve of the unknowable" is not to be found in any other current theory—especially within Jacques Derrida's deconstruction, where analysis seems not only to touch but to celebrate and enjoy the limits of theory's, and its own, ability to produce knowledge.

within the theoretical conception developed in this book, provides an instance for a way of thinking that may have broader value in addressing problems beyond poetry.

Chiefly, however, I hope that the theory offered in this book may help address the problem of the decline of poetry. Providing a central place for rhythm in theorizing about poetry can help to restore the market specificity, so to speak, of poetry—that is, the pleasures and experiences that poetry alone offers.

As I have mentioned, this book does not present a historicist theory in the current sense. At the same time, the theory makes it possible to bring history and culture into the reading of poetry without losing sight of some transhistorical sense of what poetry is. Historicity can be found in the specifics of a poem's attempt to address the sublime power of its rhythm—the particular terms, images, and concepts it uses. At the same time, the poem subverts those terms, images, and concepts as they are used and valued in the surrounding culture, by demonstrating their inadequacy before physical reality as it is instanced in poetic rhythm. The unhistorical element within the theory of poetry as telling rhythm is thus like the unhistorical element within deconstruction. For deconstruction demonstrates how texts signal the gap between their signifiers, which are culturally and historically specific and meaningful, and the physical reality to which they purport to refer—which is by definition outside of discourse. But unlike some practices of deconstruction, the present theory makes room for history in relation to this unhistorical element. If I may speak, moreover, of a transhistorical sense of poetry, it is because all theories rest on some level upon transhistorical, universal concepts. These concepts may be thought of as mere fictions, but they are enabling fictions. Without them, none of the specifics of history or culture studies would be available to knowledge.[8]

Meanwhile, this book presents its own history of the Nietzschean tradition and of my own place in that tradition within the context of postmodernism. But the book is not altogether arranged in chronological order. It falls into three sections, which follow an argumentative structure.

---

8. For an analogous point about the uses of essentialism (which is also universalizing) in contemporary feminism, see Fuss 1989, especially chapter 4, "Luce Irigaray's Language of Essence" (55–72).

The first section attempts to arrive at a working definition of poetry. After a brief exposition of the theory in chapter 2, chapters 3 through 7 investigate definitions of poetry, leading in a logical rather than chronological order to Russian formalism and then away from it to bring up the questions that might best be addressed by the Nietzschean tradition. Within this portion, chapter 4 reviews concepts of poetry especially with the benefit of modern linguistics; some readers may find this material too elementary and may want to skip ahead. Chapter 7, on Roman Jakobson's structuralist model of poetry, attempts to justify my own approach to poetry as self-directed allegory on the basis of Jakobson's theory. This may be thought of as either a reader-oriented or a text-oriented argument for my approach, and it may be of interest even to the reader who is otherwise generally familiar with Jakobson's work.

The next section focuses on the Nietzschean tradition. It traces within this tradition the notions that I find most useful to bring to bear in the reading of poetry today: the allegorical relation between that which is accessible to knowledge and culturally mediated through language, and that which is inaccessible to such knowledge but which provokes or calls forth the very production of knowledge. It is my hope that these, as well as the earlier chapters 4 through 7, can be of use to students who may wish to refer to specific discussions on particular theorists or issues. Quite apart from any benefit the present theory may derive from historical context, some of these other theories, especially those of Nietzsche and Kristeva, are notoriously hard to read, and I hope that this discussion may provide some help. Others, such as Abraham and Lacoue-Labarthe, have not to my knowledge been discussed much in print. In addition, chapter 8 attempts to show how Nietzsche provides another basis for my theory of poetry as allegory—here, as a genetic, or writer-oriented theory.

A word of explanation is due about my exclusion of several important thinkers about poetry, even though they are prominent in contemporary theoretical discourse. These include Martin Heidegger, whose sustained and vital interest in poetry made it a prevalent subject matter in such essays as "Language," "What Are Poets For?" "Language and the Poem," and others collected in *Poetry, Language, Thought* (1971c). Another is Paul de Man, whose career-long devotion to poetry is well known. One simple reason these two have been omitted is that neither has anything to say about rhythm in poetry, which I believe characterizes the experience of poetry and should receive attention if theory is to help rediscover the special pleasures poetry has to offer.

Another reason for their exclusion is that, although both Heidegger and de Man respond directly to Nietzsche in various ways, neither of them quite fits into what I conceive in this book as the Nietzschean tradition—that is, a tradition of thinking that goes back to *The Birth of Tragedy*. What I take as the hallmark of that tradition is a structure for understanding the world crystallized in the binary opposition between the Dionysian and the Apollinian—in which each principle is entirely defined in relation to the other and is thus an effect of the other. Of chief interest for me in this structure is the idea that the known world, which is the world of language, is both a revelation and an illusory veiling of an unknowable reality; that reality is, itself, the negation of the principle of individuation or difference, and thus of language. It is crucial to my argument about poetry that this nonlinguistic reality be made manifest through the physical experience of rhythm. While the Nietzschean tradition I trace here includes such a concept of rhythm (or, in the case of psychoanalysis, of the drives, which I connect with rhythm), neither Heidegger nor de Man includes rhythm in his account of poetry. I have included such thinkers as Freud, Lacan, and Kristeva, who seem to me to develop and elaborate this structure.

In a more general way, I must warn the reader that my book touches on many ideas, concepts, experiences, and impressions that may in turn resonate for them with philosophies and theories that are far beyond the scope of this book or my limited powers to discuss. On occasion, I have tried to make gestures in the direction of some of these theories in comments and footnotes; more often, unfortunately, out of ignorance or given my present limitations, I have had to pass over them in silence. I can only plead that, were I to discuss all of the theories having any relevance to my present topic with sufficient depth to do them justice, my book could never be finished. Certainly, the questions raised in this book should be seen as leading to further questioning.

The last section returns to my own theory. Chapter 13 sets forth the theory in some detail, and further develops its potential repercussions not only for the reading of poetry but for some larger issues in contemporary theory, along the lines of the foregoing comments in this preface. Finally, chapter 14 illustrates how the theory can bring together the historically and culturally specific with the transhistorical notion of a relation to the unknowable, through close readings of four ballads from different eras and cultural provenances—medieval and modern; English, Anglo-American, and African-American; folk, literary, and commercial. Supporting and anticipating these readings, I hope, will be the reading of the popular commercial rap, "The Funky Cold Medina," in the second half of chapter 8. It is placed there in order to help point up the differences between my use of psychoanalytic theory and Abraham's use, which I would regard as more conventionally oriented toward the bringing of affect into consciousness, the conquest of the unknown by knowledge. Insofar as this rap is in ballad form, it could also easily have fit into the last chapter.

The reader may thus benefit from some repeated comparing and contrasting of various strands of theory with the one offered here, leading to several applications of the theory at the end. In this last chapter, I hope that my illustration of the variety of readings that the theory can produce will help dispel fears of the reductiveness that so often attends theories that succeed only too well at making sense of complex texts. The poems discussed in chapter 14 are different enough: the traditional medieval "Lord Randal," Emily Dickinson's "Because I could not stop for Death—" Gwendolyn Brooks's "the ballad of chocolate mabbie," and the modern popular ballad "The House of the Rising Sun." By introducing such variety, I hope at once to demonstrate the range of applicability of the theory developed here and the specificity of each possible reading. If the theory provokes further experiments in the reading of various poems with equally various results, I shall consider this venture a success.

Part 1:
Questions for a Theory
of Poetry

2

Telling Rhythm: A Poetic Paradox

This book attempts to redress the neglect of poetry in contemporary literary theory.[1] While the past three decades of literary and critical theory have provided a multitude of approaches and insights into narrative literature and related artifacts—such as historical, philosophical, and scientific discourse—major contributions to the understanding of poetry have been fewer. The thrust of poststructuralism

---

1. In these comments I do not mean to underestimate such contributions as the work of Anthony Easthope. See my comments on what I hope to be the relation between his work and my own in the Introduction. Many other recent theorists, including Harold Bloom, Paul de Man, and Geoffrey Hartman have written about poetry, but they have not addressed what I shall argue to be the distinctive features of poetry *as poetry*. Their approach has generally been rhetorical—that is, they conceive of what characterizes poetry as a certain rhetorical strategy for expressing meaning, and they consider sound and rhythm in poetry chiefly as rhetorical devices for contributing to the expression of meaning. I shall discuss the problems with this approach later in this chapter and again in chapter 6. Julia Kristeva certainly contributes to a theory of poetry; but, as I hope to show in chapter 11, she tends to efface the distinction between poetry and prose in order to make her theory work. One exception is Nicolas Abraham, discussed in chapter 12, but his theory does not include the benefits of poststructuralist insights.

The essays in Hošek and Parker's collection, *Lyric Poetry: Beyond New Criticism* (1985), apply recent theoretical approaches to the study of poetry, but here, too, those approaches are basically rhetorical analyses, so that there is no coherent new theory to address what makes poetry special and different from prose, or that takes account of poetic sound and rhythm without simply reducing these to another rhetorical device. Jonathan Culler makes this point eloquently (Hošek and Parker 1985, 40–41). As he later observes, "Recent criticism has not developed an alternative theory of the lyric, but it has produced changes in the study of the lyric" (43).

seems aimed rather at kinds of discourse whose artificiality is liable
to be ignored and truth value to be assumed—that is, expository
prose and realist fiction. Meanwhile, the investigation of such matters
as how one knows that a poem is a poem and what the relation may
be between poetic form and other aspects of poetry is more congenial
to the structuralism of the fifties and sixties. Although the insights
of that theoretical movement continue to have some value, it is time
to move beyond them while retaining their specific focus on poetry.

Deconstruction as such has little to say about poetry as such:
deconstruction treats poetry as more or less just one more form of dis-
course without any special value or privilege.[2] But in so doing, the
spirit of deconstruction—the recognition of difference in language—is
not realized in the practice, which tends to make all texts pragmatically
interchangeable. This may be at least in part because deconstructive
practice concentrates on the relation between theme and rhetoric (what
the text says and how it says it), leaving little or no room for a discus-
sion of form (what the text looks like and sounds like).

But poetry usually *does* look and sound different from prose, and
it has done so for most of its recorded history. Arguably, the poems

---

2. A noteworthy exception, perhaps, is Jacques Derrida's polyglot book (short
essay), *Was ist Dichtung* (1990), which suggests that poetry is characteristically
learned by heart, and which compares poetry to the figure of a hedgehog on a
highway in danger of being run over—a kind of self-contained mystery that draws
attention to its secret self. Nevertheless, even here, I find it hard to tell whether
Dichtung (*poésie* / *poetry* / *poesia*) is meant in the inclusive, Aristotelian sense—
for example, imaginative literature—or in the narrower sense of verse, except that
the importance of memorization faintly implies something of the latter. The mystery
of poetry includes the question of what poetry is, which provides as much the
focus of this essay as the answer to the question. Derrida does not provide here
the sort of answer that leads to a thoroughgoing theory of how poetry is to
be read.

Paul de Man devoted much of his career to the study of poetry, especially late
Romantic and early modern (see, e.g., *The Rhetoric of Romanticism* [1984]). But
here, too, the limits of *poetry* are hard to tell. De Man's focus in poetry is entirely
rhetorical, as was Cleanth Brooks's overt definition: a matter of metaphors, figurative
language, irony ([1951] 1989). My point is that it is hard not to find such figures
of speech in most prose fiction as well, so that these qualities cannot be considered
the distinguishing marks of poetry.

Elsewhere, de Man defines poetry as "the foreknowledge of criticism" (1983,
31)—in other words, as a text that anticipates interpretation. Can this definition
not apply to any properly literary text?

in prose and free-verse poems in the modern period have their deliberate effect only because the audience expects that poetry and prose are distinct. It therefore behooves us to discover what the differences between poetry and prose are. Such an investigation may give rise to new and interesting ways of reading poetry.

A revitalization of poetry theory is needed in view of the current relative unpopularity of the critical and theoretical study of poetry, compared to that of prose fiction. Indeed, in much of the First World, people hardly seem to be reading poetry any more. A new approach to poetry may provide a link between the reading of poetry and the sorts of pressing social and political ideas that have already been brought into the discussion of prose. And although any model of poetry, like any theory, is framed in universalizing terms, we can develop one that will, paradoxically, make possible readings of individual poems that are historically and culturally specific—yet deeply relevant to current political discussions.

In reviewing several modernist theories of poetry, including Roman Jakobson's structuralism, Nietzsche's theory of the lyric, and various versions of the psychoanalytic model of dreams, we shall in fact find emerging a remarkable—one might almost say uncanny—coherence of ideas, like teasing but telling variations on a single theoretical theme.

The theoretical model to be presented here comprises two basic ideas: (1) poetic meaning can be understood as an interpretation or representation—an *allegory*—of the bodily rhythmic energy of poetic form; and (2) poetic form itself, as rhythm, is beyond meaning and is therefore, when taken by itself, uninterpretable and sublime.

I use the word *sublime* throughout this book for the effect of physical rhythm with respect to language, without any necessary, specific reference to other theories of the sublime. For me, the sublime is a sense of infinitude, or excess, specifically in relation to language—that which exceeds one's ability to put it into words and thus fills one with a sense of speechless wonder. Nevertheless, this concept *may* be thought of as an extension of Edmund Burke's and Immanuel Kant's definitions of the sublime, but in terms that make sense after the linguistic turn in theory that characterizes postmodern thought.[3] For

---

3. The relevant passages of Kant's *Critique of Judgment* are book 2, sections 25–29 ([1790] 1987, 97–140). Pluhar's translator's introduction in his edition of Kant

both Burke and Kant, sublime experiences are those that pose a challenge to our understanding—and for both, as a result, there is both a discomfort and a pleasure in the experience of the sublime. Things of vast measure or of immense power—what Kant calls, respectively, the "mathematical" and the "dynamic" sublime—put us ill at ease because, as Kant would say, the imagination cannot present them or provide for them the sort of perceptual packaging that makes discrete objects normally accessible to the operations of reason. Instead, these experiences enable us to feel our own urge to find a wholeness in them, which is the activity of reason itself—and it is this self-discovery, for Kant, that is pleasurable. Somewhat similarly, for Burke, sublime experiences are painful but distant enough to cause a "delight" (rather than a positive "pleasure") in their very disruption of comfort, simply because they exercise the mind and thus keep us from the melancholy or deadness of lethargy (E. Burke [1758] 1958, 39–40, 134–35).

Whereas Kant emphasizes the relations between sensation, imagination, and reason, I prefer to focus on the relation between *language*, as the "presenting" function, and the world of sensation. The world is understandable to us insofar as it is mediated by language, but at any moment, owing to the finitude of any particular utterance, language is exceeded by the infinitude of the world. The world as such— as a world of sensation for which there are no meaningful categories as supplied by language or culture—can be an object of terror when we witness the falling apart of our ways of understanding. It can evoke *wonder*, accessible to us through such ecstatic practices as meditation. Nothing can be said concretely about this world of wonder, but much can be said about the experience of language breaking down before it, and of the sorts of experiences that bring us in contact with both the world and the breaking down of language. In poetry, music, and dance, the physical sensation of rhythm is an insistent manifestation of the physical world. Words, as meaningful signs, can *describe* rhythm or *define* it, but cannot *replace* it—that is, be it. This relation between words and the world holds true for *any* instance of physical reality, but rhythm is special insofar as it continues to draw

---

is extremely helpful. See also Jean-François Lyotard's useful discussions of the sublime, Burke, and especially Kant, in "The Sublime and the Avant-Garde" (1991c), "Answering the Question: What is Postmodernism" (1984b, 77–79), and *The Differend* (1988, 165–67).

our attention and to recruit our participation, through its catchiness, so that, so long as we perceive it at all, it does not disappear into its "meaning"—that is, its significance as constructed by the representational work of language. The experience of rhythm is pleasurable both because it enables us to witness the energetic struggle of language to find terms adequate to it—this would be akin to the pleasure of the sublime in Kant and its delight in Burke—and also precisely because the challenge to language confers upon us a momentary feeling of freedom from any particular, finite construction of the world. This freedom accounts for the exhilaration people feel when chanting, dancing, listening to music—Bach or Afro-Carribean music, for example—with a powerful and intricately elaborated beat, and sometimes when they hear or read poetry.[4]

The effect of poetry derives from the tension between the meaningful, historically and culturally specific themes and images and the meaningless power of rhythm that these more conscious elements attempt but fail fully to encompass. Rhythm is only secondarily a meaning effect: clearly, specific rhythms, such as the English unrhymed iambic pentameter, or blank verse, may and often do allude to certain traditions and authority figures, such as Milton's *Paradise Lost*. But there is also an effect of rhythm that goes beyond signs, beyond meaning in a semiotic sense. That effect is what makes it possible for rhythm to appeal to the *body* first rather than to the imagination or the intellect. And it is the play of tension between that appeal to the body and the intellect's efforts to put it into images and ideas that will work for us as a fairly inclusive and yet subtle definition of poetry.

This tension has direct relevance to contemporary political issues in a number of ways. For example, it is somewhat analogous to the tension between socially encoded meanings attached to the body, such as race and gender, and the body itself, whose reality always somehow exceeds such meaningful, value-laden social constructs. *Poetic meaning is to the rhythm of poetic form as social constructions of the body are to the*

---

4. For an interesting corollary in interdisciplinary anthropology/brain-science studies, see Lex 1979. This approach may beg many philosophical questions about the relation between positivistic science and the theoretical paradigms that construct and enable its truths—questions that are, in this particular reference, beyond my present scope.

body itself.[5] The specific ways in which the body is constructed are historically and culturally (and individually) specific, whereas the simple fact of social construction and its inevitable inadequacy before the excessive, infinite complexity of life itself—these things are, more or less, the ahistorical constants that make any history of the socialized body possible.

An example of how it might work to draw an analogy between poetic rhythm's relation to meaning and the body's relation to its construction is William Blake's "The Tyger" in his *Songs of Experience.* Here, the hysterical tone in which the speaker hurls his questions at the Tyger, and the way in which those questions equivocate perfectly between the rhetorical (giving precisely the answer of which the speaker is most afraid) and the sincere (in which the wrongheadedness of the questions prevent the speaker from seeing the obvious) both point to the idea that the speaker is creating his own Tyger without knowing it. The animal himself, on the other hand, although physically present, always escapes the radical classification—and damnation—imposed by the rhetoric of the speaker's questions. Much of the power and thrill of this poem comes from the insistent repetitiveness and parallelism that gives the poem a strong, relentless beat. It makes sense, then, to see the Tyger himself as a local habitation and a name for that powerful rhythm which comes into existence at the same moment as the language and images of the poem, but with which the language of the poem is also trying to come to terms—and failing in the effort. The result is a feeling of the awesome ineffability of reality itself— of God's creation. At the same time, we become more competent to criticize the inadequacies of prejudice—and to recognize that all per-

---

5. This relation between social construction and "the body" somewhat resembles that posited by moderately constructionist feminist theorists such as Gayle Rubin, who in "The Traffic in Women" (1975) suggests that there are real, physical differences between the sexes but that societies construct meaning upon these differences, exaggerating their contrast and homogenizing each side. More recently, Judith Butler has criticized the very notion of a real or natural body—nothing natural is outside of the social system of meanings, which controls and informs perception itself. But Butler's critique only presents a problem to my system if the real body is assumed to have definable content. On the contrary, for me, the body is there as a mystery that challenges any social constructions or definitions of it. Here, Kathryn Stockton's recent work (n.d.) on the body as "God" in postmodern feminism is closely akin to my approach.

ceptions that have meaning and can be reflected in words are somewhat tinged by those very inadequacies. In high Romantic terms, the very inadequacy with which we speak of the sublime world is a characteristic of our fallen state within it. Yet even our fallen speech invokes, precisely through its imperfect struggle, the sublimity accessible to us through the rhythm that appeals, not to our limited intellect, but to our bodies. To use Blake's terms, rhythm cleanses the doors of perception.

Likewise, in the traditional African-American ballad of John Henry, the chief images of the poem—John Henry driving the steel with his hammer, the race with the steam drill, and, in some versions, the trains passing the historic spot after his death—all of these images evoke strongly the notion of an overpowering rhythm. Even the sexually suggestive terms in which John Henry is mourned by his "woman" and in which, more generally, he hammers a drill within a tunnel—these reinforce images associated with physical rhythms. From a purely thematic point of view (and using structuralism conventionally to read the thematic content), the poem is clearly based on an opposition between John Henry and the steam drill—and thus, more generally, between worker and boss (in the first instance—or perhaps between individual worker and the impersonal, profit-motivated industrial machine), between black and white, human individual and capitalist industry.[6] But beyond this opposition, the force of rhythm drives all of the characters and all of the machines—the very same force of rhythm that is realized by the ballad stanzas, whose relentlessness is pointed up by, among other features, the repetition of each last line as a refrain. John Henry's inferior social position, which sets up his spiritual heroism as well as his martyrdom, is part of a system of values assigned to people that is constantly undermined by the sublime realities of being human. The equivalence of stanza to stanza and of hammer to steam drill (roughly—the hammer *does* temporarily beat the steam drill, but the steam drill, of course, wins out in the long run) and the equivalence of moment to moment in the same rhythm—these equivalences ironize the surface inequality of John Henry to his boss or to the industry. Indeed, the very failure

---

6. For a more detailed, historically specific reading of this ballad as well as a discussion of its sexual overtones, see Levine 1977, 420–27.

of each tool in turn, first the steam drill and then John Henry's
hammer, may be read as a figure for the failure of either image to
translate in full the underlying power of rhythm, the unspeakable
reality in which we are no longer individuals in a social and hierarchical
sense.

The above two operations on texts are, broadly speaking, *allegorical*
readings of the poems' thematic surfaces. An allegory is a coherent
series of signs that function as figures of speech to indicate an equally
coherent series of things or ideas in some other realm of experience.
Unlike usual allegories, however, in this case the figures of speech
indicate something that itself cannot be brought into speech directly—
the physical experience of the sublime power of sound and rhythm.
Insofar as the unrepresentable cannot by definition be represented,
allegorically or otherwise, these texts also allegorize their own failure
fully to represent the nature of their object. Furthermore, this object,
the power of rhythm, is produced by the very material that also forms
the signs constituting the allegory. In several different senses, then,
the readings suggested here describe self-reflexive allegories—in which
the self that is reflected in allegory is not merely conceptual but
material—not merely the idea of allegory but the material being of
the poem's rhythm.

Insofar as poems may be read as allegories of themselves, they
are also riddles that must be solved. This may help to explain the
general riddling quality of poetry, its tendency to present its situations,
images, and ideas in a way that requires some work to decipher them.
This tendency is a mere extension of the fundamental nature of the
poem, which is already allegorical.

The foregoing readings, furthermore, suggest that at least some
poems can be thought of as self-reflexive allegories of their own failure
to speak their own message, which is the energy of their rhythmic
being. Such poems present a paradox—a speaking of the inability to
speak the unspeakable. The model of poetry presented in this book
will be called poetry as allegory of the sublime power of rhythm, or,
more briefly, poetry as telling rhythm. It is to be understood that
such an allegory is doing the paradoxical work of representing the
unrepresentable (and its own failure to do so). This is brought out
in the double meaning of the phrase, "telling rhythm": an allegory
that attempts to tell rhythm and a rhythm that tellingly cannot be
allegorized into imaginary terms.

Poetry's allegory, telling rhythm, may be compared to deconstruction, and some of the same terms may be used, although poetry's allegory allows for the existence of something outside of language, rhythm. By contrast, deconstruction tends to emphasize how we live in a world that is already a world of language. There is a sense of infinitude in deconstruction, too—how language leads on to more language. But in the present theory, there is also a vitality outside of language, challenging it, calling it forth, and also provoking the revelation of its defeat—which is the very moment that ensures its freedom and its continued life.

Thus, in the reading of the Blake poem and the traditional ballad, the binary oppositions upon which the thematic surface is constructed in each case—good and evil ("The Tyger"), black and white ("John Henry")—are undermined or deconstructed by the revelation that both sides are types of signs attempting to indicate, each in its way, the power of rhythm. At the same time, rhythm itself is manifest in the poem, and its presence dwarfs and ironizes any representation of it, in a way that suggests a more general insight about representation or signification: reality is always greater, more powerful, more sublime, than any representation of that reality through signs, even though the signs are more manageable and calculable, especially within (so to speak) a calculus of prejudice. The poem at once presents this calculus and nullifies it by realizing through sound the sense of an overpowering reality. As we have seen, moreover, that very disruption of a prevailing (and specious) order is itself figured in the poem's allegory: in the case of "The Tyger," by the manic insistence of the questioner; in the case of "John Henry," by the successive failure of the rival drilling tools and by the tragic death of the hero.

Within the confines of language, which codifies prejudice, that overpowering reality is absolutely nothing—since it is *not* language. But poetry enables us to feel that what is nothing in language is nevertheless something, something whose power is felt precisely in its challenge to language. And precisely herein lies the difference between telling rhythm and deconstruction: the fact that, in telling rhythm, something is there beyond language. The allegory and deconstruction are comparable in their unmasking of prejudices, ideologies, or other apparently fixed beliefs, as mere functions of language that betray their own inherent instability. But poetry as telling rhythm offers something ecstatically beyond language that makes the outcome of unmasking better than a mere foregone conclusion within the always already constructed.

While the function of telling rhythm is in some respects comparable to deconstruction, it presupposes an initial theoretical *structure* that does not disappear later: the structural relation between the realities of sound and rhythm and the signing of language, borrowed and adapted from Saussure.[7] Likewise, earlier I spoke of several different theoretical paradigms—Jakobson's structuralism, Nietzsche's theory of the lyric, and psychoanalysis—having a surprising coherence. Obviously, when we speak of a single theoretical theme or a general model of poetry, aside from specific references to structuralists such as Jakobson, we are on the whole treating the question of poetry in structuralist terms. Yet structuralism per se has largely been abandoned as a critical practice for some time. Why, in the case of poetry, was it ever dropped, and why should we now consider taking it up again?

The chief prevailing caricature of structuralism is that it is ahistorical and generally aims toward the universal rather than the specific, thus producing a relatively static and perhaps dangerously ethnocentric or otherwise prejudicial view of reality. In the specific case of poetry, Henri Meschonnic's essay, "La Poésie est critique" (1979), may be taken to typify the case against structuralists such as, say, Jakobson.

For Meschonnic, the meaning of poetry is inextricably bound up in history; an individual poem's meaning cannot be separated from its historical and social contexts. This concept of meaning is certainly different from that associated with some of the New Criticism, where meaning is assumed to be more or less universal. Nevertheless, a generation of modern critics and theorists has thoroughly rejected that position, and their critique of the rigid and blind universalizing found in elements of structuralism is leveled a fortiori against the New Criticism. A structuralist linguist and literary theorist like Tzvetan Todorov is clearly able to develop particular structures uniquely suited to the respective texts under study, and therefore potentially responsive to history and culture (1977). But the possibility Todorov offers is generally not taken up by poststructuralist criticism, which has moved in the last decade toward the New Historicism and cultural studies.

---

7. How this initial binary opposition is special and is not subject to deconstruction in the prevailing sense is a matter to be taken up in chapter 8, with regard to Nietzsche's version of that opposition, the duality of Apollo and Dionysos.

Underlying the quest for the historicity and cultural specificity of meaning is, of course, the assumption that meaning is to be sought in poetry. If one refuses to apply historical and cultural contexts to reveal meaning, and at the same time one insists on a more rigorous reading of a poem than that afforded by the New Criticism, one is left with no option but to limit oneself, positivistically, to what is clearly, even scientifically observable; meaning in poetry becomes less appealing to discuss than form alone. Thus Meschonnic's real problem with Jakobson seems to be that structuralist readers of poetry like Jakobson seem only to be able to analyze the *surface* features of the poem and then to demonstrate how these surface features form patterns that conform to, and confirm, proposed theoretical structures.

Nevertheless, this charge as leveled against Jakobson is unjust. Jakobson presented a universal principle for understanding, at least initially, an aspect of the relation between meaning and form—what Jakobson calls "the principle of equivalence," which will be further discussed in chapter 7. But the larger point is that a theoretical structure does not *have* to remove itself from history and society—as we can see, for instance, in Anthony Easthope's theory of poetry as "social phantasy" (1989). Indeed, a theoretical structure such as telling rhythm, which posits a way of understanding the relation between form and meaning, can help us to highlight the historical and cultural specificity of meaning, in its effort to allegorize the power of poetic rhythm for its own specific audience and to tie that power to the web of immediate and ever-changing historical issues.

Even to make this relatively ahistorical theoretical observation is in fact an historical possibility of the present age, of postmodernism—and therefore a postmodern way of reading poetry in general. I am using the term *postmodernist* to cover several related and important trends observable today in politics and theory. These trends include the crossing of disciplinary boundaries—such as, in this discussion, the boundary between linguistics and literary theory—as well as a certain pragmatic eclecticism with regard to earlier theories. In politics, likewise, there is a crossing of boundaries that have separated various "one-issue" social movements, such as feminism, gay/lesbian liberation, and the liberation movements of racial and ethnic minorities. It has been possible to cross these ideological boundaries and yet still maintain the specificity of each individual's or group's political experience in part because of the development of constructionism (as opposed to essentialism) in theories of race, gender, and sexuality—and, beyond constructionism, the general theoretical shift toward an orientation around the *reading* of social reality as a *text*. All of these developments may be seen as responses to modernism, either developments from it or reactions against it, and hence postmodernist.

The theory of poetry as allegory of the sublime is no exception. Indeed, given the reader- and text-orientation of both modernist and postmodernist theory, this book does not present a theoretical model to explain *postmodern poetry* but rather a theory in a certain postmodernist spirit that will be applicable to the reading poetry from various periods, especially more metrically traditional poetry.[8] But "a certain postmodernist spirit" is hardly precise. The next chapter will explore in further detail the ways in which the theory of poetry as telling rhythm makes sense within the context of postmodernism.

---

8. In this regard, it is important to note that one of the most recent developments in current poetry, perhaps in reaction against the extreme modernism of L = A = N = G = U = A = G = E poetry, is a return to traditional metrical forms and to innovation *within* rather than against those forms.

3

Becoming the Postmodern Reader of Poetry

This book does not attempt to make more readable postmodernist modes of poetry in particular. Rather, it suggests that the *theory* of reading poetry in general, as allegories of the physical effect of rhythm in all its sublime power, can be seen meaningfully in its historical context—that is, the present moment of postmodern culture. This is important because, as postmodern readers of theory, we today expect to find a certain relation between a specialized theory of reading and a conception of larger social, political, and philosophical issues. In other words, a theory of poetry today must make poetry more readable for us, and must help us to find the pleasure in reading it; but in addition, it cannot work by removing poetry entirely from any of our other concerns in real life. This chapter will briefly argue for a particular view of postmodernism that will, I hope, make sense of my claim for a postmodern theory of poetry.[1]

It has been suggested that deconstruction can be seen as a last move of modernism (Aronowitz 1988). Both structuralism and deconstruction are modernist insofar as they propose fundamental approaches and reveal fundamental principles that are claimed to have universal applicability—stripping the complexities of a text down to its essentials, either to produce the underlying structures or to demonstrate

---

1. In what follows, I make no distinction between *postmodern* and *postmodernist*. My purpose is not to present a coherent theory of either so much as simply to locate my own theory of poetry in the current theoretical environment, which I see as one that historically follows from and also breaks from modernism.

the instability of those structures. Thus the deconstructive critique of structuralism is, just as much as the version of structuralism it criticizes, a theory that claims to have universal validity without much alteration in any particular circumstance and without much variety in the end results. To get beyond this problem, and thus to be able to look at poetry in a way that allows for its difference from other modes of discourse, we must go beyond the modern as well. The only way to do so without repeating modernism's problems, however, is to enlist selectively the elements of modern theory that could help us the most in the formation of a new theoretical paradigm. As I hope to show, my own theoretical paradigm is designed to include *both* the universal and the particular, the historical and the ahistorical, as a *relation* between the known (images and ideas in poetry) and the unknowable (the power of rhythm).

A theorist of poetry today might well gather the tools left by modernism, selecting the most useful ones pragmatically, in order to bring poetic theory in line with the evolving concepts of discourse and ideology in other areas. Such a postmodern approach to poetry should at once recognize the usefulness of structuralist insights into the universals of poetic language, while at the same time making possible an appreciation of the specific differences among poets, among poems, and among moments within a poem, especially as these differences bear upon meaning in the political and social spheres. If I propose a theoretical paradigm of avowedly limited use as a construct in order to make possible an inclusive definition of poetry, that should not be construed as the negation of meaningful differences or the reduction of specific pragmatic contexts in poetry. Linguists try to do the same thing, and their theories about the universals of language likewise should not be taken as merely reducing the universe to sameness in order for the theories to succeed.

On the contrary, theoretical paradigms framed in universal terms are both necessary and inevitable in order to make the historically and culturally specific elements of a phenomenon accessible to perception. And every time one makes a statement or observation of any kind that seems to be quite specific, there is always, lurking behind it as it were, some theoretical structure that is itself conceived, if it is brought to consciousness at all, as transhistorical and transcultural. This is a quality of the rhetoric in which theories are framed, and, in a more general way, it is a quality of language itself. Todorov makes this clear in practice in his *Poetics of Prose* and also points out explicitly how language by nature tends toward a certain unavoidable universality.

> Our exigent reader will say at this point, . . . [y]ou were to speak about a tale, about what is specific and unique in it, and here you are again, constituting a genre . . . of which [this tale] is merely one of the possible illustrations.
>
> And whose fault is that, if not the fault of language itself, essentialist and generic by nature. As soon as I speak, I enter the universe of abstraction, of generality, of concepts, and no longer of things. How to name the individual, when the names themselves, as we all know, do not belong to the individual himself? . . .
>
> Or else, for the individual to be heard, the critic must fall silent.
> (1977, 189)

This does not mean, of course, that this transhistorical or transcultural structure, whether explicit or assumed, is actually as limitless in its application as it may claim to be—indeed, as it *has* to claim to be on a rhetorical level, in order to be a theory at all. Nor should we deny that any theory, however universal its terms, is itself a product and an integral part of the specific social and historical contexts surrounding it. In Todorov's case, his practice implicitly addresses the question of the limits of the applicability of any given structural theory by altering the structure to suit each particular text, including its own cultural and historical provenance. In the present case, the theory of poetry as allegory of the sublime seems to work best for poetry composed in strict, metrical verse forms—although it may also yield some interesting insights into some free-verse poetry.

As for its own intrinsic historical specificity, the present theory is an avowedly *postmodern* way of reading poetry from various historical periods and origins. It is an attempt to address a side of formal poetic traditions that has been neglected by modernism both in theory and in practice, an element of radical energy that is not so much revolutionary as evolutionary, and that connects the popular culture of ballads, rock lyrics, and rap with the high culture of sonnets and odes. It is this radical energy, moreover, that I maintain is the *differentia specifica* of poetry, what makes poetry distinct from other modes of discourse.

Admittedly, the appropriateness of the term *postmodern* for this project is by no means self-evident. The word has become exceedingly popular in recent times, and its meanings seem almost as various as its appearances. But particularly noteworthy are the conceptions of postmodernism proposed by Jean-François Lyotard, who has devoted several works to this topic. It will therefore be useful to place our present use of the term in relation to his.

In one essay, Lyotard defines the postmodern age as one characterized by the new information technology (1986). In the economies of the most developed countries and, arguably, of the whole world under the new network of multinational corporations, competition and growth do not take place in the realm of production so much as in the area of decision making about investments and policies, an area dependent on and governed by access to information of all sorts. This information must be acquired quickly and must be reduced into forms that can be easily processed and manipulated. The controlling model here is, of course, the digital computer, for which all information must be reduced to the form of binary bits of data.

We may infer from Lyotard's analysis, in a neo-Romantic vein, that this reduction naturally leaves a great deal of the human world out of consideration simply because it cannot be so reduced. Human emotions and feelings, and especially that unique feeling of wonder or awe with which we apprehend precisely what is untranslatable and unrepresentable about reality (e.g., "you should have been there!")— these are aspects of life that must go on if life itself is to continue, and they have been viewed, since the Romantic period, as locked in a struggle for survival against the conquering force of industry and its mechanical reductions. The area of the irreducible, then, would become the field of resistance to consumption or domination by multinational capitalism and its inhuman demands. This reading is supported by Lyotard's own observations in his introduction to *The Postmodern Condition*:

> [The decision makers] allocate our lives for the growth of power. In matters of social justice and of scientific truth alike, the legitimation of that power is based on its optimizing the system's performance—efficiency. The application of this criterion to all of our games necessarily entails a certain level of terror, whether soft

or hard: be operational (that is, commensurable) or disappear.
(1984a, xxiv)

But surprisingly, what is important to Lyotard is actually that
this resistance to the absolute reducibility of everything is necessary
for the system as a whole to continue functioning. If challenges to
the rules of the game are not brought forth, and if new rules are
not constantly developed (a few at a time), then the game merely
repeats itself and stagnates. Capitalism as a *metaphysical* principle (1986,
215) demands that its procedures constantly change or "progress" in
order for it to survive.

In the second part of the essay, Lyotard focuses particularly on
literature, including poetry, which, in the postmodern age, must take
on the role of such resistance in the realm of discourse. Insofar as
any literary convention, and especially conventions of poetic form, is
identifiable and therefore can be reduced to one or another calculable
category, poetry in Lyotard's framework must now resist any kind
of recognizable convention. Likewise, in his better-known essay clos-
ing *The Postmodern Condition*, "Answering the Question: What is
Postmodernism?" Lyotard attacks Jürgen Habermas for complaining
of postmodernism's effect in "destructured form" (1984, 72). Again,
we might infer, traditional poetic form would be considered as some-
thing that can be identified, labeled, and hence reduced and controlled.

Lyotard's views seem readily to explain—indeed, perhaps to
boil down or reduce—such current practices as minimalist $L = A =
N = G = U = A = G = E$ poetry (see McGann 1987). No wonder the
poems are not in complete sentences and there is no recognizable
sense in them, in any ordinary meaning of the word. The poems
are there to keep the reader from making sense of them—they are
resisting the empire of reason in its latest manifestation, quantifiable
information. But if such poetry resists the reader, it also resists
most potential audiences for poetry, save a small elite who is in
the know about the politics of its practice. Hence, ironically, such
poetry actually may help to uphold and to serve a hierarchical class
structure by appealing almost exclusively to a small subset of bourgeois
intellectuals. Meanwhile, the most traditional aspects of poetry, far
from being attacked, are powerfully affirmed by the raps and other
quotable lyrics engaged in by a great many people outside of this

elite. Among most educated people as well as the underclass, meter
and rhyme continue to delight and fascinate; and among educated
people who are not in school but still enjoy written poetry,
Shakespeare, Keats, Elizabeth Barrett Browning, Langston Hughes,
Robert Frost, and even Fitzgerald's *Rubaiyat* retain their popularity
far above free verse and minimalism.

(The elitism of the modernist, antimetrical poetic avant-garde
should not really meet with any objection from Lyotard, since, for
Lyotard, the whole purpose of the language games of art is ultimately
to insure the continued survival of capitalism and its underlying
metaphysics—that is, the metaphysics of conquest and mastery. But
things become even more difficult to keep straight because of Lyotard's
use of terms like *reactionary*—in opposition to Habermas's use of the
same terms differently—when Lyotard criticizes any intellectual or
artistic movements directed away from the institutions and values of
modernism—which values, of course, he calls "postmodern.")

The position of this book is that there is nothing necessarily
reactionary or undemocratic about the continued popularity of appar-
ently traditional verse. On the contrary, what is wrong is the theory
that writes it out of democracy. Indeed, a deeper consideration of the
relation between poetic meaning and poetic form will show that,
although various vanguardisms in poetry can easily be co-opted and
work well in an economy of disposability and planned obsolescence,
the opposite goal of resistance to reduction and consumption can be
achieved at least as well, if not better, by poetry whose physical
rhythms are obvious—that is, traditionally metrical poetry—as by
those which represent an assault on the reader's expectations. This
position entails a few further implications.

First, democracy and some notion of tradition do not necessarily
conflict. On the contrary, recent writers on the postmodernist concept
of "radical democracy" such as Ernesto Laclau and Chantal Mouffe
stress the importance of cultural and political traditions as the very
means by which historical, cultural, and individual difference can be
acknowledged and empowered (see, for example, Mouffe 1988, 38–
41). The notion of breaking a tradition down in order to be free is
implicitly based on the fundamental Enlightenment conception of the
universal individual to whom are attributed the natural "rights of
man." The problem is that such a model only accepts a certain type
of individual as qualifying for status as free subject, and there is thus

an implicit hierarchy to every revolutionary plan of this sort. By contrast, people who acknowledge their own positions within inherited traditions can also acknowledge the ability of traditions to change and grow and their own overall equality as individuals with respect to the impossibility of a single truth (see also Feyerabend 1988).

The metrical rhythms of poetry, moreover, are what appeal to the body in its fundamental existence, prior to or outside the ideologies that construct the body within any social code. In this sense, there is a certain universal element in poetry. But such universality does not rule out the individual differences of traditions, of readers, or of poems. In the theoretical model of poetry to be presented here, poetic meaning can be allegorized as an effort to represent, interpret, or rationalize the physical energy of poetic rhythm—while at the same time, in some way, acknowledging that it can never fully translate that energy into language. The *language* part of poetry, poetic meaning, is always historically and ideologically specific. But its specificity is possible precisely because it attempts to speak about something that is outside of itself, outside of language (that is, the rhythm of poetry), and it therefore attempts to identify that rhythmic force with something more familiar within the realm of specific symbols and meanings. Just because the phenomenon of rhythm is outside of language (in the present, restricted sense) does not mean that it does not exist or that it is not worthy of discussion. Indeed, the current general lack of attention our society pays to poetry and poets (despite the underclass's poetic and rhythmic vitality) is traceable to our society's privileging of the mental over the physical and of meaning over being, of quantifiable value over life and pleasure.

This analysis of the current situation of poetry in our age is directly in line with Lyotard's critique of the information age and the privilege it accords to things whose reducible meaning and value can be clearly defined and manipulated. Rhythm (and more generally the sensuous appeal to the ear and the body) is the one thing that cannot be translated or paraphrased: it is only real when it is actually experienced. Given the importance of rhythm as already resistant to reduction, clearly, the more powerful the rhythm and the more strongly it resists being coopted into meaning, the more effective it will be in achieving the postmodernist goal. By contrast, certain free-verse structures can be (and are) read as rhetorical presentations of the meaning of the words. The general shift in practice (which has

by no means been universal) from conventional meters in the nine-
teenth century to free verse in the twentieth has been analyzed as a
replacement of the basis of metrical organization from sound to syntax
(Kristeva 1984). If this is so, then free-verse poetry as a rule would
tend to allow for reduction to paraphrasable meaning much more
readily than traditional verse. Good poems in traditional meters are
memorized, recited, chanted, and set to music; their performance
reiterates and reinforces the fact that there is something in them—
the rhythm—that can only be realized by repetition and cannot be
replaced by any sign.

These observations on the difference between traditional and free
verse should not be taken too dogmatically. The qualities I attribute
to traditional verse, with its predictable rhythmic patterns, are true
to some degree, greater or lesser, of virtually all poetry in any formal
style. But my comments describe general tendencies. The degree to
which free verse has actually cooperated with the reductive consum-
erism of late capitalism helps to explain the urgency of modernist and
more recent poetry to resist meaning on the level of *content*—the
poems are hard or sometimes intentionally impossible to understand.
Yet, at worst, there is an irony in this strategy: for the reader simply
becomes "educated" to accept incomprehensibility as itself a sign for
resistance and thereby reduces the poems. What we are moving away
from instead of toward is the sense of human reality—such as the
rhythms of the body—having an essential being beyond any attrib-
utable meaning; a being that can only be experienced, not defined,
and that resists any social construction.

In suggesting that we develop a way of *reading*, not just pro-
ducing, that is appropriate to the postmodern condition, and in sug-
gesting that such a way of reading would actually honor rather than
dismiss the traditional practices of poetic rhythm, I share with Lyotard
an impulse to revive the term *sublime*. Unlike Lyotard, however, I see
sublimity as a quality of experience that comes from a recognition of
the very ineffability of being, the degree to which reality always
exceeds the limits of its construction through language and social
codes of value. For Lyotard, the sublime seems to emerge through
an overt conflict with social convention. But the trouble with Lyotard's
concept of sublimity is that it leads to the overriding problem of his
entire essay, "Answering the Question: What is Postmodernism?"
(1984b): it does not answer the question. Lyotard speaks of the need

of artists to oppose socially endorsed correctnesses of taste, and therein would lie the source of sublimity. But such a statement is appropriate to impressionism and cubism—in other words, it is *modernist* through and through, in any ordinary sense of the term. Are we to understand Picasso and Schönberg as postmodernists because they created a sublimity through an assault on conventions? But then how does our own time, which Lyotard himself defines as coming after about 1950 (1984a, 3ff.), differ in any meaningful way from the period usually considered to be high modernism?[2]

Since our present concern is to develop a way of reading poetry that, while benefiting from various modern theoretical developments hitherto, would focus in a new way on what poetry specifically has to offer us, we must necessarily think of the present as different from the immediate past, the postmodern as different from the modern. For one thing, there have been significant apparent changes in the reception of poetry. In the earlier decades of the twentieth century, Keats and Fitzgerald were popular, and volumes of their poems were commonly given as gifts, while poets like T. S. Eliot were real celebrities, quoted in writing and in party conversation, admired almost as only movie stars are today. (Then we had Eliot and Rimbaud; more recently, Rambo.) Thus it becomes the more pressing to find a way of reading poetry of various periods, not only of our own, that would help us in our own day to rediscover what poetry has to offer. And in order to do so, we must recognize in some sense how we are no longer living and thinking in the modernism of Eliot and Picasso, nor, for that matter, in the modernism of formalism, structuralism, or the American New Criticism. But modernism continues to have enormous influence on our thinking, especially in academic circles, and, while that influence is often benevolent, it can sometimes

---

2. These and the following criticism's of Lyotard's definition of postmodernism are well anticipated by Fredric Jameson's trenchant and useful foreword to the English translation of *The Postmodern Condition* (Lyotard 1984a). While Jameson criticizes Lyotard by placing him in several indispensable philosophical and political contexts (and makes some references to architectural style), my focus, of course, is more particularly on the question of poetic form. In addition, Jameson does not go far enough, in my view, to show what is not only impractical but dangerously reactionary about a wistful return to high modernist values—especially in terms of the class relations that, despite their rhetoric, they uphold in their pragmatic effects.

hamper us considerably from moving on, say, to read poetry in a way that will enable ourselves and our students to find poetry more than mere assigned reading in an English class. The problem is, in part, that the modern poets and artists themselves benefited from, and to some degree *created*, a critical machine that would promote them and legitimate them. (Think of Eliot's essays and of the New Critics who were also poets.) And this critical machine has the unfortunate effect of excluding both creative work and, especially, methods of reading that emerge from a different worldview or experience. Yet at the same time, since it is modern, the machine always poses as if it were the latest thing and there could not be anything newer. This is precisely how it excludes new ideas. An example of this procedure, and a useful one for us, is in fact the work of Lyotard on the postmodern. Although he provides substantial insights into the postmodern, Lyotard's attempts to address the question of the differences between the modern and the postmodern exemplify the subterfuge of the modern posing as postmodern theory, of sameness posing as difference; it is therefore appropriate for us to pause over his work at this point, on our way toward a stronger sense of that very difference.

In "Answering the Question," Lyotard avoids answering this particular question entirely by explicitly disavowing any attempt to define historical periods—such as the postmodern as opposed to the modern period. Rather, postmodernism is more like a state of mind, or a moment in the Hegelian sense.[3] "A work can become modern only if it is first postmodern. Postmodernism thus understood is not modernism at its end but in the nascent state, and this state is constant" (1984b, 79). This turn of thought is surely the most frustrating point in Lyotard's book—for why do we even bother with books such as his, if not to find out what is going on now that modernism seems to be over? Indeed, Lyotard himself takes this way

---

3. In Hegel's *Phenomenology of Mind*, a moment is both a stage and a *movement* of the mind along its path toward absolute knowledge. Thus we have the ironic situation where Lyotard relies on a structure of thinking inherited from Hegel, which depends for its legitimacy upon a larger structure like Hegel's grand narrative of the mind's enlightenment, in order to explain what happens when such grand narratives of legitimation are no longer credible—but I leave discussion of this irony for another day.

out in bad faith. For in the beginning pages of the essay that composes the bulk of *The Postmodern Condition* (1984a), it is quite clear that postmodernism *is* what comes after modernism—that is, after the heritage of the Enlightenment, including Marxist utopianism, is no longer fully credible.

In the area of the arts, the problem of defining postmodernism in Lyotard's terms goes even further. While Lyotard opposes current attacks on the avant-gardism that has developed through the modernist period, he fails to acknowledge how modernism itself, with all its avant-garde fervor, has established a new orthodoxy that is just as repressive to new expressions in the arts as any classicism has ever been, if not more so. Literary magazines not only accept poetry without an audible or palpable rhythm (if not without sentences), they often accept such poetry exclusively.[4] Along with the drive for free verse comes a restrictive stereotyping of theme: nostalgia for a rustic, homespun past, tales of exotic travels, and the glamor of emotional confession.

The modernist orthodoxy exerts a canonizing and exclusionary force not only in poetry but in other arts as well. In choreography, for example, the prevailing canon favors the suppression of readable formal structure. Many well-established contemporary choreographers follow in the tradition of Martha Graham, in which structure is subordinated to expressive representation, pushing dance in the direction of expressionistic theater. At an opposing extreme, Merce Cunningham and his followers take pains to insure the utter randomness of movement and to avoid any clear relation between movement and music. But both of these tendencies are modernist in their avoidance of readable structure and their distance from popular culture, in which formal structure is crucial. Exceptions to these tendencies, such as Twyla Tharp and Garth Fagan, are few, and their recognition is still limited. Dance that is too clearly structured or too close to the vernacular practice runs the risk of being criticized as "unoriginal,"

---

4. Poet Vikram Seth's *The Golden Gate*, a novel set in today's world and composed entirely in neat, rhyming tetrameter stanzas, has character Janet Hayakawa, an artist, roundly condemned by established critics as "derivative": "Are Moore's and Calder's use of medium / Unknown to her?" (1986, 10). Clearly, for these critics, there is only one, already well-trodden path to originality. It is easy to see Janet, at least here, as a surrogate for the poet himself confronting the regime of modernism.

no matter how completely novel it in fact is. The parallel with poetry is clear: poetry is more acceptable to modernist prejudices if meter is effaced either (analogous to dance theater) to benefit expression or (analogous to Cunningham) simply to undermine the reader's communion with it.

Another example is music, although here, the venues of distribution are so various that it is harder to generalize. But if we focus on the prestige value conferred upon music by its performance in classical concert halls, we may note what has become the standard practice of placing the twentieth century music slot, so to speak, as the piece in the middle of the program, so that audiences are held captive and compelled to hear the work, which is typically dissonant and atonal. Prizes are given repeatedly to composers such as Eliot Carter. Meanwhile, jazz composers, who are also very innovative and who often work with elements of the classical tradition, have only recently begun to receive any such prestige—as in the new jazz programs at Lincoln Center in New York. In the past, jazz seems to have been considered too close to popular traditions to merit the special value assigned to avant-garde innovations within what was deemed classical music.

What is important in the analysis of this exclusionary modernist orthodoxy is that we do not draw the line of opposition as one between avant-garde and traditional—that has become a kind of double-speak, because it always makes a convention of the unconventional and makes real originality impossible. Rather, if anything, the real opposition is between art whose appeal is almost exclusively conceptual—in an elite context—and one that is more closely connected to ongoing vernacular practice—rap and blues in the case of poetry, street and social dancing in the case of dance, and so forth.

Furthermore, to return to Lyotard, the fundamental question is how we conceive of the social function of art practices such as poetry and dance. If, on the one hand, we are to view these practices as ways to keep challenging the rules of the game precisely so that the game—that is, capitalism—can keep going on as usual, then we can agree with Lyotard, but we must also recognize that there is an intrinsic bad faith in the purpose of an art that is made at the outset, but unavowedly, in order to be co-opted. Avant-garde for the sake of avant-garde fits in well with this ideology, and, in fact, the double-speak of avant-garde art that claims to be democratic but actually only appeals to a heady elite squares well with this bad faith. If, on the other hand, we see the arts as in some cases expressions of forces at once beyond the metaphysics of capitalism and yet intimate and vital for many people both alone and in their social relations, then the modernism that Lyotard champions is hardly the only way for art to keep its responsibility to its public.

The object of Lyotard's harshest criticism, in opposition to the postmodern, is what he refers to as realism. What I am proposing is not a reassertion of realism in any common sense—such as social realism or nineteenth-century realism—including the sense in which Lyotard uses the word to attack what he considers to be a betrayal of postmodernism. Yet, in a certain sense I advocate a fresh sense of the *real* in poetry—that is, not any *representation* of the real, but the reality of physical rhythm: that aspect of poetry which stimulates representation as it is allegorized in poetic images and statements, but which at the same time escapes any possible representation and causes even the images of poems to acknowledge and celebrate that excess of reality. This sense of the real has a closer kinship to Lacan's order of the real, on the one hand, and to the devastating truth of Dionysus in Nietzsche's *Birth of Tragedy*, on the other. These connections will be traced further below. At the same time, the way of reading poetry advocated herein falls well in line with Fredric Jameson's sense of postmodernism's dismantling of the high modernist opposition between high and popular culture—since, until the rise of modernism, both high and popular culture shared a sense of the physical, musical rhythmicity of verse and the connections among poetry, music, and dance. Here, too, the present theory acknowledges a certain *social reality* that is conveniently ignored or even villified by Lyotard in a way that only too strongly suggests an unwitting perpetuation of bourgeois class alliances.

A postmodernist theory of reading poetry must begin, it would seem, by making it possible for us (as postmoderns) to read the kinds of poetry that are popular among readers today and that have been so for most of history. In addition, such a theory must pay especial attention to what makes poetry poetry. For it has been modernism's legacy to break down genre distinctions to such a point that poetry *as such* has become virtually unreadable. (That is, poetry can only be read as prose, with certain disposable rhetorical effects superadded.) This gesture was once liberating, and, in more recent times, it has had a beneficial effect on theory itself, which has become increasingly interdisciplinary and eclectic. Indeed, the present discussion participates in the eclecticism in postmodernist theory. But at the same time, in the area of literary genres themselves, if we are to move on from that aspect of modernism that has meant a new orthodoxy and a reduction to the mere fetishism of avant-garde, we need to discover anew the *differentia specifica* of poetry.

4

What Is Poetry?

A crucial element in any theory of poetry, postmodern or otherwise, will be its definition of its object, poetry. A postmodern theory will have to get beyond the modernist definitions of poetry, such as Cleanth Brooks's concept of poetry as irony or as metaphor. This approach suggests what I shall call a *rhetorical* model of poetry, in which poetry is conceived as a communicative message in a distinctively expressive form, which consists of rhetorical devices such as metaphor. The rhythm of poetry, when mentioned at all, tends to be included as just another rhetorical device to express the message more effectively. This chapter will attempt a different approach to the definition of poetry. In doing so, it will risk taking recourse to what are hoped are fairly well-shared perceptions and intuitions among a reading and listening audience today. Insofar as these perceptions are not shared, perhaps at least the structure I suggest for understanding and categorizing whatever the perceptions are will retain its validity. The model of poetry to emerge will be one in which rhythm is central.

Rhythm is the more or less regular repetition through time of a sensory experience, especially auditory or tactile. As such, the experience of rhythm involves both cognitive apprehension—the recognition, expectation, and completion of patterns—and physical involvement or participation. Rhythm is thus at once physical and mental, affirming a nonlinguistic continuum of body and mind (Lex 1979). Rhythm is a source of pleasure, and, upon reflection, it inspires a sublime wonder. Rhythm exerts a force of catchiness that engages the listener's desire to participate, a kind of drive toward rhythm. It is in this sense that I refer to rhythm as having a sublime power. The present theory of poetry is based upon this sense of rhythm as a sublime force, a pleasure and a power. Rhythm is realized in poetry primarily as meter, and the term *rhythm* as used in this book refers thus to meter in the first instance. Ornaments such as rhyme and alliteration may be used in a poem to foreground the meter or, in some instances, to provide a counterpart to the rhythm realized as the meter. Also, these devices, like meter, contribute to an opacity about the physical qualities of the poem's language which will be discussed in this chapter. This opacity is one of the chief effects of metrical rhythm in language relevant to this book's theory. The most important effect, however, is the catchiness that obtains most clearly in meter.

Questions like "What is art?" or "What is poetry?" lead to inevitable difficulties in discussions today, because of the modernist urge to transcend or break down generic categories. Almost everyone who reads English will recognize that Shakespeare's sonnets and Keats's "Ode to a Nightingale" are poems. But very quickly, someone will praise Henry James's novels for their "sheer poetry." Such a claim, if made in earnest, would be a bit disingenuous, since the comment is essentially a figure of speech—and thus only has meaning precisely because Henry James's novels are *not really* poetry, but only resemble it in some way. But the distinction obviously becomes more difficult in a case such as Baudelaire's *Petits poèmes en prose* and imitations thereof. There, the ambiguous nature of the writing—they are poems *in prose*—is made explicit in the title; but is it not just a little less explicit in Lautréamont's *Les Chants de maldoror*—where the *chants* are clearly in prose? Walt Whitman's verse presents similar problems. With its syntactic parallelism and repetitions, in the absence of meter, how does it differ from the sermon or other oratory rhetoric, which is normally regarded as prose?[1] And what about Gertrude Stein? *Tender Buttons* and *Bee Time Vine* may strike the reader as *a kind of* poetry (here whether we mean *poetry* loosely or strictly is hard to decide). But is *Ida* prose or verse? What about *Three Lives*?

As the above cases make clear, the question of what poetry is has become virtually inseparable from the question of the difference between poetry and prose.[2] It is easy to define prose, as it has been

---

1. See Hollis 1983 for a demonstration of the relations between Whitman's style and oratory.

2. One could readily point out that the opposition of poetry to prose is relatively

defined traditionally, as the writing or speech that is *not poetry* (OED, s.v. "Prose")—more or less the way nonfiction is whatever is not fiction. It would be inappropriate, however, to define poetry as what is not prose. As old as the tradition is of defining prose in a way that depends on a notion of poetry is the notion that the nature of poetry itself is somehow self-evident or at least that one should always know poetry when one hears or reads it. Yet it seems at this point useful to pursue the opposition prose/poetry in order eventually to shed light on whatever definitive, if not necessary, features characterize poetry.

In view of the difficulties immediately encountered in the effort clearly to distinguish poetry from prose, however, it makes much better sense to do with the opposition poetry/prose what Robert Scholes et al. do in a college textbook (1986, 115–17) with the similarly problematic opposition between fiction and history: consider these to be two poles at opposite ends of a spectrum.

---

modern—perhaps that it comes into play only when prose itself gets to be considered a viable mode of literary expression, which might come hand in hand with the advent of writing and the transition from orality to literacy, or, even more, with the advent of printing and the wide circulation of the written word. Prose is usually considered less easily memorized than verse.

My argument should still have some validity, since I do not claim to be setting out a way that poetry always has been read and always will be read, but rather a way of reading poetry that makes sense for us today and might help to renew the value of poetry in an age in which poetry has fallen from favor. Thus I can concede any historicist claims as to the concept and value of poetry in other ages without necessarily having to alter my way of reading poetry, or at least many poems, today—including poetry from other ages whose concept of poetry differed from our own present one.

There are reasons not to rest so easily with this historicism, either, however. Throughout antiquity, as in modernity, terms of music and dance were applied to epic, lyric, tragic, and elegiac poetry and not to history or oratory in prose. Aristotle (*Poetics* 1) attacks the notion that poetry is to be identified by the presence of meter; but this very attack acknowledges the prevalence of that notion in his day. Likewise, Socrates' insistence in Plato's *Phaedrus* that oratory be considered as a kind of poetry, and his playful proposal of a "palinode" to his own oration, as well as his equally playful references to inspiration for his own philosophic speeches, make best sense if they are considered jokes against the background of an assumption that prose oratory is a mode of discourse opposite in nature to poetry. Finally, it would not be necessary or interesting for Horace to insist that his *Sermones* are not poetry unless people, observing that they are composed in the epic meter, thought them such.

poetry <————————————————————————————————————> prose

Note that unlike Scholes, I do not even suggest these two items to be points along the spectrum, but rather hypothetical directions defining the line. Thus I can evade the possible problem of having to situate any particular work along the line as poetry par excellence. I can, however, place a number of literary texts (or rather groups of texts) at points along the line relative to each other.

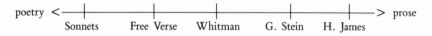

Perhaps not every reader would agree with me in my placement of the above kinds of writing relative to the poles of poetry and prose, but surely most would agree that, given the task of distinguishing poetry from prose, sonnets are more characteristic of poetry than are the novels and stories of Henry James; and that, conversely, James's novels and stories typify prose better than do, say, Shakespeare's sonnets.

In this spectrum, there is no real pure poetry or pure prose. The spectrum is an attempt to represent in a coherent way the impression we may have that some texts are more characteristic of poetry than are others. Ultimately, we can hope to isolate the qualities that serve as criteria for what is more poetic or less poetic, and therefore to formulate a notion of the definition of poetry.

If one text can be more poetic than another, then so, perhaps, can one poem show the predominant qualities characteristic of poetry more strongly than another poem. This idea is already represented in the above spectrum by the position of free verse (i.e., unmetrical poetry) slightly further from poetry and closer to prose than are sonnets. Thus within the broad category poetry, various individual poems in sundry styles can be placed on the spectrum relative to each other, all assumed to be within a narrower band of the spectrum, so to speak, which would be positioned toward the left in the above larger spectrum.

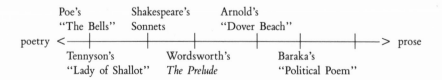

Naturally, different readers again may diverge somewhat on the relative placement of these texts, but the general model may still make sense. It may be difficult for some readers to imagine anything more poetic than Shakespeare's sonnets—especially if I propose that something to be Poe's "The Bells"! But if one examines the sonnets for lines or passages that, taken out of context, could be mistaken for prose (as critics used to do before modern critical practice developed), one would be more likely to find such passages there, I submit, than one would in "The Bells." Whether this makes "The Bells" not more poetic but simply more of a caricature of poetry is not immediately relevant here. For indeed, a caricature is made precisely out of the exaggeration of the qualities that characterize its original, and therefore would be very useful to us here by showing the qualities that define poetry with such intensity as to be hyperbolic.

Furthermore, clearly, not only might individual readers differ as to which text to place where on the spectrum, but readers can be assumed to differ across historical periods, according to the tastes and concepts of poetry prevalent in different ages. At this point, what is most important is simply that we grant that at any particular time, for any particular reader, some kind of spectrum is possible. The mere possibility of a spectrum from a hypothetical pure poetry to a hypothetical pure prose is more important than the specifics of any individual's spectrum.

Nevertheless, it is hoped that many or most present-day readers will also grant the possibility of a kind of test, in which works are deemed more prosaic if, out of context, parts of them cannot readily be identified as poetry, and vice versa. Related to this test would be one whereby the relative difficulty or apparent pointlessness of making a prose paraphrase of the text helps to identify texts that are more like poetry.

Although the spectrum model avoids the concept of a specific point or state of being to be considered as poetry itself, it still necessitates some idea of what poetry is, what the predominant qualities of poetry are, as distinguished from those of prose. Poetry and prose have in common the fact that they are made out of language. Therefore, to distinguish them, we must note the differences in the qualities of language that they comprise.

Roman Jakobson's essay "Linguistics and Poetics" attempts to define poetry in terms of qualities of language. For Jakobson, the poetic quality of an utterance is the degree to which attention is paid (presumably by both the utterance's producer and recipient) to "the MESSAGE as such"—the "poetic function" is a "focus on the message for its own sake" (1960, 356). This definition in and of itself would seem to work for prose fiction just as well—indeed, for any work of *literature*—since the reader's attention should be focused on the text itself and not, presumably, on the author or on the reader herself or himself. In Jakobson's terminology, moreover, the message does not include the specific context in which the message has meaning. Thus the message itself is, in effect (although Jakobson does not say so), deprived of its communicative meaning in proportion as attention is focused upon it exclusively. The model seems to be—especially as it appears in Jakobson's own schematic diagram—something like a conveyor belt moving along from the addresser to the addressee. The message is the individual item on the conveyor belt; but to the degree that our focus is shifted away from the context from which the message is derived, the item on the conveyor belt becomes increasingly mysterious, like a decorative but empty carton.[3]

The peculiarity of the relation between message and context in poetry can be understood, moreover, in terms of another relation, that between signifier and signified in Ferdinand de Saussure's model of the sign (see Ducrot and Todorov 1979, 14–19). The distinguishing quality of poetry lies in the particular attention accorded the signifier— if not over the signified, which depends on context for its very existence, then at least over the amount of attention ordinarily accorded the signifier relative to the signified.[4]

Analogous to the signifier-signified relation are, of course, the

---

3. See Paul Goodman, *Speaking and Language* (1971), for a classic critique of the conveyor-belt theory of language from the point of view of pragmatism. Pragmatism offers a great deal of insight into the function of poetry relative to its audiences; but it does not, I believe, address the central questions at hand, namely, What makes poetry distinct (i.e., from prose)?, and What is the relation between meaning and form in poetry?

4. Just as pragmatism has questioned the usefulness of the proposition-oriented or code-based descriptive model of language, so have deconstruction and especially its notion of *différance* greatly complicated the binary opposition between words themselves and what they say, rhetoric versus theme, or form versus content. For now, it will be useful to maintain the distinction, however, and even to bear in mind that deconstruction does not obliterate it but merely complicates it by problematizing the notion of reference.

traditional distinctions, respectively, between rhetoric and theme and between form and content. By *rhetoric* I mean the use of specific features of an utterance in order to express meaning effectively—in other words, rhetoric is language as seen from a utilitarian perspective. What rhetoric gets across to its audience is its theme. *Form* is slightly different. Form is language as considered independently of meaning— how it sounds, how it looks, how it is organized and arranged. When one says, as many have done throughout the history of criticism, that form expresses content, one is in effect viewing form as rhetoric, rhetoricizing the formal object by making it appear to be a means to an end—that is, the expression or conveyance of content. In this view, rhetoric and form, at least at first glance, are easily subsumed into one category, as descriptive features of the signifier; whereas theme and content, in this connection, are both attributes of the signified.

Given the distinction, then, between form and rhetoric on one side and theme and content on the other, we may make some general observations about ordinary language that should lead us to an understanding of its difference from poetic language. A great deal of language, including the language in which this text is written, is not supposed to draw one's attention to its rhetorical features (style, images, figures), nor to its formal features (how it sounds), but rather to its thematic content (what it says). Such language is said to be *transparent*. Expository writing is carefully formed and revised with the object in mind of the most perfect transparency possible. Scientific language, as well, is designed to be relatively transparent, and mathematical language follows strict rules and conventions for the sake of transparency. At the other end of the spectrum, we have opaque language: one cannot understand it, because one's attention is so strongly drawn to the mere sounds. This language is almost not language at all, since it doesn't mean anything; only its place within the larger system of signs that are *potentially* and *conventionally* meaningful allows it to be viewed as language. Opacity is not only a fixed feature of certain utterances. A given utterance can easily be rendered opaque. Such is the situation when an ill-behaved child gets the better of an elder by repeating everything the latter says, including even the command to "shut up." The imperative utterance is then no longer meaningful language, but meaningless sound; the child has succeeded in removing from the adult's language its power of reference.

The two extreme kinds of language, transparent and opaque, are possible because of the dual nature of the linguistic sign, as first clearly set forth by Saussure (1916). The sign is composed of a signifier and a signified. The signifier has only a purely arbitrary relation to the signified, and can only be a signifier in that (*a*) it is *different* from what it signifies, (*b*) it is *different* from other signifiers, and (*c*) it is consistent with rules that define a system of signifiers—rules such as the allowable phonetic inventory within a given language. Thus transparent language focuses our attention immediately on the signified— we can hardly notice or remember what signifiers are used; whereas opaque language is somehow designed to focus our attention on the signifiers, so that at one extreme it is difficult or impossible to give heed to what they signify. Opacity can be achieved through repetition, because repetition tends to undermine rule (*b*)—it causes signifiers to become alike. And repetition is the basis of rhythm as we have defined it. Signifiers are in and of themselves meaningless, although they are full of potential meaning because of their adherence to the three rules given. They only mean something, however, insofar as they are attached to their meanings by convention and usage. The relations between signifiers and signifieds are, of course, by definition problematic, since they are conventional and not natural: signifiers always mean more than just one thing—they depend on other signifiers in an infinite network of contexts for their definition—and, as we have seen, they can easily be made to revert to meaninglessness.

Poetry is not meaningless language—far from it. But the surface features of the signifiers in poetry demand a great deal of attention, more or less as much attention as the meaning that they signify. It is this tension between opposing forces, between the transparent and the opaque, between sense and mere sound, between the meaningful and the meaningless, that characterizes poetry. Whereas in prose, the surface features of the language (that is, how the words sound, etc.), if they are noticeable at all, are expected to *support* the content of what is expressed, in poetry, meaning does not clearly dominate. It is not entirely the case that mere sound dominates a poem, either, although perhaps in some poems it does. For the most part, there is a balance between the two—not so much a harmonious balance as a tense conflict, a conflict that places the reader in a certain state of distraction in which new possibilities of meaning seem to emerge from latency. In a slightly different context, Roman Jakobson describes this tension as poetry's "organized violence against language" ([1923] 1973, 40).

The objection may be raised at this point that the present definition of poetry, making reference as it does to Saussurean semiology, presumes a code-based theory of language, which has been superseded by more recent, pragmatically oriented theories of language—speech-act theory and the like. But these theories do not affect the basic distinction between what language is made of (phonic or visual signs) and what it is used for (meaning or, in pragmatics, action). Speech acts, implicatures strong and weak, and relevance (Sperber and Wilson 1986) are all matters that would thus fall under the larger category of rhetoric, because they address questions of how language works, not what it is physically made of. These theoretical concepts would only affect semiology by shifting the observer's attention from the basic nitty-gritty facts of language to the effects of language in its actual use in communication, within a somewhat narrowly conceived social context. The present analysis of poetry represents something of an effort to note at once, and inseparably, both the structure of the poetic sign and the effect achieved by such a sign when received by an audience that is competent to recognize that sign's potential as poetry.[5]

A poem, then, is an utterance designed to draw the reader's or listener's attention simultaneously in the opposed directions of mere sound and meaning, and thus to afford a sustained feeling of tension. How does a poem achieve this effect of sustained, divided attention? Are there any general rules that characterize poetry's method?

The above example, drawn from everyday life, of the child besting an elder through the reduction of language to mere sound, helps us by graphically illustrating the answer to this question. Whether as a natural corollary to a certain stage of cognitive development, or as a result of learning by chance experiment, almost any child knows that language is rendered meaningless through repetition. The more regular the repetition, the more the language is made opaque and restored to its origin as pure signifier, mere physical sound. A child who says "no" to every question, no matter what its tenor, clearly no longer means to negate. Nonsense words themselves are in many cases, though by no means all, characterized by sound repetition: baby talk's "dada," "googoo," and so on—as are their close allies, onomatopoeic words

---

5. On the notion of literary competence, see the discussion below on Jakobson's principle of equivalence, as well as Culler 1981.

such as *choochoo* and *murmur*. Finally, predictability pushes language toward nonsense—predictability, whether operative before the utterance fulfills expectations or only in retrospect, after the utterance makes it obvious that it could have been anticipated. Hence clichés, because they are automatic and predictable and thus exhibit an inappropriate repetition of a previously heard sound pattern, are avoided in certain modes of discourse because they may seem to be devoid of meaning and therefore to threaten the ability of the entire utterance to mean anything.

An interesting play on this principle, in poetry, can be found in the raven's uncannily meaningful repetition of "Nevermore" in Poe's "The Raven": the repetition itself pushes in the direction of the meaningless, contrary to the bizarre appropriateness of the word as an answer to the speaker's distraught questions. In another case, a sonnet by sixteenth-century French poet Joachim du Bellay (1910, 5-6), the repetition of the name *Rome* over the course of the poem reduces this sign to a mere sound and thus rhetorically dramatizes the poem's theme, the irrevocable loss of Roman civilization as a living force:

> Nouveau venu, qui cherches Rome en Rome
> Et rien de Rome en Rome n'apperçois,
> Ces vieux palais, ces vieux arcz que tu vois,
> Et ces vieux murs, c'est ce que Rome on nomme.
>
> Voy quel orgueil, quelle ruine: & comme
> Celle qui mist le monde sous ses loix,
> Pour donter tout, se donta quelquefois,
> Et devint proy au temps, qui tout consomme.
>
> Rome de Rome est le seul monument,
> Et Rome Rome a vaincu seulement.
> Le Tybre seul, qui vers la mer s'enfuit,
>
> Reste de Rome. O mondaine inconstance!
> Ce qui est ferme, est par le temps destruit,
> Et ce qui fuit, au temps fait resistance.
>
> [O newcomer, you who seek Rome in Rome
> and perceive nothing of Rome in Rome,
> these old palaces, these old arches that you see,
> and these old walls are what is called Rome.

See what pride, what ruin: and how
the one who put the world under her laws,
to tame everything, was [herself] sometimes [at last] tamed,
and became prey to time, which consumes all.
Rome is the only monument of Rome,
and only Rome has conquered Rome.
The lone Tiber, which runs away towards the sea
remains of Rome, O earthly inconstancy!
That which is firm is destroyed by time,
and that which flees puts up a resistance to time.

                                    (My translation)]

The more the word *Rome* is repeated, the more it is emptied of meaning, transformed from an ancient palace to a monument in ruins. The word as a functioning sign can offer no resistance to the process of time, for its very persistence through that process results in its depletion of meaning.

On an abstract, theoretical level, it makes sense that nonsense should be attainable in language by means of the repetition of sound patterns. Language works by means of two opposing principles: repetition and difference. Words impose categories upon reality, categories that assert a likeness among all their respective members (Eco 1979, 66–81).[6] Those same categories work, however, by distinguishing themselves from each other. If every word in a given language is different and no word is ever repeated, we do not have a language at all: we would have no way of ascertaining the meaning of any word, since it would not represent a category drawing more than one element together. Theoretically, this would be one way of achieving nonsense. But it is practically impossible: the very phonetic structure of language, with its limited set of phonemes, requires an eventual repetition of sound patterns. Thus the alternative, repetition, is a practical and readily available mode of making language into nonsense.[7]

---

6. This construction of reality by language includes the illocutionary force of language as conceived pragmatically—as in, for example, an imperative. If I tell someone to wash his hands, my words achieve their imperative effect because of the categorical analogy of the desired act with countless other washings of countless other hands at other times and places.

7. The forms of nonsense discussed here are achieved by means of the manipulation of syntax, if that term is understood very broadly to mean the sequence of sounds

In order for sound repetition to be perceptible, it must involve some alternation of elements. The sound *lllllll* (imagine beginning to say the word *lamb* and holding the first sound) is not a repetition of the sound, since it is not a repeated execution of a discrete sound unit *l*, but rather a single, elongated unit. By contrast, *lalalala* repeats the *l* sound; the repetition is perceptible because of the intervening *a*, the alternation between repeated *l* and repeated *a*. The most thorough manifestation of sound repetition, therefore, is the regular alternation of elements of sound—that is, rhythm. And whereas sound repetitions of one sort or another, usually accidental, are inevitable in any language and therefore generally do not by themselves distract the hearer or reader from the meaning of the utterance, rhythm, and only rhythm, is sufficiently evident, sufficiently different from the nature of meaningful language, to make possible the sustained tension between the meaningful and the meaningless dimensions of language found in poetry. In short, then, poetry is characterized by rhythm. Rhythm in poetry primarily takes the form of meter. Other features, such as rhyme and alliteration, may support the meter. In an unmetrical poem, such devices may contribute some effect approaching rhythmicity, pushing the utterance toward poetry on the poetry-prose spectrum.[8]

---

or signs assembled together to form an utterance. Nonsense can also be achieved through semantics, as it is, for example, in marked "nonsense verse" such as Lewis Carroll's *The Jabberwocky*. Whereas repetition works to make nonsense in syntax, in semantics, the opposite principle is used: *The Jabberwocky* is nonsensical because so many of its important words are unique to that text and thus have no outside linguistic context to give them meaning. The same is true, of course, of Edward Lear's line "He weareth a runcible hat"—where, while on the semantic level, "runcible" is nonsensical because it is unique, at the same time, on the syntactic level, the use of "weareth" to make meter rather than to express any appropriate archaism subordinates the semantic field of the words to the repetitive structure of the verse rhythm.

8. Some recent theorists, such as Henri Meschonnic, resist the definition of rhythm used in this book. Appealing to Emile Benveniste's etymology (archaeology) of the pre-Platonic meaning of *rhythmos* as the shape of a moving being such as a dancer or a stream of water ([1951] 1966), Meschonnic rejects identification between rhythm and meter (see Meschonnic 1982, 69–73; 1989, 20–22) and between poetry and verse, insisting that rhythm is a characteristic of all discourse and criticizing any fast distinction between poetry and prose. Of course, the purpose of this book is quite contrary to this last point. Instead of doing away with the conventional

Throughout this discussion, by design I have referred to rhythm as a kind of nonsense, aware of the deprecatory feel of this term. From the point of view of normal, rational language—that is, language as a system of signs used to mean things other than themselves, rhythm *is* nonsensical, it has no meaning at all. Rhythm from this point of view is empty. But from another, hypothetical point of view outside of language, rhythm would seem very full—not of meaning, but of pleasure and power.

So long as we are speaking rationally, in language, in order to analyze and understand the experience of poetry, then such a point of view must remain entirely a hypothetical fiction. In fact, in any event, a point of view would require some kind of subjectivity, which ordinarily is inextricable from the social network of language. But rhythm certainly is experienced, physically—at the same time as it is cognitively experienced as the raising and satisfying of expectations through repetition. Rhythm is recognized and can be named in language, but rhythm *is not* in and of itself language—except in the rare cases in which some special meaning is assigned to a particular rhythm as a code. Rhythm can be enjoyed without any such meaningful associations.

The enjoyment of rhythm should not be thought of as a trivial, frivolous luxury, like the enjoyment of a rare and expensive delicacy. Rather, it makes better sense to understand the prevalence and importance of rhythm in poetry and music within the context of a basic human urge which we might postulate as a drive toward rhythm. In other words, the pleasure of rhythm might be assigned the same degree of fundamental importance in explaining activities such as poetry as the pleasure principle has in Freud's theories of human activities in general. A poignant example is the woman whom I observed dancing to the rhythm produced mechanically by a washing machine in a laundromat, already mentioned. Anthony Easthope, in his *Poetry as Discourse*, also presents rhythm as an instance of the pleasure principle—"an intense and original pleasure" (1983, 33) or a "pleasure in nonsense" (Freud, quoted in Easthope 1983, 33)—and

---

definition of rhythm and the idea of meter as rhythm in poetry par excellence, this book attempts to deal with literary works that do not fit the standard of metrical verse by placing them on a spectrum between poetry (verse) and prose.

thus a kind of fundamental source of vitality. One of his best examples is the chorus of Little Richard's famous "Tutti-Frutti" (33). And, as Easthope points out, the rhythmic, formal devices found in verse are instances of the same pleasure as is found in jokes according to Freud's *Jokes and Their Relation to the Unconscious* (Easthope 1983, 34; Freud [1905] 1989, 149). For Freud, as Easthope points out, rhythm would then be an instance of the exercise of infantile and unconscious urges with the result of a pleasurable release of psychic energy. Such release is also a relief from the pressure of conscious life and its repressions, which are the very mechanisms that make social life possible. Hence the pleasure of rhythm has the power, not only to seduce the listener to participate, but to cause the participants to regress to a state before the constitution of the social subject—the clearly demarcated individual who shares in social codes of value and judgment.

The hypothetical point of view of rhythm is not accessible to us in the *meaningful* aspect of poetry, which is, after all, made out of language. By making use of its own material self as an instance of rhythm and as the object of its meaning, poetry is a use of language that gives us indirect access to this power that is inaccessible through ordinary, prosaic language.

If one could take rhythm, this poetic principle, so to speak, and push it to the extreme, one would have nothing but the meaningless alternation of repeated sounds to form a rhythm. Although this form of nonsense is often found as a musical effect in portions of poems and especially of song lyrics ("Hey nonny nonny," etc.), it could not occupy a poem completely, or that poem could no longer be considered an utterance at all: its material would now be pure music and no longer language. At the opposite extreme, one could imagine language so transparent as not to have any noticeable shape of sound at all—that is, no repetitions of phonemes; no sound, just pure meaning. This is an evident impossibility. Thus either end point of the spectral line from prose to poetry with which we began is really not a point but an asymptote: each in its way is impossible. As a result, since poetry, as language, must have meaning (or something approaching meaning, at least), it always has something akin to prose; since prose, as language, must have some sound patterns, accidental or intentional (rhetorical), it always shares something with poetry. This kinship by no means renders impossible a definition of the qualities that distinguish poetry from prose.

Poetry, accordingly, is an utterance designed in such a way as to draw attention simultaneously to its dimension of pure sound and to that of meaning, creating a sustained tension between the two forces; and which achieves that effect of tension by means of structuring its language according to rhythm. It is useful to compare this definition of poetry with the observations of the Russian formalists, who had taken on many of the same basic theoretical questions.[9] Elements of our definition of poetry were present in formalism, but the formalists did not manage to assemble a coherent theory in which all of their principles could be logically connected or derived one from another (see Erlich, esp. chaps. 10 [171–91] and 12 [212–29]). They tended to proceed empirically, intuitively, and inductively. The idea of a non-sensical dimension to poetic language, moreover, although quite evident in the Russian formalists' early interest in futurist poets such as Khlebnikov, was never systematically integrated into a general theory of poetry. Rather, as the definition of poetry became more rigorous, mostly in Jakobson's turn toward structuralism in the 1930s, rhythm came to the fore, and nonsense seems to have dropped from the picture. The formalists appear never to have seen how these two effects might be very closely related.

Yet formalism has contributed significantly to modern theorizing about poetry, and its contributions should not be ignored. In order better to understand the differences between my presentation and the original formalist insights, it will be useful to review some of the latter. More importantly, a brief critical review of formalist concepts of poetry will help clarify precisely what this critical movement left yet to be conceptualized. The theory of poetry as allegory of the sublime may be thought of as a return to the questions that the formalists left unanswered, in the hope of defining and answering them with even greater precision.

---

9. For example, the experiments in evocative sounds of the early-twentieth-century Russian futurist poet Victor Khlebnikov. See Erlich 1981, 45–46.

5

Russian Formalism

It will be important to place the theory of poetry as allegory of the sublime power of rhythm, as a postmodern theory of poetry, within the historical contexts of other literary theories whose elements continue to inform literary discussion. In so doing, I hope to show how the present theory continues a line of thinking that may be called the Nietzschean tradition, adding to it and modifying it in ways that make the present theory particularly suited to postmodern demands. But before we turn to Nietzsche, it will be useful to see how the theory of telling rhythm responds to certain problems to be found in other modern theories, such as Russian formalism and the structuralism of Roman Jakobson. At the same time, an examination of each of these theories will show useful elements that should be kept in a viable postmodern theory. We begin with formalism, which in certain ways is at the root both of the development toward today's poststructuralism and, conversely, of the American New Criticism. As was suggested in the previous chapter, the primary importance of the opacity of language in poetry, and therefore of rhythm and repetition, was a tenet of Russian formalism. As I hope to show, one serious problem in Russian formalism was how to integrate this primacy of rhythm or physical, opaque sound with the facts that poetry still usually has meaning and that reading or listening involves some interpretation or understanding of that meaning. This is an area that the theory of poetry as telling rhythm may be seen to address, while retaining some useful and attractive insights from formalism.

The question with which we began the last section, How does poetry differ from prose? is a typically formalist question. The formalists were concerned with discovering the definitive difference, or

differentia (singular), between literary and nonliterary modes of dis-
course. As a rule, they regarded that differentia to be a quality of
self-directedness or self-containment: the work of literature draws
attention to its own devices rather than merely to an outside world
to which it may purportedly refer. *Devices* seem to include any features
of the literary work that appear on the surface and that do not require
the importation of a coherent outside context in order to be recog-
nizable. Figures of speech such as metaphors and antitheses are literary
devices, as are patterns of ordering events in a narrative. In poetry,
these would presumably include meter and other formal features.
Clearly, the idea raised above that poetry draws attention to its own
material being would accord with this notion of self-directedness. The
principle holds just as well, however, for literary prose.

It must be acknowledged that early formalism made use of an
ambiguous vocabulary that is rather unhelpful to our purposes. Often
the terms of opposition are not poetry and prose, but poetry and
ordinary (i.e., nonliterary) language. Since our present purposes
include precisely an understanding of the differences between poetry
and prose, it is an unfortunate fact that the use of the term *poetry*
to refer vaguely to all imaginative literature of whatever genre is a
hallowed tradition going back to Aristotle and even earlier.

In ancient contexts, it was arguably unnecessary to develop a
theory specific to poetry qua verse. Literary prose in Aristotle's Greece
was not a developed genre, probably at least in part because very few
people were literate and imaginative literature had therefore to reach
its audience primarily through oral recitation and memorization. Here,
verse offers advantages we can now appreciate within the framework
of an explicit theory: verse is well suited to oral delivery because its
formal (pure sound) dimension makes it appealing even if its meaning
is not immediately understood; and verse is memorizable because of
the interplay between the sounds, which follow their own, somewhat
predictable, patterns, and the meaning or thematic content; each can
then reinforce the other as prompts for the memory. Accordingly,
imaginative literary prose emerges only in the Hellenistic period and
again in the second-century Roman Empire—in both cases in the
form of prose romances (novels) such as the Greek *Apollonius of Tyre*
and the Roman *Satyricon* of Petronius and *Metamorphoses* of Apuleius.
Otherwise, prose is reserved for oratory, history, science, grammar,
and philosophy.

Accordingly, a close reading of *Poetics* (1 and 4) reveals that, while Aristotle takes pains to argue that not all discourse in verse should be called poetry, he never in fact suggests that anything in prose could qualify as poetry. The presence of metrical verse is more or less assumed. For both Plato and Aristotle, the important issues are oriented toward content and revolve around the effect and value of poetry as "imitation" or representation of the truth. And although Aristotle does suggest some principles of decorum in the relation between various meters and subject matters (e.g., iambics for satire), neither he nor Plato before him suggests any theoretical reasons why meter or rhythm and imitation should be related on principle. One could only guess that, for them as for us, the presence of a regular rhythm in language causes the utterance to be bracketed off from ordinary communication and thus to become a second order of discourse in which, say, an expression of sadness is an *imitation* of an expression of sadness—which, as Aristotle observes, gives the reader pleasure because of its effectiveness. One could also speculate that the predominantly metaphoric nature of poetry (i.e., verse), and its tendency to juxtapose one image against another so as to make it clear that those images *are* metaphors, give poetry as a whole the impression of being at one remove from direct expression and thus an imitation. But these speculations can only be made with the benefit of modern formalism; they are applications of modern, post-Aristotelian terms back to a reading of Aristotle and Plato.

In the context of a modern theory like formalism, which claims to proceed empirically from the *surface* features of texts rather than from their relation to truth, society, history, and so on, the continued use of the term *poetry* in its slippery post-Aristotelian sense seems less to serve the rigor of linguistic theory than to provide a theoretical rationale to support modernistic innovations that break down the barrier between poetry and prose. In fact, formalism took root as a supportive critical response to the futurist avant-garde in Russian literature, especially poetry, at the beginning of the twentieth century. But from today's perspective, we may reconsider these modernist experiments precisely as the artistic equivalent of the formalist project that followed them: that is, the reduction of important differences in language and literature to the absolute minimum so that they could be more clearly defined. If poetry is made to be more like prose, then how far can one go, a poet might ask, before the work is no longer conceivable as a poem? In other words, these poets themselves were discovering the differentia that constitutes poetry, but they were doing so through artistic experimentation rather than through explicit theory.

A later phase of formalism developed the notion of a *dominant* feature, or *dominanta,* that distinguishes one mode of literary discourse from another. In the case of poetry, the dominant feature is the repetition of patterns, or rhythm. Rhythm pervades every aspect of the poem, governing not only the meter but also alliteration, rhyme, stanzaic forms, and so forth, presumably insofar as these latter either support the meter or provide a counterpoint to it.

The evolution of formalism from an early, somewhat hyperbolic phase that lacked theoretical rigor to a later, more sophisticated phase can also be seen in its treatment of the vexing question of meaning. What relation is there in poetry between the literary differentia, self-directedness, and literary meaning? If rhythm is the dominant feature of poetry, how do we assimilate this all-important feature to our overall interpretation of poetry, our impression of its meaning?[1] The question of meaning has obvious relevance to our present discussion, since the model of poetry as allegory of the sublime power of rhythm is a theory that accounts for meaning in relation to poetic form, even as the latter is understood in ways that resemble formalist theory.

And the relation between form and meaning is precisely the weakest area of formalist theory. In its radical early phase, formalists such as Victor Shklovsky asserted the primacy of the literary device over all other considerations, such as emotional or ideological content. Indeed, according to Shklovsky and others, themes and other aspects of what would normally be regarded as content should be seen rather as *motivations*—that is, excuses that enable the writer to deploy various artistic devices in the work while still holding the reader's attention. As such, these matters of content could be dismissed from serious literary analysis, which could apply itself primarily or exclusively to the devices themselves.

---

1. The formalist-structuralists themselves often seem to have answered the question of the relation between rhythm and meaning by merely dodging it and analyzing a poem as a rhythmic "structuring" of a message that, in and of itself, need have nothing whatsoever to do with rhythm. Such, for example, is Jakobson's famous collaboration with Levi-Strauss in the "reading" of Baudelaire's "Les Chats" (1972).

Although the formalists did not express themselves in directly political terms, this subordination or dismissal of content could be understood to have important political implications. In the tense atmosphere of revolutionary Russia and later communist Czechoslovakia (and, frankly, from then until glasnost), it was a matter of great urgency for Russian and East European intellectuals to demonstrate the value of literature and art aside from being a mere vehicle for the most overt propaganda. The Russian formalists were in the very serious business of trying to save traditional and nineteenth-century Russian literature, which was, of course, hopelessly "feudalistic" or "bourgeois," against the heavy-handed censorship of communist philistinism. In order to do so, and to save themselves (for the moment) from the accusation of being, themselves, bourgeois holdovers and enemies of the people, they would have had to demonstrate the possibility of social and political value in literature aside from, or even in spite of, an apparently reactionary overt message. This strategy certainly continues to have value for us today; but it must be balanced by a more inclusive theory of how poetry works.

If the devices of the literary work do not function as representations or conveyors of meaning, then what is their function? For formalism, the chief function of literature is to make the familiar experiences of life, including language itself, appear strange and unfamiliar, and therefore, in a sense, freshly perceptible after the senses have been dulled by familiarity. In a general way, then, formalism took the prevailing hierarchical relation between content and form—where form serves content by representing it—and stood it on its head: content is a mere occasion for the workings of form, while form, in the broad sense of literary devices, achieves its own end of defamiliarization. For the formalists' immediate audience, this principle preserves a sense of social value in all literature, despite its apparent political position, so long as it is technically effective. Defamiliarization makes democracy and class consciousness possible, since the invisible workings of ideology thus become visible and can be changed.

For us, the theory of defamiliarization also offers at least some kinship with our own theory, wherein poetry brings to our awareness the unspeakable sublimity of material reality through the workings of its rhythm and through its allegorical representation of the power of its rhythm. In both cases, the reality around us is in danger of falling into a kind of blind spot. For formalists, the blind spot is familiarity; for the theory of poetry as telling rhythm, it is conventional codes of language and meaning. In both cases, poetry revitalizes reality and saves it from that blind spot. In formalism, poetry does this by means of devices such as images and metaphors. In the theory of poetry as telling rhythm, poetry valorizes and energizes reality by using its own material reality, its own material being—pure rhythmic sound. Poetry then allows us to witness the failure of language to address the power of the very material out of which its signs are made—the rhythm is telling.

Meanwhile, the theory of poetry as telling rhythm will attempt to redress at least two very serious problems with the formalist approach.

The first problem has to do with the notion of motivation. Since it suggests that the apparent meanings of literary devices are actually trivial compared to the devices themselves, we have no clearly theorizable relation between devices and meaning, which is theoretically unsatisfactory to say the least. Furthermore, if by *devices* we mean to include figures of speech such as metaphors, we have the problem that the device itself cannot be defined or imagined without some sort of reference, that is, the various levels of meaning at work in a metaphor, and so on. How can the reality to which the literary work refers be defamiliarized if we assume that same reality to be a trivial motivation for the display of devices?

The notion of motivation can best be understood not even as an attempt at a rigorous concept, but rather as a somewhat hyperbolic reaction. In the first instance, that reaction is occasioned by the political pressures toward a naive reading of literature as message mentioned earlier. More abstractly, the reaction was against prevailing critical practices in the late nineteenth and early twentieth centuries, in which works of literature were read as evidence for the lives of their authors or the ideologies of their social milieus—matters that, from a formalist perspective, are external to the text. It should be possible, not only for the formalists but for most critical practices since their day, to read the text without immediate recourse to specialized contexts not presented within the text itself.

Most of us today share the prejudice that the text itself has something worthwhile to say or to do. Conversely, treating the text as a means to attain knowledge of something else, such as the author's life, historical circumstances, or the thought of his or her circle, runs the risk of fallaciously ignoring the possibility of individual imagination, while it effectively devalues the text as an object of interest and pleasure. Formalism inaugurated these attitudes of reading for our age.

Even as we appreciate the formalist turn away from external considerations, we should probably also bear in mind that the historicism of the late nineteenth century could have served, among other things, the very real and practical purpose of educating readers as to the texts' historical contexts in order to make meaning possible. We live in an age when many students come to literature with virtually no historical background in which to contextualize their reading, and the academy has responded, in part, by integrating the postformalist insights of structuralism and poststructuralism into the new cultural materialism.

Nevertheless, the old history and biography also served, at times, to fetishize authorship and to narrow and oversimplify the possibilities of meaning to such a degree that reading became obtuse and judgments were passed based on naive impressions of complex texts. To this state of affairs formalism reacted, and, in fact, formalism had much more to say about what makes poetry interesting and special than either the old or newer historicisms have done. Having eliminated external considerations, however, formalism could not resolve the resulting question of the relation between content and form, and, again, resorted instead to the untenable notion of motivation.

The second problem with the formalist view of devices and meaning touches upon the problem of defining figures of speech already noted. To begin with, the literary text is defined as self-directed. To borrow Jakobson's considerably later formulation (1960), the poem is a discourse in which we find the "set [i.e., the writer's and audience's focus of attention] toward the MESSAGE (356)," wherein the message is defined, more or less, as the conveyor of the context (i.e., the referent or content). But what does the poetic message convey, if the focus of attention is not on the content? If meaning is trivial relative to the devices themselves, if the devices are not primarily there to convey content, then how can the message, the devices, be defined at all?

Formalism attempted to resolve these dilemmas, understandably, by challenging the assumed opposition between form and content. But in proposing an alternative, the formalists only aggravated the general lack of rigor of their theory. In place of the form/content dichotomy, several formalists insisted upon a "unity of form and content" and accordingly replaced *content* with the term *material*. The model of a distinction between form and material here was somewhat Aristotelian: the form is what gives the shape to the material so that it is perceivable and recognizable. As is the case with the formalist use of the Aristotelian concept of poetry, this notion only seems to lead us into a muddle when it comes to understanding the nature and working of a poem.

As to the first point, the "unity of form and content," obviously there must still be some definable relation between these two elements, no matter how unified they are conceived to be—so the question remains as to the nature of this relation. In fact, there is only one way that one can speak of such a unity, and that is precisely if the perceptible form of a work of literature is understood as the rhetorical means by which the content is expressed. The devices are *rhetorical* devices, and as such are of course subordinate to content—the very situation the formalists were trying to get away from.

The form/material model borrowed from Aristotelian physics only clouds the picture further. If the material out of which a work is made—by which, presumably, is meant the imaginary experiences and events themselves—if this material is to be compared to clay and things like rhyme and meter to the mold that forms the clay—or actually to the *shape* of that mold, then obviously material and form are two completely heterogeneous categories: clay on the one hand, a drinking cup on the other. How then can one speak of a unity between them? They have nothing in common. This criticism leaves aside the even more basic problem of how there can be such a thing as literary material that is not already formed—that is, a story that has no words. At least in more recent times, partly because of the legacy of structuralism and poststructuralism, we are disinclined to accept such a notion as possible.

Meanwhile, even as formalism exerted a powerful influence on the emergence and development of the American New Criticism, many of the problems associated with the relation between form and meaning can be seen repeated there. Many modern critics roughly in the tradition of the New Criticism tend to see sound and sense as echoing each other—or, more precisely, to see sound, or poetic form, as a *vehicle* of meaning. In other words, poetic form is subsumed within the category of *rhetoric*—it is among other rhetorical devices used to present the theme effectively. Critics commonly speak of this relation as the "unity of form and content," even though, as we have seen, the rhetorical model of form quite clearly subordinates it to content.

We have seen how this subordination contradicts other elements within formalism. But aside from what may be seen as an internal problem within that particular theoretical school, and despite its extraordinary popularity and its heavy use from the eighteenth century onward, there are many problems with the rhetorical view of form.[2] From the point of view of production, in the most obvious case of traditional poetic forms, it seems obvious that the form—the meter, the stanzaic arrangement, the rhyme scheme—must be at least provisionally chosen by the poet before the particular words are written to realize the form. Insofar as most of the articulate meaning is carried by the words, then, and insofar as the words are chosen to realize the form, poetic form comes into the poet's mind before the precise meaning—even if the theme is as traditional as the form. The form's demands take priority and exert a determinative force over meaning, since the originality of the poem in such cases is expected precisely in the area of specific meaning--the treatment of the theme—and *not* in the degree of compliance (or lack thereof) with formal rules set by tradition.

This is clearly the case with song lyrics within vernacular traditions. Popular ballads of the past and raps and country western songs of today are obvious examples. But then so are poems whose forms are in conscious imitation of those vernacular practices or are derived from them. These categories would cover a very large area in the history of Western poetry and probably much other poetry as well, though probably not all.

Furthermore, the poet's struggle to make good sense under the prior constraint of formal conventions contributes greatly to the effect of overdetermination observed by readers of a wide variety of poetry. An interesting and satisfying interpretation of a well-known poem almost invariably notes several lines of intersecting meanings among the words, and implies that all of those possible meanings are somehow intended. The richest poetic texts seem to be the ones that offer us

---

2. See Derek Attridge's trenchant critique of "imitative form," centered around Samuel Johnson's cutting parody of this critical method (1982, 287–88).

the most possibilities for such intricacies of meaning and for some coherency among them. Nor is this appreciation only modern—the assumptions of a coherent polysemy and an infinitely meaningful text underlie midrash, the oldest of Jewish traditions of biblical interpretation. And in poetry, this experience of coherent polysemy or over-determination seems directly related to the fact that word choice is to begin with not immediately determined by a simple message, but rather constrained by the nonmeaningful demands of form. Since the poet cannot simply use any word that would carry meaning across, there is always already a break between the simple message and the words actually used, a break or gap that opens the way for polysemy. The poem's words, furthermore, are simultaneously determined by the heterogeneous demands of form and message; thus every word gives the impression of having to be there and of meaning more than it appears to mean on the surface.

The priority of rhythmic form in the production of poetry was observed by the German Romantic poet Schiller, when he remarked that he composed poetry after the onset of a "musical mood."[3] We may wonder, however, whether the very example of Schiller might suggest a limitation in the notion of the priority of rhythm and therefore in the theory of the poetry as allegory of rhythm itself: Could this theory really be not so much postmodern as neoromantic? Might it work preferentially for romantic poetry? Does the same notion of the priority of rhythm have any relevant application to, say, the neoclassical poetry of the eighteenth century?

If we compare the famous poems and lines of, say, Keats and Shelley to those of Pope, it does seems as if the Romantics are at least much more obviously concerned with the *theme* of music. We have Shelley's

> Music, when soft voices die,
> Lives within the memory...

---

3. "With me the perception has at first no clear and definite object; this is formed later. A certain musical mood comes first, and the poetical idea only follows later." Quoted by Friedrich Nietzsche in *The Birth of Tragedy* ([1872] 1968, 49). This sentiment has been expressed by many other poets throughout history; most recently it found a voice in some remarks by the contemporary poet and novelist Vikram Seth in a radio interview.

and Keats's

> Where are the songs of spring? Ay, where are they?
> Think not of them, thou hast thy music too . . .

as well as the whole "Ode to a Nightingale." Indeed, Romanticism and the age of sensibility immediately preceding it went beyond the neoclassic "Horatian Ode" to make popular the greater ode and hymn as poetic forms alluding to Greek models that are presumed to have been musical. The Romantics, in short, seem to be nearly obsessed with the music of poetry. By contrast, heroic couplets in the age of Pope are devoted to topical social criticism, the exposition of moral philosophy, and satire. But must these observations mean that Pope, say, did not work with a musical paradigm of verse? Or rather, more to the point, does Pope's work defy the notion of the priority of rhythm over theme in poetry?

Certainly, as some of Pope's most celebrated lines make clear, Pope's conception of the relation between meaning and sound in poetry is strongly rhetorical:

> The *Sound* must seem an *Eccho* to the *Sense*.
> *Soft* is the strain when *Zephyr* gently blows,
> And the *smooth Stream* in *smoother Numbers* flows;
> But when loud Surges lash the sounding Shore,
> The *hoarse, rough Verse* shou'd like the *Torrent* roar.
> When *Ajax* strives, some Rock's vast Weight to throw,
> The Line too *labours*, and the Words move *slow* . . .
> ("Essay on Criticism," ll. 365–71; Pope 1965, 155)

But we also have from Pope's autobiographical comments the image of the young poet pacing back and forth in his chamber, reciting aloud his "numbers" until they attain the perfection worthy of the written word. How could such a poet *not* have the constraints of the heroic couplets in mind first, acting prior to the very sense of his message—the message that he would nevertheless succeed in uttering in such a way as to satisfy those constraints without any distortion of its sense? In fact, the project of making heroic couplets that manage as well to serve expressive rhetorical needs could be seen as a way of making an art that hides its artifice. This is a value in Western poetry of many periods, from the *sprezzatura* of the Italian Renaissance to the "language of the common man" of Wordsworth. Thus, in Pope, the *thematic surface*—the images and statements of the poem—are concerned not so much with the musical power of the lines as with the need to suppress the irrational in favor of the rationality and decorum of pure rhetoric.[4] At the same time, the audience anxiously awaits the close of each couplet as it manifests the wit of this voice of supreme reason, an optimistic voice, however sarcastic its immediate tone, which can reveal the underlying perfection of the order of nature as understood rationally.

There is an irony in such a poetic style, an irony that comes out in its predilection for satire. On the one hand, the triumph of reason over folly that informs the faith of this poetry is tantamount to the domination of the unruly body. Yet on the other hand, the rhythm of this poetry manifests the body not as unruliness but as the most perfect order, the order to which the rational sphere of the poem's statements and attacks can only aspire. So still, to a degree, we have a poetry that recognizes the ways in which the world of speech and ideas falls short of some sublime principle that is manifested physically in the poem—even if that same poetry tends to *represent* the body *thematically* as a source of corruption or a threat to order. We see something of this ambiguity in Pope's approach to nature, which can be viewed either as morally unregenerate or as the instance of divine order revealed in the world, a complete lack of affectation, as in the "Epistle to Arbuthnot." In a sense, we have two bodies: one the lower-class, unruly, vicious body that must be criticized thematically; the other, the perfect, orderly, natural body that responds to the perfection of Pope's rhythms. The wittiness of his couplets makes possible a perfect coincidence of this latter body with the intellect that constructs it.

---

4. In pure formalist terms, the predictability of heroic couplets may begin to become its own automatism. Pope is simply fighting the automatism imposed upon his language by the heroic couplet form by keeping a balance between the demands of rhetoric and rhythm—an automatism that to begin with results from an effort to defeat the automatism of ordinary speech by defamiliarizing it with the rhythm of poetic meter. These terms work as far as they go, but they do not come near the matter of the relation between poetic rhythm and the body, a relation I consider crucial.

But if these are feasible approaches to Pope (as well as Boileau and others), they still may place the satirical use of verse, the essay in verse, as something of a limiting case for the theory of poetry as telling rhythm.[5]

The cases of modern free verse and metrical experimentation are complicated as well. Here, the selection of a departure from tradition seems to be a choice made at the outset. If so, then rhythm would still have priority in composition, only in these cases rhythm takes the special form of a meaningful absence.[6] Whether rhythm has

---

5. It may be interesting to note that the Roman poet Horace claims in his *Satires* (or *Sermones*, as he more aptly calls them) that those works are *not poetry*—even though they are composed in dactylic hexameter, the high-style meter of epic. The term *poetry* Horace reserves for his *carmina* ("songs"), the *Odes* and *Epodes*, written in imitations of traditional ancient Greek lyric meters. The *Sermones* differ from these latter in style and theme as well as in meter. Horace's *Sermones* and *Epistolae* ("letters," also in dactylic hexameters) are the avowed models for most of Pope's verses in heroic couplets and for their analogues in the same period in England and France. The meaning of claiming in verse that that verse is not a poem is an intricate issue of both genre theory and literary history (and cultural and linguistic history) that is unfortunately too complex to be broached here.

My comments comparing Pope's poetry to the Romantics' may be placed in the context of Barthes's much more forceful opposition in *Le Degré zéro* between the two categories, by now fairly conventional in French literary criticism, of *classical* and *modern* literature ([1953] 1972a). For Barthes, a classical poet like Pope uses meter as a mere ornament to get across a message that is prior to any of the poem's language. By contrast, modern poets allow multiple messages to emerge accidentally from the mysterious polysemy of words. Thus, in brief, the focus in classical poetry is on the content, while the focus in modern poetry is on the form. Perhaps Barthes is right, but this analysis seems to me vastly to underestimate the depth and complexity of eighteenth-century (or French seventeenth-century) semiology as well as the continuities in poetry from that age to our own. In addition, Barthes seems to forget how richly polysemous and form and rhetoric conscious is verse of the seventeenth century and earlier. What better exemplifies the "density of the Word" ([1953] 1972a, 37) than Shakespeare's sonnets or the lyrics of Marvell and Donne? Here, as so often elsewhere, the problem is that the *critic*'s focus is exclusively on words and meaning, and so the rhythm of meter becomes a matter of mere decorum, ornament, or rhetoric. Yet Pope could have written prose and chose not to. How do we account for the fact that Pope's message is *in verse*?

6. In fact, a great deal of free verse actually has some kind of rhythmic pattern, often a prevailing strong-stress orientation of either two, three, or four beats per line, with enough regularity so that exceptions can be thought of as departures from a prevailing paradigm. Nevertheless, the arrhythmicity of "L = A = N = G =

priority in such forms of verse comes down once again to the question of the difference between poetry and prose—that is, whether these forms are poetry to the same degree as are the metrically strict forms against which they should probably be seen as meaningful departures. If relatively unmetrical poems are thought of as merely the most perfect rhetorical presentations of their meaning, the perfect "unity of form and content," then we must wonder how they really differ from prose, which readily makes equal claims to such rhetorical expressiveness, and therefore what meaning there is in calling them poems at all.

From the point of view of the reader, the rhetorical approach to poetic form poses the problem of undermining the difference between poetry and prose. Every claim that can be made for the efficacy of particular sound features in poetry in the presentation of the theme could be made just as well for prose—in either case, we are assuming that the transparency of the message is desirable, since otherwise effectiveness of presentation would be out of the question. Yet it is clear, at least in poetry that anyone would easily recognize as poetry (e.g., Shakespeare's sonnets), that the work is designed in such a way that transparency of the message is *avoided*. This same feature can at least arguably be demonstrated in all sorts of poetry, not only the metrically regular but various forms of free verse. If, conversely, we were to counter that metrical regularity—the repetition of certain sound combinations or qualities—were rhetorically effective only in the presentation of those certain themes that are specifically appropriate to poetry, we would be making two questionable assumptions: (1) that clear distinctions could easily and readily be made or found between themes that occur in prose and those that occur in poetry— an assumption that the history of poetry would seem to argue against; and (2) that the reader turns to Shakespeare's sonnets to find out what Shakespeare, or Shakespeare's speaker, has to say, rather than to read fine sonnets. But again, what Shakespeare's speaker has to say is precisely what could be (and always is in literary critical essays) *retold in prose*.

U = A = G = E poetry" and other modern and postmodern genres, at least as far as the ear is concerned, seems undeniable. Even here, perhaps arguments could be made for visual rhythmic paradigms, which can be associated indirectly with the rhythms of visual art in West African culture. See Thompson 1979.

Granted, in reading poetry, a certain reduction to prose is necessary; at a certain point in the reading process, the reader must demote the rhythmicity of the poem from the area of primary focus. Getting the meaning out of poetry generally first involves reading the poem as if it were prose. This, of course, is how most of us have been taught to read poetry, and it is a mainstay of the New Criticism. The problem lies in whether one stops there and goes no further. If one does, then poetry is merely a prose message with some formal baggage adding to its rhetorical effectiveness (at best) or merely distracting us from the message (at worst). Alternatively, one *returns* to the poem and becomes aware of the power of the poem's formal being presenting an experience of infinitude as compared with the limited meaning one has derived from the prosaic manner of reading. And one is simultaneously reminded of the sublime pleasure of reading poetry, the reason one has turned to poetry to begin with.

The problem with the usual way in which poetry is discussed and taught today (and even sometimes the way it is produced) amounts to a question of reducibility. As soon as we allow ourselves to speak of poetry as an effective presentation of the theme, we are asking for the replacement of the poem's signs with others of the same value, even while at the same time denying, as the New Critics would, the possibility of such replacement. All the features that add to rhetorical effectiveness can easily be summarized as such: the poem means x— but add extra rhetorical effectiveness. Such a theory would have no reason to privilege rhythm over any other rhetorical feature. And yet, as I have suggested, rhythm does have a certain primacy in the experience of the poem, at least in the case of those poems whose rhythms are audible, but perhaps even for others as well. Rhythm is not a trivial member of the class of rhetorical effects in poetry; rhythm is an important element in the definition of poetry, as the chief method whereby the reader's or hearer's attention is drawn to the physical material of the utterance and is thus divided between meaning and pure sound.[7] How we are then to understand the relation between form and meaning in poetry cannot contradict this definition by

---

7. In the terms provided by Russian formalism, we could say that rhythm is not only one of the important sorts of *differentia* in the genre of poetry but the *dominant differentia*. See Erlich 1981.

allowing form to collapse into meaning as a rhetorical aid in its presentation. Therefore we must find a means of understanding that relation other than the rhetorical model implied by the New Criticism.

At the heart of formalism's conception of the literary work of art, and especially of the poem, lies a basic contradiction. On the one hand, poetry is "self-directed speech"; as in the theory of poetry as allegory of rhythm, poetry is discourse that draws one's attention to its physical features as much as to its meaning. (Jakobson: The "set" is to the "message.") On the other hand, the formalists conceived of form along quasi-Aristotelian lines as a shaping or forming of the material, which was pre-aesthetic (Erlich 1981, 188–89). Like the New Critics (who borrowed many of their ideas), they insisted on the unity of form and theme. How could this unity be possible unless surface features are conceived as meaningful? And if this is the case, then in what way could the reader's attention be said to be directed toward the surface features? In other words, if the surface features are understood to be meaningful and therefore to contribute (rhetorically) to the message, then they are no longer "on the surface"; they immediately are taken to indicate something other than themselves. Either one can have pure sound, which does not indicate anything whatsoever and which has some effect to be discussed in terms other than meaning, or else one can have meaningful signs. One cannot pretend that the one is definitive and then define it by means of the other.

The greatest weakness in the Russian formalist approach to poetry, from beginning to end, is the failure to distinguish between form and rhetoric. When the formalists refer to the surface of the text or to its devices, they refer ambiguously to its patterns of pure sound and to its images, metaphors, and so forth. If by *devices* we also mean rhythm in poetry, then it becomes impossible to tell why rhythm should be particular to poetry and should not be found anywhere where forms are used to convey meaning—in prose as well. And yet the formalists seemed to agree that rhythm was the *dominanta* of poetry.

But there is another problem as well. It is possible, indeed necessary, to speak of a unity of rhetoric and meaning, precisely because the nature of rhetoric by definition is the use of signs to get meaning across. By the same token, it is just as necessary to maintain an opposition between form and meaning; for this is analogous to the opposition between signifier and signified in the Saussurean model of the sign—where they are only arbitrarily associated. To assert a unity between form and meaning is to collapse the two sides of the poetic sign, each of whose definition depends upon its distinction from the other. The signifier is what it is precisely because it *is not* that with which it is arbitrarily associated; likewise for the signified. Thus, while the formalists insisted on a unity between form and content (or material), on the one hand—a claim that only makes sense if form is reduced to rhetorical device—on the other hand, they observed how form follows its own laws and plays its own games, leading the formalists to resort to the notion of motivation to explain the presence of content at all. The two views of form, pure and rhetorical, are simply incompatible.

6

After Formalism: The Impasse of Rhetoric

In the last chapter, we saw how Russian formalism greatly contributed to our understanding of poetry in modern times by focusing on the opacity of language in poetry and especially on rhythm as the chief device for achieving this opacity. We have also seen, however, how formalism reached an impasse in resolving this insight with the need to find some appreciable relationship between form and meaning: in its attempts to do so, formalism would tend to slide into the view of form as a rhetorical device. The problems raised by viewing poetry according to a rhetorical model are worthy of further exploration, because they provide a crucial context for the significance of the theory of poetry as telling rhythm. For the present theory will attempt to address these problems precisely by offering a nonrhetorical model while still preserving a structural relationship between form and meaning. This chapter will review, briefly and somewhat polemically, the problems that the rhetorical model of poetry provokes. In addition, we shall see the beginnings of a way out of the impasse of rhetoric by means of the concept of the metrical *set,* a mental function of raised expectations with close ties to the physical experience of rhythm. The focus of this concept is thus on the effect of rhythm outside of meaning.

Throughout this discussion the question of what to make of rhythm is crucial. The problems raised by the rhetorical model will in following chapters provide the grounds for recourse to two other models. First will come Roman Jakobson's sophisticated stucturalist model, which issues out of formalism but which deals with the question of the relation between form and meaning in poetry in a more sophisticated way. The Jakobsonian model may be thought of

as an elaboration of the concept of the metrical set by means of his
"principle of equivalence." We shall then move on to the Nietzschean
tradition, which offers an entirely other and deeper way of seeing
the relationship between rhythm and meaning. The theory of poetry
as allegory of the sublime power of rhythm brings together insights
from both Jakobson and the Nietzschean tradition, as well as elements
of formalism itself.

Before we examine the problems inherent in the rhetorical model,
we must recognize that there is a sense in which poetic form *is* a
kind of rhetoric—in which, indeed, it is a system of meaningful codes,
which contribute to the poem's rhetorical configuration just as do
such stylistic features as level of diction and tone. That is, chiefly as
a genre indicator, a given poetic form, and more specifically a particular
meter, will condition the reader's or listener's reception of the content
of the poem. If a twentieth-century American writer composes a
sonnet in the Shakespearean form, one of the effects of this poetic
form is in fact an allusion to the tradition of Shakespearean sonnets,
going back to Shakespeare's own. The form in this case functions as
a sign of Shakespeareanness, as its denotation, and connotes the various
values associated with this category: tradition, Englishness, canonicity,
the aristocratic milieu, and so forth.[1] These connotations color the
reception of the poem's thematic content.

An extreme form of this connotative coloring can be seen in
Roland Barthes's comment on poems written in the traditional or
classical French form, the alexandrine. Such poems, according to
Barthes, can provide *plaisir* (pleasure) but not *jouissance* (ecstasy)—in
other words, and to use an older critical vocabulary, poems in this
metrical form can be beautiful but not sublime. Barthes's emphasis
in *Le Plaisir du texte* (1973) is on the personal, subjective response to
the text, but his position in that essay is continuous with that in his
Le Degré zéro de l'écriture ([1953] 1972a). Indeed, many of the French
theorists writing in recent times about poetic form—such as Barthes,

---

1. By connotation here I especially have in mind the concept of signification
found in the mythic signs analyzed by Roland Barthes in *Mythologies* (1957, 202;
1972b, 117). In the second essay, "Les Romains au cinéma," Barthes' speaks of the
"Romanness" (*romanicité*) connoted by the single lock of hair dangling over the
brow of every actor in older historical movies representing Roman antiquity, such
as director Mankiewicz's *Julius Caesar* (1957, 27–30; 1972b, 26–28).

Julia Kristeva (1984), and Henri Meschonnic (1988)[2]—are remarkably unanimous in their insistence upon the permanent loss of viability of classical forms since the onset of the modern (i.e., modernist) age. Kristeva writes of the "fetishism" of these forms, their reification of certain processes with which the rhythms of poetry should in general engage the reader's spontaneous participation. All of these writers seem to assume—without fully arguing it—a polemical stance that upholds modernism in poetic form and that rejects the classicism of traditional forms. Underlying this polemic, this modernist ideology, is a smooth and complete identification of traditional forms with their conventional associations, their connotative meanings.

But the effect of audible, metrical patterns cannot be reduced to the mere fetishism of convention. It may seem so reducible when a reader in the late twentieth century looks back to seventeenth-century French works in alexandrines, such as the tragedies of Racine, the comedies of Molière, the fables of La Fontaine, and the satires of Boileau.[3] But even in the first of these cases, say, Racine's *Phèdre,* the sense that there is some power in the pervasive repetitions, the poignant wordplays, and most of all the insistent rhythm—some power that escapes the category of mere "alexandrineness" even for the modern reader—and that sense of power is itself virtually inescapable. Indeed, if, as we saw earlier (chap. 4), insistent repetition has the effect of weakening meaning, then in the *Phèdre,* this power can be identified with fate itself, the great rhythm of the universe, which reduces the signs of individual will to the wailings of tragic pathos.

In the history (and current state) of English-language poetry, the inadequacy of the prevailing modernist view of traditional meters should be even more obvious to its readers. While recent theorists, such as Barthes ([1953] 1972a), Kristeva (1984), Easthope (1983), and

---

2. See also Meschonnic's collection of essays, *Les États de la poétique* (1985), especially "Les Sens de 'rythme'" (86–92) and "La Poésie est critique" (182–91). Noteworthy exceptions to this tendency are some works of Philippe Lacoue-Labarthe and Nicolas Abraham, to be discussed in later chapters.

3. Or, indeed, it may seem so reducible to one who has been brutalized by a certain system of education that provoked confusion between the artificial scansion of meter and meter itself (or its normal performance) and that seems to crush the life out of poetry for all but a few—as appears to have been the case for English students in the nineteenth and earlier twentieth centuries and perhaps for French students in the elite track to this day. For the former, see Steele, 1990, 7–8 and 58–68.

Todorov (1987), continue to support the revolutionary and liberating claims of free verse, of forms that result (it is claimed) from the smashing of restrictive conventions and that undo their fetishism, the poems that continue to play the most vigorous and active role in the *practice* of democratic movements are in fact traditional in form: the chants of picket-line marchers, the hypnotic rhymes of street raps, and the vernacular blues and ballad forms—both in their traditional forms and as modified in rock and roll lyrics.[4]

It may be objected that these modes of poetic expression are the products of the uneducated and should not be compared to their own favor with "high art" poetry nor even addressed by the same theoretical approach. To say so, however, would be precisely to fall into the modernist trap, to accept the modernist dichotomy between high and popular art uncritically, and to forget that those very terms were devised in order to legitimate and promote modernist art and poetry precisely by attempting to distinguish it artificially from the vulgar rabble—in short, it would be a failure to historicize modernist critical tastes. It must be owned that modernism's most overt rebellion was against the culture of the middle class, its conformity and its lack of imagination. But in effecting this rebellion, modernists tended not to sympathize with the underclass, but rather to take the pose of an elite hankering for a return to feudal aristocratic values. (Think of Yukio Mishima's private army, Ezra Pound's prophetic voice of fascism, and T. S. Eliot's high Anglican royalism.) Artifacts of underclass traditions were seen as an assault upon the power of the noble individual and were thus hardly different from middle-class commercialism or moralism. Vernacular art was imitated—how could it not be!— but often in an ironic tone as if to point up its vulgarity:

> O O O O that Shakespeherian Rag—
> It's so elegant
> So intelligent

> (Eliot 1970, 57)

Of course, the spirit of Russian formalist sympathy for futurist poetry does not fit this pattern well, since many of the formalists were

---

4. Timothy Steele (1990, 279–94) provides a cogent dissenting argument against the continued view of free verse as liberating in a conclusion that harmonizes well with the present arguments.

revolutionary leftists. In this regard, it is noteworthy that as Jakobson further developed his insights, he tended to shift toward a practice of including examples of poetry from all provenances, both high and popular, and in fact emphasized folk tradition.

In the present context, an effort to devise a *postmodern* theory of reading poetry and thus, in effect, to democratize poetry theory, Jakobson's combination of inclusiveness and sensitivity stands as a model. For the purposes of this book, a theory that works for a great deal of poetry of diverse provenances and class alliances is more powerful than a theory that succeeds only by narrowly circumscribing its scope on the basis of critical prejudice. Accordingly, the insistence among critics in recent times that traditional poetic forms are as a rule effete and passé, and therefore should be written out of theory altogether, may now be seen—ironically—as an elitist bourgeois view, limited by its own class provenance, and blind to what should be obvious in the poetic scene beyond the confines of that class.

Not that poetry experienced in a working-class milieu should now be seen as the exclusive province of theory either. Certainly, we cannot ignore the fact that iambic pentameter, as heroic couplets and as blank verse, does not prevail in such popular contexts, and that the form calls to mind a body of poetry available primarily through formal education.[5] But then, all rhythmic expressions are in part learned behavior, products of the education of the body that already experiences rhythms in some less pronounced way. Thus Celtic folk dances are full of triple meters, while Baltic rhythms include odd numbers such as fives, sevens, and even thirteens; West African rhythms both there and in Brazil and the Caribbean include brilliant and dense polyrhythmic counterpoints. No one can deny that rhythm is a culturally mediated human experience. The point is that pronounced rhythms are not verbal, are often learned directly through the body, and are usually immediately appreciated through an individual's body even if they are new to that individual.

And even given the relative upper-class provenance of nontetrameter rhythms such as iambic pentameter, one must also bring to mind such outwardly radical political poetry as Pablo Neruda's retelling of modern history in the Western hemisphere—from a Latin-American

---

5. See Easthope 1983 for the historical development of iambic pentameter in relation to bourgeois ideology and subjectivity.

perspective—in the ironically titled *Canción de Gesta,* a narrative poem
in consistent and elegant hendecasyllables (iambic pentameter), with
occasional rhyme.[6] The style of this work as well as the general
reception of Neruda in Latin America (and the popularity and prestige
of poetry and poets there) bespeak an audience that extends beyond
the ruling elite. The point is not that such conventional associations
do not exist or are not important. Rather, these connotative values
simply do not define the limits of even the most "conservative" verse
forms. A certain margin of less conventional, less controllable energy
persists, not only as pleasure but as power and ecstasy, in sonnets
and raps, in ballads ancient and postmodern, in blank verse and the
blues.

In thus juxtaposing such diverse traditions as the high-style sonnet
and the modern commercial rap, canonical blank verse and the popular
blues, I do not mean to undermine important differences. But wherein
do the differences lie? For too long, the assumption has been that
anything taught or read as poetry has no relation to popular musical
and dance forms—even though the poems themselves often affirm that
connection, overtly and repeatedly. Likewise, the assumption has been
that folk forms, sometimes sung by illiterate composers, could not
be worthy of contemplation and interpretation. But postmodernism
encourages us to understand that there is no rational basis for such
gross and unfair distinctions. It is probably more to the point to say
that, given the division of attention between the opaque and trans-
parent aspects of poetic language, between form and meaning, the
balance is different in different modes of poetry. Poetic traditions
whose connection to the popular musical idiom is more highly
abstracted, such as the highly literary forms (sonnets, blank verse,
etc.), may generally have the weight shifted toward the side of trans-
parency and meaning, with a greater emphasis on rhetorical play (puns,
anagrams, etc.). "Subliterary" folk forms may emphasize music more

---

6. Clearly, there is an ironic side to Neruda's form in this case: the form is thus
a sign, used ironically, to refer to the chanson de geste tradition. But surely a work
on such length and scope cannot be reduced to a single gesture of irony. If it were
so, the triumphantly clinching ironies in individual couplets that close chapters
would work against the irony of the form overall—one irony would work against
another, and the work as a whole would find little political sympathy in its readers.
This is far from the actual situation.

strongly over meaning. But these observations do not hold true in every case, and the differences in any event are subtle. They do not necessitate entirely different methods of reading. In every case, popular as well as literary, reference to an already existing formal tradition may have some influence on meaning; but it is equally true that such reference cannot exhaust the topic of the role of form in poetry.

Especially in dealing with canonical literary poetry in the academic setting, it is relatively easy to theorize about the effects of poetic form in relation to poetic meaning if we reduce the former to its aspect of mere convention. This is because such mere convention is itself already a meaning effect. This fact has probably given modernist theories of poetic form a special advantage in the academic context. (Here, as elsewhere, theory is in part the artifact of its conditions of production: academics are paid to find meaning in phenomena and to teach languages, so meaningful signs always tend to take priority over nonmeaningful but nevertheless powerful phenomena.) By contrast, it is more challenging, but also much more important, to begin to address the question of that other aspect of poetic form—the aspect of an energy that escapes the conventions of meaning. This latter task is important because it helps us to understand why people bother with poetry at all; it brings us much closer to the special properties of poetry than do exclusive considerations of rhetoric and convention.

In addition, the very fact that the rhetoric of modernism, with its tireless promotion of free verse, dominates discussions of poetic form today to the exclusion of other points of view represents an inherent contradiction within modernism: modernism is a rhetoric of liberation and novelty, but it has become the prevailing institution and is thus neither liberating nor novel. Meanwhile, the modernist tenets underlying poetry criticism are all but invisible: they are almost never questioned and not even recognized as particularly modernist or as serving any particular interest. These very facts should make us question the possible ideological grounds of modernism and attempt other approaches.

The reduction of poetic form to either mere rhetoric or to a mere sign or fetish: these tendencies can be seen, to a greater or lesser degree, not only in modern literary criticism and theory but in the treatment of poetry by linguists. Proceeding in part on the basis of the groundwork laid by the formalists—much of which, as we have seen, is still quite solid—linguists in more recent times either have continued to fall into the same conundrums or, at best, have indicated the need to move away from them. A number of linguists recently have devoted interesting studies to poetry, emphasizing in particular (as one might expect) either meter or the semantic issues surrounding figurative language. Of the latter studies, Lakoff and Johnson 1980, Lakoff and Turner 1989, and parts of Leech 1973 are noteworthy; figurative language alone, however, occurs in all kinds of verbal expression and can hardly be used to characterize poetry. Linguists have also turned their attention to meter, which has been used more successfully to define poetry, even in some cases to include some free-verse poetry. Linguistic discussions of metrics in this century are far too numerous for me even to give cursory consideration to them.[7] But these discussions do not tackle the problem of bridging the gap between such theories of metrics and the question of meaning. Some discussions do attempt to draw connections between meter and meaning.[8] But in order to do so, they must draw upon some theory of literary meaning or some approach, either original or already in place— and in this case, as in many others, the theoretical approach is either a version of the New Criticism, a rhetorically oriented reader-response criticism, or some combination of these. In other words, meter is still treated as a *rhetorical device*.

An important exception to this rule, and an essential book on many counts, is Derek Attridge's *The Rhythm of English Poetry,* which presents the concept of the metrical set within a theoretical discussion of the effects of rhythm in poetry. After a superbly persuasive presentation of a new method of metrical analysis for English poetry, Attridge devotes a chapter to "The Functions of Poetic Rhythm." Here, Attridge begins by distinguishing

> between *semantic* and *nonsemantic* functions of poetic rhythm, that is, between those aspects which operate within the same space as the meanings of the poem's words, whether to reinforce, limit, expand, or modify them, and those which operate on some other

---

7. Attridge 1982 gives an exemplary overview of metrical theories, both in earlier times and in the more recent history of linguistics. See esp. part I ("Approaches"); the second chapter is on modern linguistic approaches.

8. Such as Fussell 1965 and several of the essays collected in Freeman 1981.

axis, contributing to the total working of the poem but not to
its "meaning" in the narrow sense. (1982, 286)

Attridge's distinction is somewhat similar to my own between the
rhetorical model of poetic form, in which form merely assists in the
expression of content, and some other model in which the power of
rhythm would be foregrounded. (The types of effect he places within
each category result in a somewhat differently organized analysis.)
Diplomatically, Attridge acknowledges both semantic and nonsemantic
functions of poetic form as legitimate at the outset. Of course, we,
too, may admit the appropriateness of occasionally noting the use of
form within a poem for obviously rhetorical purposes; but such rhe-
torical uses cannot, as we have seen, be allowed to characterize the
function of poetic rhythm.[9] Accordingly, in commenting on what he
calls the "iconic functions" of poetic rhythm—that is, local and
noticeable rhetorical effects in which the rhythm palpably imitates
some thematic idea (such as the regular beating of a clock) or emblem-
atically represents some concept (such as using triple rhythm to rep-
resent the Trinity)—Attridge points out:

> Precise imitation of the external world offers the reader little more
> than amusement and admiration, like realistic bird-calls in a sym-
> phony or *trompe-l'oeil* details in a painting; the most powerful
> rhythmic functions in verse exist at a less conscious level, and it
> is an attractive thought that the rhythms of poetry may harness
> those deeper dispositions towards the patterned retardation and
> release of energy that underlie the expression of emotional states,

---

9. Readings of the semantic effect of a poetic rhythm can reach a degree of
subtlety and complexity that edges beyond the rhetorical model altogether. Such is
the case, for example, in John Freccero's brilliant commentary (1983) on the meter
Dante devised specifically for the *Divine Comedy*. For here, the ultimate significance
(i.e., semiotic value or semantic effect) of the meter is to dramatize an idea that
itself is utterly unrepresentable: the beatific divine vision. Freccero also points out
a parallel between the mystical paradox of representing divine truths and the literary
paradox of writing a (fictional) autobiography, a narrative that accounts for the
steps leading up to the writing of that account, in which the closure of the account
would contradict the nonclosure of the writer's life while writing the account.
Likewise, the mystical paradox involves the clash between the temporality of poetic
rhythm and the eternal present of the divine.

whether they are interpreted as features of an imagined speaker's utterance or as an affective colouring without a personal locus. (1982, 299)

It is something like this second group of functions that calls our present attention here; these are what Attridge calls the "affective functions" of poetic rhythm.[10] Attridge observes that the emotional energy involved in the affective functions of rhythm are not necessarily specific or even clearly definable:

Although for convenience we can refer to these characteristic patterns and dispositions of energy as *affective rhythms,* we must remember that they lie deeper than specific emotions and mental states (as is indicated by the powerful but unparticularised emotional quality of much nonprogrammatic music). (1982, 298)

We must note in particular Attridge's reference to the undifferentiated emotional power of abstract music—a comparison that will be useful to keep in mind throughout our discussion. Interestingly, Attridge also points out that the kind of poetry most likely to evoke this power is precisely not modern free verse but verse that follows more traditional, regular rhythms (300), which he logically and persuasively associates here and elsewhere with the biological rhythms of neural and muscular, bodily activity (76–79).

Given the fact that poetic rhythm appeals relatively directly to the body, we might say that the other features of poetry such as images and ideas, by contrast, appeal more to the mind. Thus we may draw an analogy: poetic rhythm is to poetic meaning as body is to mind. This analogy rests upon the traditional body/mind dichotomy of Western metaphysics, which is hardly unproblematic and which has been subject to many powerful critiques. For our purposes, though,

---

10. Because Attridge's lines of distinction are drawn differently from mine, Attridge conceives of these "affective functions" in somewhat more narrowly emotional sense, and thus includes them among the semantic rather than the nonsemantic effects (1982). The latter term is only reserved for the more abstract aesthetic functions of causing the poem to appear as a coherent whole and of causing language itself, through poetry, to be defamiliarized (in the formalist sense) and made freshly striking.

the mind may temporarily be distinguished from the body as the aspect of the human being that deals in symbols and symbolic manipulations. Yet these symbolic manipulations themselves may be seen as ways of attempting to make sense out of the world in which the body lives—indeed, in which the mind lives insofar as it is part of the body. To return to poetry, then, we may consider reading the ideas and images of a poem as, in like manner, attempts to make sense out of the physical being of the poem—an aspect of the poem that, itself, as we have seen, is not exactly verbal, since it is not a sign at all in the semiotic sense, that is, not a meaningful sign for anything.

Let us consider what is at stake in the reader's apprehension of the rhythm of poetry itself—for how the poem then makes imagistic and rational sense out of its rhythmic energy will be experienced by the reader as the poem's representation of the reader's very experience in reading the poem. The apprehension of rhythm involves a richly complex combination of imagination, learned behavior, physical or quasi-physical activity, a mental and physical predisposition or readiness to interpret certain cues the right way, a process of self-correction, adjustment, and confirmation, and rapid learning. To be more precise, rhythm is principally a *physical experience,* either in the sense of a bodily movement or of an imaginary readiness for or recreation of bodily movement; but it is made possible in part by a degree of *mental focusing, expectation, readiness, conscious recognition, and will.* To this latter, more mental side of the complex interaction of rhythm, which is probably far too complex ever fully to be defined, Attridge applies the term *set,* a term that has come into fairly common use in linguistics. The metrical set bridges the gap between mind and body in the experience of poetic rhythm.

The metrical set enables the reader to perceive the rhythm in the poetry that engages that set. The poem makes it possible for the reader to raise certain expectations, which it then may or may not perfectly fulfill. But what expectations are these? How do we define that aspect of poetry that engages the reader's set? The work of the linguist Roman Jakobson provides an elegant and very effective theoretical model to describe what we expect to find in poetry, once our set to poetic rhythm has been engaged. A consideration of Jakobson's theory in addition will give us some insight into the central problem, the problem of how poetic rhythm is related to poetic meaning.

7

Roman Jakobson's Structuralist Model

The metrical set is the mental condition that makes the experience of rhythm in poetry possible. But since the metrical set is mental, learned, and thus culturally mediated, might it serve as a clue to lead us out of the rhetorical model of the relation between poetic rhythm and meaning, and toward some other, more satisfactory model? Roman Jakobson's theory of poetry, centered around the "principle of equivalence," serves to elaborate on the nature of the metrical set and at the same time to begin to make connections between rhythm and meaning that are not rhetorical.[1] This chapter will focus on Jakobson's contribution to the possibility of such a nonrhetorical treatment of poetic rhythm. Near the end of the chapter, I shall venture a further development on the basis of Jakobson's insights that provides justification for my own model of poetry as allegory of the effect of its own rhythm. As I suggested in chapter 1, the reader already well familiar with Jakobson's theories may wish to skip ahead to that discussion.

Jakobson's approach may be understood within the context of

---

1. Jakobson uses the word *set* with a slightly different meaning from that of Attridge and other linguists. Jakobson suggests that it translates the German *Einstellung* (1960, 353), presumably meaning "attitude" or "approach" (with *zu*, "toward"), and thus the emphasis is on how the set *focuses* one's attention on one or another aspect of an utterance—such as its meaning as a transparent conveyor of meaning ("context") or its physical shape as an opaque object ("message"). I find my own use of such terms as set, context, and message clearer in relation to today's critical discussions, and I hope that it will not cause undue confusion that I therefore use them differently from Jakobson, while attempting to explicate Jakobson's theoretical structure in my own terms.

Russian formalism, a movement in which Jakobson was active early
in his career. Several of the formalists tried to overcome the pitfalls
of thinking of poetic form as a rhetorical device to express poetic
meaning by observing correlations among various strata of poetic
language, including sound, rhythm, and syntax. This approach would
relate form to meaning without subordinating one to the other. Roman
Jakobson eventually crystallized this notion of poetry in his essay
"Linguistics and Poetics" (1960) with his well-known principle of
equivalence, a theory whose elegance signals its place in the emergence
of structuralism out of its formalist roots. For Jakobson, the principle
of equivalence, the mental process involved in parallelism and com-
parison, as well as in contrast or opposition, characterizes the language
of poetry *at every level,* not only in the repeated elements of metrical
organization and the repeated sounds of rhyme and alliteration but
also in the repetition or contrasting of images, themes, and meaning.

Jakobson describes poetic form as the "projection of the principle
of equivalence from the axis of selection onto the axis of combination"
(1960, 358)—that is, the expression of the principle of equivalence
(e.g., one iambic foot is equivalent to another, or one noun phrase
is equivalent to another) applied to the progress of temporal phenomena
in language (whether purely auditory: one metrical foot follows
another; or more syntactic: one phrase follows another). The principle
of equivalence is the kind of thinking that normally governs the
selection of one word over other words for a particular meaning,
while a quite different kind of thinking governs the placement of one
word after another and makes syntax and logical order possible. In
poetry, the principle of equivalence is allowed to govern both the
selection *and* the combination of elements to form the sequence—the
line, the sentence, the stanza, and so on.

Take for example the first line of a well-known nursery rhyme:

Jack and Jill went up the hill

This line has a total of seven syllables. We mean by this that the
procession of connected sounds that makes up the line as spoken aloud
can be divided up very easily and intuitively by a competent English
speaker into seven units. While the individual sounds that make up
the various syllables obviously differ, the abstract notion of *syllable* is
such as to make all the units equivalent to each other—otherwise they

could not be counted together. The syllable is the lowest stratum of organization of the verse line. Next we note that the stress pattern of the line follows a regular alternation, which can be represented by S and W, for strong and weak stress, respectively, written above the line:

S   W   S   W   S   W   S
Jack and Jill went up the hill

Here, every S syllable has the same value for the purposes of meter as every other S syllable, and the same for the W syllables. Note, for example, that we could rearrange the order of the words, and the metrical effect would be pretty much the same:

S   W   S   W   S   W   S
Up the hill went Jill and Jack

Insofar as there are only two elements whose combination constitutes the metrical pattern, S and W, and they alternate evenly, we could easily group the syllables into units of two each, which would still be equivalent—except for the last one, or the first one, depending on how we form our units.

Either:
{S W} {S W} {S W}{S}
Jack and Jill went up the hill

or:
{S} {W S} {W S} {W S}
Jack and Jill went up the hill

It really does not matter which way we group the syllables. The point is that, either way, except for the lone syllable on either end, the units of two syllables each are again equivalent to each other.

"Jack and Jill" is a familiar children's song chanted to a musical beat. Each line takes up four beats. The beats fall, generally, on the strongly-stressed syllables (S), while the weak (W) syllables take the offbeats, the musical time between the beats. Together these form an even alteration. Following Attridge's innovative example, I shall use the symbol B under each syllable that takes the beat. The offbeat syllables may be marked *o* for offbeat or simply (as in the next example) left unmarked. Beats and offbeats are respectively different from *S* and *W* syllables for a few reasons. Sometimes, a *W* syllable may take the beat if it is surrounded by other equally weak or even weaker syllables, and the same goes for *S* syllables taking offbeats when in certain environments. In other languages, such as French and Japanese, the distinction between *S* and *W* may not obtain, and yet there may be a musical dimension to meter. *S* and *W* are markings of the stress attributes of syllables in languages such as English that have meaningful stress distinctions, whereas beats and offbeats are attributes of the musical structure underlying a meter and realized in a particular verse instance by means of the particular words with their stress features. In the second and fourth lines of our example "Jack and Jill," moreover, we may follow the musical tradition to organize these beats in a way that we would not expect by simply reading stress patterns of the words: *wa-ter* and *af-ter* (which rhyme to reflect an archaic pronunciation) are sung so that both syllables take beats—the first syllable in each case is drawn out to take the time of both the beat and the following offbeat, and the final syllables, unstressed in normal speech, are artificially given musical beats.

Jack and Jill went up the hill,
B   B   B   B

To fetch a pail of wa- ter;
   B   B   B   B

Jack fell down, and broke his crown,
B   B   B   B

And Jill came tumbling af- ter.
   B   B   B B

Note, in addition, how the first and third lines are arranged around the beat in the same way; that is, there are *S* syllables on each beat and *W* syllables between beats, but neither before the first beat nor after the last. Likewise, in the second and fourth lines, we begin with a *W* syllable before the beat, and there is no *W* syllable between the third and fourth beats—in both lines, the last word is disyllabic and is stretched out musically to cover two beats, even though the second syllable is not really stressed in ordinary speech. Thus on a higher level of complexity than that of beats in a line, we find equivalence between the first and third lines and between the second and fourth. Another way of saying this would be to say that the combination of the first two lines follows the same pattern as the combination of the second two lines, lines 3 and 4. The whole stanza is then composed of two metrically equivalent halves. Finally, each stanza is equivalent to every other stanza following the same metrical arrangement, as is the case in "Jack and Jill." Thus on successive hierarchical levels, the pure sound of the poem is structured on the basis of the principle of equivalence.

In all of the foregoing observations, moreover, we could say that the principle of equivalence, which in normal prose or ordinary speech would apply only to the selection of elements, applies in poetry to the combination of elements in sequence as well. In ordinary English speech, for example, as we utter each syllable, we naturally select whether the syllable should be given stress or not relative to the surrounding syllables, in order for each word to be pronounced correctly, and also in order that the whole sentence will have the right stress pattern to get across emphasis and even the type of sentence (declarative, imperative, etc.). This process is mostly or entirely unconscious for the competent English speaker, but if we could bring it to consciousness, we could say that a basic principle governs the process, whereby at each moment we must select the appropriate amount of stress from all the possibilities. Insofar as all the various possible stress levels on any given syllable are just that, possible, they are equivalent, but only one is the most appropriate for selection, based upon the requirements of the word and of the meaning of the sentence. By contrast, in poetry, the equivalent strong stresses and their contrasting weak stresses are selected to begin with to conform to a pattern that extends over time, and words must be found that will make sense with that pattern. Here, stresses are not so much selected from a pool of possibilities as determined to form a pleasing combination at the outset. Hence, "the projection of the principle of equivalence from the axis of selection to the axis of combination."[2]

---

2. Obviously, the term *axis* suggests that Jakobson conceives of any utterance as something that could be mapped out on a two-dimensional graph, more or less

The principle of equivalence can manifest itself not only in the organization of sounds but also in the formation of rhetorical devices. In its normal, prosaic manifestation, the principle of equivalence makes possible the figure of speech known as metaphor, since a metaphor is a word used to mean another word by virtue of some implied similarity or comparison (equivalence) between the two meanings. What is strikingly useful about Jakobson's simple and yet powerful formulation, then, is that it thus touches on both form and meaning in poetry and therefore begins to suggest some principle of relation between the two. That is, the kind of thought process that goes into the creation (and comprehension) of a metaphor governs the making of poetry *at every level*—not only in the selection of words as signs of meaning but even in the stringing together of sounds or grammatical structures. Comparability is the rule everywhere: one poetic image is to be compared with another in order to decipher its meaning; one rhythmic unit is to be compared with another in order to perceive the general rhythmic pattern; and, indeed, one rhyme word is to be compared with its complement in order both to mark patterns of regular sound and to suggest patterns of association in meaning.

To turn to our example of "Jack and Jill," we can see the principle of equivalence at work on the level of meaning in the form of likeness between the subjects as well as a contrast between the events in the first two lines and those in the second half of the first stanza:

Jack and Jill went up the hill
To fetch a pail of water;

---

like a curve in mathematics. I have chosen to explain Jakobson's principle first in relation to the phonology of meter, even though it is easier to imagine it working in the area of words in a sentence. Thus each word is selected from a pool of "equivalent" words—they don't all mean the same thing, but they all could take the same syntactic place in the sentence and are thus grammatically equivalent. This could be thought of as the vertical coordinate of the word. The horizontal coordinate is the word's place in the sentence—subject, object, and so on—where, obviously, selection from a pool of grammatically equivalent possibilities is not the guiding principle, but rather a necessary place along a determined sequence. Of course, types of sentences are selected from a pool of possibilities—shall we begin with the subject, or with the object?—but once that selection is done, within the sentence itself, the word order is a sequence of dissimilar elements, whereas each word is the product of a selection from among similar elements.

Jack fell down and broke his crown,
And Jill came tumbling after.

In the first half of the stanza, likeness is immediately drawn between the two subjects, Jack and Jill—in sound, in syntax, and in the roles they play in the tale. *Jack* and *Jill* are both monosyllables beginning with *J*. A small contrast is felt between the hard stop *ck* at the end of *Jack* and the continuant liquid *ll* at the end of *Jill*, a contrast easily associated with the notion of difference and complementarity between the genders—that is, on the level of what is represented, or meaning. In the first line, the goal of motion is given: the hill. In the second line, the goal of the action is announced: a pail of water. *Hill* and *pail* both end in the liquid *l*; furthermore, since Jack and Jill are together—their togetherness is emphasized by·their sharing a single verb—the compound noun that they form together also ends in *l*. The entire action represented in the first two lines is held together by the repeated terminal *l*, according with the general harmoniousness of the action, the similitude of Jack and Jill.

While likeness seems to rule the first two lines, contrast, the other variant of the principle of equivalent, dominates the second half and the stanza as a whole. Whereas in the first half, Jack and Jill are together, they are separated in the second half—not only physically within the tale, but syntactically as well: Jack falls down in line 3, and Jill tumbles in line 4. Even the verbs mark this contrast: a single verb for the compound subject "Jack and Jill" in line 1 versus two different verbs, one for each distinct subject, in lines 3 and 4. Of course, the characters are going *up* in the first half and *down* in the second, a process that seems to accord with the pattern of tension and release associated with binary musical forms such as this two-part stanza. If at this point we were applying the theory of poetry as telling rhythm rather than Jakobson's principle of equivalence alone, we could say that the up-and-down action in the stanza's tale actually *represents* allegorically the tension and release created by the binary musical form. But for Jakobson, images do not allegorically represent form or rhythm; Jakobson's point is simply that all levels of the poem's language, from sound to syntax to images to events, fall under the sway of the principle of equivalence.

Let us concern ourselves first with a few of the implications of Jakobson's theory as it bears strictly on poetic form alone. Later we shall consider the idea of the principle of equivalence, or metaphoric thinking, as the link that joins form to meaning.

First of all, Jakobson's theory suggests a certain position of the reading or listening subject in relation to the poem. Jakobson presents poetry as the complete or intentionally incomplete fulfillment of generic expectations raised by conventional formal cues. The principle of equivalence applied to combination, since it describes the experience of formal conventions—and, indeed, of poetic forms of a great variety, from Walt Whitman's repetitive anaphora to the variations of Russian folk chants—is understood as a determination in the reader's reception of poetry *prior* to the poem itself. In other words, the reader comes to the poem ready to look for forms of equivalence, whether they be more or less consistent replications of familiar conventions (from prior reading or listening) or whether they be new and thus require discovery. This sense of the poetry reader's expectations conforms to the notion of literary form set forth by Kenneth Burke—"an arousing and fulfillment of desires" ([1931] 1964, 1)—but it is at once more empirically descriptive and more rigorous. The reader of any language, poetry or prose, is always ready to understand semantic selection in the context of the principle of equivalence. In poetry, this expectation is merely extended to an area where it is not otherwise ordinarily encountered, manifesting that act of violence that Jakobson had noted in a much earlier paper as characterizing poetic language: poetry is "organized violence exercised by poetic form upon language" ([1923] 1973, 40). We have seen earlier how mere repetition can work against the ability of language to mean, to function transparently to convey meaning. Jakobson furnishes us with a more subtle analysis of this process. Clearly, the application of the principle of equivalence to the process of combination in language produces that certain relative opacity that characterizes poetic language over prose and other forms of discourse. The more the meaningful combination of words is subordinated to the requirements of equivalence in field of reference, syntax, or sound, the more opaque the language becomes.

The reader of poetry must infer and then apply the specific manifestations of the principle of equivalence and is therefore required to approach the poetic text with a combination of eagerness to organize elements into a coherent pattern and flexibility to give that pattern up for another one, should it prove inadequate to accommodate important elements of the poem. A Jakobsonian reader thus enters the hermeneutic circle on the level of form rather than theme, or rather on both formal and thematic levels at the same time.

Thus when we read the opening line of Wallace Stevens's "Blanche McCarthy," say, we must select a few tentative inferences about both meaning and meter, which will then either be confirmed or contradicted by further reading.

Look in the terrible mirror of the sky. . . .

(1971, 3)

In the area of meaning, we note that the opening verb is an imperative, and we might thus infer, on the basis of the combination of that verb form and the fact that the title of the poem is a proper name, the concept of this poem as a speech delivered to the person named, instructing her to look. On the metrical level, we have either ten or eleven syllables (depending on whether *terrible* is scanned as three syllables or syncopated as "terr'ble," since this kind of contraction is historically common, especially around a liquid or nasal consonant) and either four or five relative peaks of stress, depending on whether we read the meter as strong stress (*Look, ter-, mir-,* and *sky*) or stress syllabic (the four already indicated plus *of*). The experienced reader is likely to let the weight of tradition guide her toward inferring a stress-syllabic meter, especially since the resulting iambic pentameter is often used for contemplative utterances and for speeches in a somewhat high or formal style. (In other words, inferences about meaning affect inferences about meter and vice versa.) Now, given the pattern of stresses in the first four words, "*Look* in the *ter*rible," the reader might think that the poem will be organized in a triple meter, with a pattern beginning with a beat and followed by two offbeats—what used to be called dactyls. But this inference would come into trouble by the time the reader reached the word *the* in "mirror of the sky," because she would now have to have three offbeat syllables in a row, crammed together between the beats, which is not generally allowed in stress-syllabic meter—one of the unstressed syllables, usually the one in the middle, is promoted to take the beat so that the general pace of syllables can be preserved. This would give the reader a beat on *of*, conforming to the hypothesis made just before of five relative stress peaks. This gives five beats and a pattern of binary alternation in the latter portion of the line, which supports the reading of the whole line as iambic pentameter. Given this inference of the meter, both the inversion in the first foot (i.e., beginning with a stressed syllable, followed by two unstressed syllables, followed by the normal alternating pattern—see Attridge 1982, 175–86) and the syncopation of *terrible* are allowable variations within the paradigm of iambic pentameter, but, as variations, they make it more desirable for the reader to seek confirmation of her initial inference of the metrical paradigm.

All of the foregoing steps, as well as those to follow, are conditioned by initial, often unconscious, expectations. The very shortness of the lines of print in the poem, for example, and the regularity of number of lines as well, offer a very strong signal that one should "think poetry" in making further inferences. Here as elsewhere, the inference may be wrong, but the more confirmation it receives, the more powerful will have to be the contrary piece or pieces of evidence—and the more the reader will feel disoriented at the moment when her constructed theory falls apart.

The second line of the poem then helps to confirm, or at least does not contradict, both inferences, and it thus allows them more strongly to condition the reading of the rest of the poem:

> Look in the terrible mirror of the sky,
> B   B   B   B   B
>
> And not in this dead glass, which can reflect . . .
>   B   B   B   B   B

But here, too, the iambic pentameter pattern is realized only with a variation—in this case, the displacement of stress from the fourth to the fifth syllable. The fact that the first two lines have what can be understood as allowable variations of iambic pentameter, but that the variations are different and take place in different places in the line, contributes further support to the initial inference of the meter. The third line likewise has initial foot inversion and a relatively weak stress on the sixth syllable, but the fourth line, completing the quatrain, has no inversion and thus secures the metrical inference for the rest of the poem, barring any later contradiction. And such a contradiction would have to be, by this point, very drastic in order to upset the paradigm already drawn.

Look in the terrible mirror of the sky
  B   B   B   B   B

And not in this dead glass, which can reflect
  B   B   B   B   B

Only the surfaces—the bending arm,
  B   B B   B   B

The leaning shoulder and the searching eye.
  B   B   B   B   B

All in all then, despite a few variations (which are allowable by tradition), the four lines correspond with the paradigm of iambic pentameter, and the reader thus feels reassured that the paradigm should hold throughout the poem. Again, this process is rapid, fairly smooth, and generally unconscious in the trained reader—including, even, the reader who has not learned the rules formally but has read and heard a great deal of iambic pentameter verse, such as the frequent viewer of Shakespeare plays. The process can be brought to consciousness if necessary, however, as it must be when the apprehension of meter is taught formally.

The foregoing description of the reader's (or listener's) experience of the poem's meter is not to be found in the published work of Jakobson. Rather, it is necessarily true in order for Jakobson's own description of poetry, the projection of the principle of equivalence from the axis of selection to the axis of combination, to work. In other words, Jakobson's formulation, and structuralist definitions in general (of which Jakobson's is the example par excellence), imply a phenomenological conception of the subject. This subject is not to be artificially separated from its object (in this case, the poem), for each is actually constituted in the process of interaction with the other. Neither the reader nor the poem can be considered in its pure state, the one separated from the other. Among other things, this phenomenological conception of the subject of poetry suggests that the apprehension of meter is neither a matter of mere social convention nor one of biological nature—even though perhaps both of these determining forces play some role. Meter is felt in the body or in a kind of virtual-body readiness; but the experience of metrical rhythm is made possible by virtue of a kind of rapid guessing, learning, testing, and further learning process. And it is the outcome of this process that linguists today such as Attridge describe as the metrical set. Granted, the tools to perceive enough in series of sounds to acquire a metrical set are bequeathed to an individual as part of the social baggage that may come under the heading of convention or common knowledge. But the set is then developed anew in each experience of poetry. The more experienced the reader of poetry, the better prepared she is to develop a metrical set to a wide variety of different kinds of poetry, even poetry structured according to varying principles—such as, for example, not only stress-syllabic but pure syllabic, strong-stress, or quantitative verse, or free verse structured by syntactic parallelisms or other less acoustic principles. The set is not the same thing as the actual experience of rhythm; it is the culturally mediated function that enables us to find rhythm in poetic meter and to nurture and sustain our ability to respond physically to rhythm.[3]

The set to rhythm in an individual is very powerful. In both music and poetry, it is often powerful enough to enable the hearer to normalize momentary irregularities without noticing them, and even to misread irregularities or complexities that go beyond the set. (For example, Western listeners may misread the complex rhythms of Balkan dance music to make them fit simpler Western norms.) Indeed, we must note that most people seem to feel, and to behave as if they feel, a strong and compelling *desire for rhythm* as one of the most fundamental urges in their experience.

All of this implies the fact that a paradigm of expectations plays a vital, if unconscious, role in the experience of the reader or listener of poetry. And the somewhat limited generality, or "universality," of that paradigm or set is precisely what makes possible the particularity of each realization—each poem and each moment within a poem. At the same time, the paradigm of expectation is one of the elements of nonlinguistic non-sense against which the meaning of a poem as a linguistic utterance is placed in continual tension.

---

3. Ultimately, it is impossible to say to what degree rhythm is a product of nature or nurture, nor should it be important, so long as we can agree that rhythm is experienced either as a physical sensation or as a kind of virtual sensation—that is, a state of readiness for that sensation or an imagining of it. Rhythm is probably like almost every other human activity: it seems to result from the culturally mediated activation, disciplining, and cultivation of inherent possibilities.

Thus the notions of the metrical set and the principle of equivalence deepen our sense of the poem as an utterance with two dimensions, the meaningful and the meaningless. Unlike prose, which usually aims at a transparency of meaning, a poem is designed to draw attention simultaneously to its thematic referents, or signifieds, and to the formal qualities of its signifiers—first among these being meter or rhythm. Meters and other formal devices may acquire conventional associations over a period of common use, imitation, and development. But these conventional associations do not exhaust all the possible effects of a formal device any more than do the connotations previously attributed to a word exhaust all the possible meanings of the word now or in the future. And in addition to these matters of *meaning,* form in poetry always retains a residue of the nonsemantic, the (at least for now) meaningless or nonreferential. Much of the experience of hearing or reading a poem, as we have seen, is in feeling the tension between the opaque, or nonsensical, or nonsemantic form and the more or less transparent thematic meaning.

Having returned to this basic conception, we also find ourselves anew at the problem of the relation between these two dimensions in the poem, the meaningful and the meaningless. Jakobson's principle of equivalence allows the two dimensions to have a certain coherency in that they are both governed by the same mental process, the process of comparison and contrast, the same mental function involved in the making of metaphors and related figures of speech such as verbal irony, allegory, simile, antithesis, and paradox.[4] In Wallace Stevens's "Blanche McCarthy," if we now look at the whole poem, we can readily see how metaphors dominate the central theme of the poem:

Look in the terrible mirror of the sky
And not in this dead glass, which can reflect
Only the surfaces—the bending arm,
The leaning shoulder and the searching eye.

---

4. It is interesting to note, then, the frequency with which these particular figures of speech—especially metaphor, irony, and paradox—come up in New Critical readings of poetry. But of course, this prevalence was never fully explained by a rigorous theory, nor was there any accounting for the difference among specific poems, given this apparently universal tendency.

Look in the terrible mirror of the sky.
Oh, bend against the invisible, and lean
To symbols of descending night; and search
The glare of revelations going by!

Look in the terrible mirror of the sky.
See how the absent moon waits in a glade
Of your dark self, and how the wings of stars,
Upward, from unimagined coverts, fly.

The "terrible mirror," at least in a fairly simple reading, is obviously a metaphor, for which the referent is given—"sky." This metaphor contrasts with the literal mirror, which is metaphorically a "dead glass," suggesting that the "mirror of the sky" is somehow "alive"— again, metaphorically. The basic message of the first stanza is that Blanche should turn away from her absorption with her image in the mirror and turn toward the "mirror of the sky"—so it is clear that the sky, too, has some metaphorical significance, wherein it is opposed to the mundane mirror. How precisely we must read that metaphor is not necessary for us to determine at this point.

The directive given in the first stanza is repeated in the other two stanzas, as is made clear by the repetition of the first line with its imperative verb, *look*. What follows the first line in the second and third stanzas each is an elaboration of the notion that is most mysterious and therefore most in need of elaboration: the nature of the "mirror of the sky." Thus all three stanzas are equivalent to each other, are, in a sense, metaphors of each other, all telling the same message in variant forms. In the first stanza, what follows the directive is an elaboration of the mundane mirror, the opposite of the "mirror of the sky," and metaphorically equivalent to the former term, although its real name, "mundane mirror" or "mirror of the ground," is not and need not be given. In the second and third stanzas, the material following the first line in each case is metaphorically equivalent to "mirror of the sky" and thus metaphorically equivalent to the material in the analogous position of the other of the two stanzas.

Clearly, this poem is another ready example of the working of the principle of equivalence in the combination of sounds—such as the metrical form—as well as in the combination of images and ideas. What we have, in a sense, is a model where form is no longer reduced to the role of the rhetorical expression of ideas, but where both form and ideas are together subordinated to the mental process of comparison and contrast, the mental process typified by metaphor. This notion succeeds in escaping from the rhetorical model of poetry, but only within narrow limits.

How, for example, do we assimilate the overall interpretation of the poem, its summary meaning, to the principle of equivalence? In "Blanche McCarthy," we could say, for simplicity's sake, that the poem is generally a directive not to look at the external self, but to look within for the truth. The poem recommends introspection. However we further explain this message—and certainly we can; the poem is very deep—it is not important here. The point is that we can come up with a single statement of that sort to give what New Critics used to call the poem's "plain sense." But what is this single statement (or directive) equivalent to? How does equivalence work with it?

The principle of equivalence governs the various levels of the *language* in which the poem is written, but it does not govern the poem's *meaning*. We still have a dichotomy between content and form, where form, the language of the poem, expresses meaning while it observes the principle of equivalence—a principle that itself appears to have nothing to do with the meaning. Thus while within the narrow perspective of the poem's language alone, form is no longer subordinated to any other element as a mere rhetorical flourish, given the wider perspective that includes an interpretation of the poem's meaning, we can see a return of the problem of rhetoricized form. This problem is evident in Jakobson's own readings of poems, in which the pleasure of riddle solving, which I believe is one of the things people enjoy in poetry, is generally lacking. The interpretable meanings of poems in Jakobson's readings seem to be simple, patent, and unproblematic; it is their means of expression that is of interest— that is, their rhetoric.

Another way of putting this problem is to ask, Why *should* the poem say what it says using the principle of equivalence? What does this principle have to do with what it is saying? Granted that it governs the poem's language, once it says what it says—but why that particular choice? How, once again, is the poem's form related to the poem's meaning?

In summary, on an abstract level, there are only three possible ways that we can understand the relation between form and content. The first and most common is to make form an expression of content, thus to reduce form to rhetoric, as the formalists did—while also registering some appropriate discomfort with this approach. Secondly, we may have form and content be completely unrelated to each other. This we see in the formalist notion of motivation, but the formalists themselves seem to have recognized the fact that having these two sides of the text be so unrelated is theoretically unsatisfactory. Jakobson seems to have pursued this path, limiting his discourse almost entirely to the language of the poem, conceived empirically, and thus leaving interpretation out altogether. Once interpretation is brought into the picture, this second model of the relation between form and meaning collapses into the first—form becomes rhetoric. This slide into rhetoric is due largely to the very absence of a coherent theory of interpretation that would form an integral part of Jakobson's formalism: if meaning is ignored, it must be primary and thus not subject to question or analysis the way that form is. Thus even for Jakobson, the principle of equivalence seems to characterize the "poetic" way of saying something that could also be said otherwise. Finally, the possibility of seeing the content as a representation of the form, while it may at first seem the most unlikely, is in fact the only one that relates the two terms without collapsing them into each other. It is therefore the approach taken here.

But it is also possible to support the procedure of taking content as the allegorical representation of form—that is, of the effect of rhythm—by logically extending Jakobson's own theory. For Jakobson, poetry is governed by the principle of equivalence, applied to the temporal (combinatorial) axis, *on every level* of language—phonological, syntactic, semantic, rhetorical, thematic. But might we not also conclude that there is an equivalence *among levels*? That is, insofar as each level is governed by equivalence—that is, a mental process that concerns comparison and contrast, or the question of likeness—all the levels have in common, or *alike,* their subordination to the principle of equivalence. Thus audible or palpable rhythm, which is on the phonological level, is in some way equivalent to metaphor. Wherein would lie this kind of equivalence? Metaphor and sound are *not* symmetrical from the point of view of the reader who is interpreting the poem—and, after all, a satisfactory theory of poetry must enable the reader to satisfy the demand to interpret. Metaphor is accessible to interpretation as a meaning effect; rhythm is not. Thus the images and ideas in poetry, which tend toward the metaphoric because of their own conformity to the principle of equivalence, must be equivalent to the rhythm in their own way—that is, by means of metaphoric signification. A sustained series of such metaphoric signs indicating what they are equivalent to—that is, the poem's rhythm—amounts to an allegory of rhythm. But of course these same metaphors are also limited by the fact that they are, as meaning effects, utterly heterogeneous from the phonological level of poetry. They must metaphorically represent something that is itself unrepresentable insofar as it is not a meaning effect and cannot really be substituted with words. Thus the meaningful level of poetry is an allegory of rhythm *as the sublime,* the unrepresentable—a telling (of) rhythm.

This extension of Jakobson's theory should be seen as reader oriented, even though it is put in terms that suggest an "objective" orientation toward the text in isolation from the reader. It is *because* the poem has evident patterns of phonological and syntactic equivalence that the reader more or less automatically expects semantic equivalences. It is because a poem's images are expected to be either lined up with each other as equivalent restatements or as contrasting terms—despite the fact that, on the literal surface, they may not seem to have much to do with each other—that the reader has a feeling that the poem as a whole, whether explicitly or not, works as a metaphor for something unspoken. And it is because of the poem's elaborate complex of equivalences and congruences that those images make sense if they are taken as metaphors specifically for the effect of the rhythm, something whose proper name is left out not only for the pleasure of the riddle but because it simply has no name.

The foregoing comments serve to extend Jakobson's theory so that it does more than simply point out a guiding principle on all levels of the poem, assuming that the reader *already knows* what the poem says without difficulty. This extension provides a basis for *finding out* what the poem says—for interpreting poetry.

At the same time, these comments suggest a way of bridging the gap between Jakobson's phenomenological approach to poetry and another tradition of thought in the history of philosophy and criticism, the Nietzschean tradition. Just as my description of poetry as an utterance with two dimensions, sense and nonsense, owes much to formalism, my model of poetry as an allegory of the power of its own rhythmic form emerges out of the dualistic system of Dionysus and Apollo presented in Friedrich Nietzsche's *The Birth of Tragedy*. *The Birth of Tragedy* suggests, in its own somewhat allegorical manner, a compelling view of poetry in which form is no longer seen as an aspect of the poem's rhetoric, and in which poetry therefore has something to offer that is utterly distinct from other modes of discourse. A number of thinkers in psychoanalysis as well as philosophy, moreover, have continued to use and develop the basic structure set up by Nietzsche. A brief examination of Nietzsche's text will enable us to perceive the outlines of that structure. It will also facilitate our drawing together the contributions of Nietzsche and the post-Nietzscheans to help us to articulate the theory of poetry as telling rhythm and to shed light on its historical context.

Part 2:
The Nietzschean Tradition

8

Meaning, Form, and the Nietzschean Sublime

Let us take a brief survey of the ground we have covered thus far. Poetry may be thought of as a kind of utterance opposed to prose, and therefore as a principle end point on a spectrum opposite prose, with various texts falling between the two principles. What distinguishes poetry in this abstract sense is the tendency toward opacity of language. Actual poems divide the focus of the reader's or listener's attention between the communicative content of their language and the physical features and effects of that same language. What contributes the most to this focus on the physical, nonmeaning substance of language in poetry is rhythm. For an interpreter of poetry who wishes to preserve a sense of the distinctness of poetry from prose— who wishes to avoid letting his or her interpretation obviate the whole point of the poem being a poem—the question will be, how can these opposing sides of the poem, the meaningful and the rhythmic, the transparent and the opaque, be related to each other? How can they form a unity, without one of them, especially the opaque side, disappearing into triviality?

The New Criticism would tend to disregard rhythm altogether, except for moments when it is taken as a rhetorical device to aid in the dramatic representation of the meaning of the words. The model here is rhetorical: a poem is a message, employing various devices, including rhythm, to get the message across as effectively as possible. Russian formalism attempted to avoid the opposition between form and content that would lead to this rhetorical subordination of rhythm, but it was not wholly successful in coming up with an alternative model of sufficient rigor. Emerging out of Russian formalism, however, was Roman Jakobson's structuralist model. Here, rhythm and meaning are both products of the same fundamental process, which is called the principle of equivalence, and which is associated with metaphor in rhetoric and with meter in form. But does this still mean that we start with a message, which is then subjected to the principle of equivalence to produce a poem? If so, then why should one bother converting a message this way? We seem still to be only a few small steps away from the rhetorical model, which fails to explain why meaning and poetic form should occur in the same utterance when prose might do the same thing more efficiently. This is especially true considering how difficult the metaphoric language of poetry sometimes is. Why go to all that trouble to get a message across?

To answer this question, I turn next to the theory of poetry of Friedrich Nietzsche, as expounded in *The Birth of Tragedy*. For Nietzsche, the relation between meaning and rhythm in poetry is not rhetorical at all. Poetry begins not with a message, which is then clothed in the garb of metaphor and verse, but with rhythm itself, which is then translated, as it were, into metaphors to make sense out of it. This theory may seem surprising or counterintuitive at first, so I shall explore it in some detail here. It turns out to be an extraordinarily powerful model of poetry, one that has had a strong influence on many later theorists—not only of poetry, but of language and thought in general—including psychoanalysis. These influences amount to a Nietzschean tradition, which forms a historical context for the present theory, poetry as telling rhythm.

Of course, Nietzsche's work predates that of Jakobson by some eighty years. But my presentation up to this point has intentionally not followed a chronological order. Rather, I have hoped to trace a line of internal logic in the exploration of the opening questions on the nature of poetry and ways of reading poetry. The theories presented hitherto have been more closely connected to what a contemporary reader might recognize as fairly close to his or her actual reading experience. We have come to a point now, however, where in order to answer our further questions, we must look toward a theory that at first will seem less empirically based. In the following chapters, more recent developments of the Nietzschean tradition—psychoanalysis and the theories of Julia Kristeva and Philipe Lacoue-Labarthe—will offer analogues and contributions to the theory of poetry as telling rhythm.

In order that we might appreciate the usefulness of Nietzsche's insights for the question of how form and meaning in poetry can be related, let us begin by further articulating for ourselves the possible relations between form and meaning in abstract terms. Aside from the concept of poetic form as a mere rhetorical device, we may see the relation between meaning and form (especially meter) in two distinct ways, each to be taken up in turn: (1) The form alludes to a specific formal tradition and to certain ideas associated with that tradition. Poetic meaning (images and ideas) allegorically refers to or comments on that tradition or its associated ideas. (2) The form is, beyond its traditional associations, an unreadable physical effect (rhythm and sound). The images and content of the poem attempt to read or rationalize the unreadable—or rather, to assign meanings and associations to the experience of unreadability itself. These two possible constructions of the relation between meaning and form in poetry by no means exclude each other. In fact, together they may have an ironic effect, where the rhythm of the poem is first seen as merely an allusion to a tradition, and then the degree to which its energy escapes the definition of mere tradition is revealed. Behind the familiar charm of the old-fashioned iambic pentameter lies the sublime power of a physical beat. The revelation of that sublime power ironizes the very idea of conventionality associated with a traditional meter, while at the same time it renews the immediate effect of the rhythm.[1]

Although form and meaning are often connected in both of these ways in any given poem, let us examine each way individually.

1. The form alludes to a specific tradition and to certain ideas associated with that tradition, and poetic meaning (images and ideas) allegorically refers to or comments on that tradition and its associations. As such, the form is itself a sign with a definable *meaning,* although the meaning is connotative and not denotative. This meaning depends on the mediation of conventional social codes. The overt images and thematic content of the poem can then be read as a representation, allegorical or otherwise, of the tradition and associated ideas invoked by the form, or as a comment upon them.

---

1. For an example of how rhythm's escape from social definition ironizes its own traditional association as a recognizable form, see my article "The Unreadable Black Body" (1990).

The meter of the Wallace Stevens poem quoted in the last chapter is iambic pentameter, which is one of the most prestigious traditional meters in English. The meter is often used with the high style and generally for formal speeches, narrative, and contemplative utterances—in, respectively, the dramatic, epic, and lyric modes. "Blanche McCarthy," an isolated, brief, somewhat timeless utterance addressed by a nameless speaker to a named recipient, fits generic expectations of the lyric mode on the thematic level. The presence of rhyme and the quatrain stanzaic arrangement supports the idea that this is a lyric poem. Thus the association of iambic pentameter with the personal statement and the contemplative mood, as well as with, say, Romantic-age lyrics in that same mood (such as, for example, the hortatory "Ode on Melancholy" of John Keats), would come to mind.

How do the poem's images and ideas work as a representation of or comment upon the associations attributed to its meter? The image of the mirror is one of the most traditional Western symbols for literary representation (mimesis) since Plato. The phrase "the mirror of the sky," being a literal impossibility, is clearly a kind of metaphor (catachresis), which is contrasted with the literal mirror, "dead glass," in the next line. Thus Blanche McCarthy is encouraged to do an act that involves taking the mirror in its figurative sense, as well as figuratively gazing into it. It makes sense to say that the speaker is encouraging Blanche to read, or to compose, poetry—that is, to find herself in the mirror whose possible representations are as infinite as the sky. This interpretation is confirmed, if not made obvious, as the poem continues:

> Look in the terrible mirror of the sky
> And not in this dead glass, which can reflect
> Only the surfaces—the bending arm,
> The leaning shoulder and the searching eye.
>
> Look in the terrible mirror of the sky.
> Oh, bend against the invisible, and lean
> To *symbols* of descending night; and search
> The *glare of revelations* going by!
>
> Look in the terrible mirror of the sky.
> See how the absent moon waits in a glade

Of your dark self, and how the wings of stars,
Upward, from unimagined coverts, fly.

(Emphasis added.)

If we put to use Jakobson's theoretical observation that the principle of equivalence governs both the combination of sounds (as form) and the combination of ideas (as content), we may draw an equivalence between the mirror of the sky, the symbols of descending night, the glare of revelations going by, and the absent moon waiting in the glade of the dark self. Clearly, we are talking about the revelation of something from within the listener's mind by means of symbols and images. The poem is full of images of making poetry: the listener is encouraged to join the speaker in the enterprise of poetry.

And of what kind of poetry, might we infer, is Blanche encouraged to join in the making? Contemplative lyric poetry, the kind of poetry in which revelations are made out of the dark self and symbols and images are searched for what they tell us. In other words, it is the very kind of poetry to which the meter alludes through its traditional associations. The speaker has already joined in the chorus of that tradition in his own way. This is how he knows enough to tell Blanche that the mirror is "terrible," and yet to urge her to look into it, since the very process of looking into it is also *making* it (as opposed to the real mirror, which is already made and "dead"), and that double process of making and searching in poetry is vital. The process of poetry keeps a tradition alive by renewing itself and the tradition.[2]

---

2. The notion that the content of the poem may be commenting on the ideas associated traditionally with its own metrical form has already been suggested by A. R. C. Finch 1993, with reference to Emily Dickinson, and separately by Marcellus Blount 1989, with reference to Paul Laurence Dunbar and Henrietta Cordelia Ray, two nineteenth-century African-American poets. In both cases, there is an issue of the appropriation of metrical forms—respectively, the iambic pentameter line and the sonnet—that because of the weight of tradition are associated with power and prestige and with the class (gender and race) of people who have held that power in the literary realm: wealthy white men. But neither author goes beyond the idea of the metrical form as a sign, albeit not directly verbal, for certain social values. Neither author raises the possibility that there is also a certain excess of energy generated by poetic rhythm that exceeds the social values assigned to a given form, and that the poem may address that excess as well.

2. Aside from its traditional associations, the formal rhythm of
the poem, as mentioned earlier, is that aspect of the poem that makes
its appeal directly to the body—as does rhythm in music. If this
aspect of form is to be taken as a sign, it is a sign for the absence
of definable meaning, a sort of zero grade of meaning. In other
words, the rhythm of a poem is a sign for its own unreadability
as a sign. But such a proposition is unnecessarily complex. It is
much more convenient simply to think of rhythm not as a sign at
all, but as the nonsignifying aspect of poetry; to borrow words from
Archibald MacLeish, rhythm is the aspect of the poem that does
not mean, but is.[3] The images and content of the poem are an effort
to address this power of the rhythm to escape definition.[4] An analogy
can then be drawn, as already noted, between poetic rhythm and
the body, and between poetic meaning and the social meanings that
are attached to the body (such as value-laden constructs of race,
gender, and sexuality) but that always fall short of the totality of
the real body. As suggested by our brief readings of "The Tyger"
and "John Henry," there is always a margin of unreadability or
inexpressibility about the real that defeats construction, and poetic
meaning may make use of that margin of unreadability in order to
perform (rather than to state) the inadequacy of social codes of value.

---

3. "A poem must not mean, but be." MacLeish's statement is additionally famous
because it is quoted by Cleanth Brooks in his well-known essay on Keats's "Ode
on a Grecian Urn" in *The Well-Wrought Urn* (1947). Nevertheless, although Brooks
quotes this line, its relevance to his approach is never made clear. On the contrary,
his concern seems to be with meaning rather than being—although, of course, the
exact difference is never articulated with any precision or rigor. I believe that
MacLeish's maxim offers an insight along the lines of the theory presented herein,
and that this insight eluded those practitioners of the New Criticism who paid
little or no attention to theory.

4. I defer for another day the question of whether a given rhythm can mean
something in a way that does not rely upon purely conventional associations in
the manner of a regular sign. Think of Plato's "natural" association of the Dorian
mode with desirable social values—but is this not a matter of mere convention?
One might well argue that triple meters are naturally lighter, more cheerful than
duple meters, and therefore are better suited to nursery rhymes. Even in that case,
however, it makes much better sense to note that triple meters place language under
even narrower constraints than do duple meters, differ more sharply from ordinary
speech, and therefore push the poetry more strongly in the direction of pure,
nonsensical, sound patterns. See Attridge 1982, 100–102.

Elsewhere, I have argued similarly, on the basis of readings of poems by Harlem Renaissance poets Claude McKay and Countee Cullen, that this very unreadability may be used as part of the poem's larger system of codes in ways that can be understood not only aesthetically but psychoanalytically and ideologically—as a sign for the real human being's resistance to the socially produced reading of signs associated with gender, race, class, or other politically meaningful codes (Aviram 1990).

The irreducible element of unreadability in poetic form can be identified with the principle of Dionysus presented by Friedrich Nietzsche in his *The Birth of Tragedy*, and, indeed, the relation between poetic form and meaning we have been pursuing matches up rather neatly with Nietzsche's dyad of the somewhat allegorical figures, derived from Greek myth, of Dionysus and Apollo. Nietzsche introduces these two figures by observing that "in the Greek world there existed a tremendous opposition, in origin and aims, between the Apollinian art of sculpture, and the nonimagistic, Dionysian art of music" ([1874] 1967, 33).[5]

It must be said that this contrast between Apollo and Dionysus in Nietzsche is not always so neat. Perhaps in an effort to be true to the concepts actually associated with the respective gods in ancient Greek culture, Nietzsche observes that Apollo, too, is a musician. He then differentiates the two kinds of music by suggesting that Apollo concentrates on rhythm, while Dionysus prefers melody and harmony. This makes no sense at all in relation to the more general opposition Nietzsche builds between the two principles, especially as they are supposed to be seen in the making of poetry. Although it is true that poetry in antiquity was hardly separated from sung music, we know that the Greeks, like some modern poets, would *set their poems to music,* so obviously the two must be distinct, especially in terms of the melodic realization. Yet when grammarians read the poetry in its written form, and when we read it today, we can readily see how rhythm already operates in the poem aside from its hypothetical musical

---

5. I use the Walter Kaufmann translation throughout, which follows Nietzsche's second edition (1874). The original reads: "In der griechischen Welt ein ungeheurer Gegensatz, nach Ursprung und Zielen, zwischen der Kunst des Bildners, der apollinischen, und der unbildlichen Kunst der Musik, als der des Dionysus, besteht" (Nietzsche 1984, 25).

setting. Any attribution of melody or harmony to the poem would necessarily use those terms as mere figures of speech.

In effect, Nietzsche uses the terms Apollo and Dionysus in two quite different senses. On the one hand, the two are allegorical figures. Dionysus here represents the musical element of poetry altogether, and especially its rhythm; while Apollo represents the images in which poetry speaks. The relation between them is what makes poetry possible; neither can really exist in isolation. On the other hand, Nietzsche also speaks of the two as different types *of musician*. This idea, superimposed on top of the initial allegory, that each god is a different type of musician or poet contributes to Nietzsche's overall argument in moral philosophy and therefore to his immediate, polemical purpose. But at the same time, when Nietzsche thus speaks of Apollinian as opposed to Dionysian music, he threatens to undermine his own allegorical use of the same terms. The typological sense, while it may serve a purpose in a moral context, does not contribute as much to an analysis of how poetry works as the more abstract idea that each god represents a different aspect of the same poem.

Let us then concentrate on this more abstract system. The contrast goes further than that between the visual and the auditory. While Apollo is associated with the pleasant imagery of dreams and with the cool pleasure of contemplating those images, Dionysus presides over intoxication (*Rausch*)—wild, uncontrollable, even dangerous—an intoxication that one does not contemplate but in which one is compelled to participate. And beyond music and intoxication, Dionysus offers a profound truth—a truth that, we soon discover, is so powerful as to overwhelm us if we confront it directly, face to face. We are protected from the insanity that this intoxicating truth would provoke in us in its undiluted form by a *veil of illusion* spun by Apollo.

What is this unbearable and yet ecstatic truth? Nietzsche explains it in two different ways, and the relation between the two is up to us to infer. Initially, the truth is that our very individuality as perceiving subjects, and the individuality and discreteness of everything in the world that we perceive, is in fact a product of the very veil of illusion for which the Apollinian principle is responsible. In other words, the potentially overwhelming truth is that the "real reality, behind all this show of appearances" (to borrow Walt Whitman's phrase), is a kind of nothingness, a primal unity, having no space, time, or other mode of individuation. Indeed, in the relatively recent terms provided by Derrida, there is nothing outside the text—not, however, in the sense of a *vacuum*, but rather *no thing*—no entities that could be identified as such, since the very process of identification requires such things as subjectivity and perception. In the Derridean view, these functions are aspects of the "text"—the sign system—in which we live and breathe, insofar as we are *we*. Our identities and the identifiable individual entities around us are constructs made possible, according to Nietzsche, by the veil of illusion, or, according to Derrida (in a slightly less tragic tone), by the system of language.[6] Nietzsche is not to be credited with utter originality for this perception either, since it comes directly from Schopenhauer, and it is also prevalent in a variety of very ancient philosophical systems, including Buddhism and Jewish mysticism.[7]

Indeed, the core of Nietzsche's system, a *representational* relation between the Apollinian and the Dionysian, is easily traced to Schopenhauer. Yet Schopenhauer reserved this sort of insight, not for his discussions of poetry, which tend to fall into the rhetorical approach to poetic rhythm, but in his comments on music. In poetry, for example, Schopenhauer speculates that rhythm and rhyme encourage "blind consent" and a sense of "conviction" on the part of the reader with respect to the content or message of the poem, since they fulfill expectations of sound patterns in an orderly, predictable

---

6. This is not offered as an interpretation of Derrida's theories of the subject and language. I bring Derrida in for brief comparison in the hope that his rigorous and now-familiar concepts may help clarify Nietzsche's basic framework, insofar as Nietzsche and Derrida share some fundamental philosophical traits.

7. On Nietzsche's debt to Schopenhauer, which he only rarely acknowledges and in later comments repudiates, see Soll (1988), who traces Nietzsche's indescribable primal unity, through Schopenhauer's will, to Kant's thing-in-itself (109–10). The notion that the subject of speech and thought is an illusion that divides up an originally undifferentiated world—a world that, by definition, exceeds the capacity of speech to define or describe it—this notion is hardly limited to Buddhism. Rather, it is prevalent in many, if not all, mystical traditions, including Cabala (which is probably a powerful influence in Derrida's thought), and may even be thought of as the essence of mysticism: the idea that the most fundamental reality is beyond the reach of language, and that the desire for wisdom is the subject's yearning for this reality wherein it is no longer a subject at all.

way (1966, 1:243–44). But in section 52 of *The World as Will and Representation*, Schopenhauer has comments on music that are much closer to Nietzsche:

> It arises that our imagination is . . . easily stirred by music, and tries to shape that invisible, yet vividly aroused, spirit-world that speaks to us directly, to clothe it with flesh and bone, and thus to embody it in an analogous example. This is the origin of the song with words, and finally of the opera. For this reason they should never forsake that subordinate position in order to make themselves the chief thing, and the music a mere means of express-ing the song [i.e., words], since this is a great misconception and an utter absurdity. Everywhere music expresses only the quintes-sence of life and of its events, never these themselves, and therefore their differences do not always influence it. It is just this universality that belongs uniquely to music, together with the most precise distinctness, that gives it that high value as the panacea of all our sorrows. Therefore, if music tries to stick too closely to the words, and to mould itself according to the events, it is endeavouring to speak a language not its own. (1966, 1:261–62)

We can see here, in the relation between the music itself and the words of a vocal piece, something close the relation between, respec-tively, the Dionysian and the Apollinian, and, in terms of my own theory, between the rhythm of poetry and the verbally expressed images and ideas that attempt to construct it as something socially meaningful but that fail before the sublimity of an energy that is het-erogeneous to the world of signs. Earlier, in section 34, Schopenhauer also speaks of "los[ing] ourselves entirely in [the] object" (1:178), an ecstatic emergence from normal subjective thought, comparable to the Dionysian moment. But although the "universality" of music seems close to Nietzsche's "primal unity," Schopenhauer also speaks in this passage as if music expresses *affect,* or subjective emotional energy. In this section, Schopenhauer also defines music as a representation of the will—and thus still, fundamentally, an image.[8] In Nietzsche's case,

---

8. Several thinkers since Schopenhauer have continued to propose a concept of music as representation rather than strictly as the object of verbal or imaginary

music may also be taken to represent, but for Nietzsche this represen-
tation is less a mimesis than an intimation, a fleeting and partial man-
ifestation of the primal unity.

The first way, then, in which the Dionysian truth appears in
Nietzsche is as a revelation of the fundamental nothingness that under-
lies everything, including subjectivity itself. Here, perhaps, is one of
the most basic differences from Schopenhauer, for whom the underlying
substrate of the individuated universe is the will. Although the will
is, in fact, prior to subjectivity and therefore a sort of primal unity,
the emphasis is not on its nothingness. That nothingness at the core
of being is more closely allied to mystical traditions, both Buddhist
and Jewish—although it would be surprising indeed to find Nietzsche
acknowledge a connection to the latter.

The second way that Nietzsche presents Dionysian truth is by
reference to the Greek myth of Prometheus and the Hebrew myth of
Adam's and Eve's eating of the fruit of the tree of knowledge of
good and evil in the Garden of Eden in Genesis. The point of both
myths, for Nietzsche, is—to put it simply—the recognition that, after
all, *we create the very God or gods who create us.* In other words, it is
the awesome recognition that we create our own reality and in this
sense are responsible for our fate. One can readily see how this frightful
recognition does indeed inform the catastrophic turn in many, if not
all, of the well-known Greek tragedies—Oedipus's recognition that
he has brought on the plague upon Thebes and the fulfillment of his
own dire prophecy, for example; and hence the powerful sense of
dramatic irony so prevalent in Greek tragedy, where the tragic character
awaits the falling of the illusions protecting him or her from the
knowledge of his or her own crime and fate. We can furthermore
infer the connection between this recognition and that presented
initially: we create our own reality insofar as we construct our own
subjectivity and therefore our own world. Nietzsche is by no means
an idealist: the world is real, but it is an indistinguishable (and thus
meaningless) primal unity until subjectivity, meaning, and value are
assigned to it by a creative process of construction—which is also a

---

representation. These include Nicolas Abraham, for whom rhythm represents affect
(see chap. 10); and Susanne K. Langer, in her "On Significance in Music" (1951),
for whom music expresses the "form of feeling," though not any particular feeling
itself.

process of illusion. Thus the Apollinian illusion has, apparently, two functions: to make possible the construction of subjectivity and the life of the individual, and to sustain that life by protecting us, most of the time, from recognizing or remembering that our individual lives were to begin with made—*by us*—out of whole cloth.

Nietzsche tends to speak of the primal unity represented by Dionysus as also a "primal contradiction" and a "primal pain." These terms may possibly make sense if they are taken to describe the latter paradox: we create the gods who create us, and our very lives as individuals are constituted by our failure to recognize our own part in the construction of our fate.

Nietzsche's notion that the veil of Apollinian illusion is necessary to protect us from the horror and danger of the Dionysian primal unity appears to be in some measure an unnecessary and excessive element in his argument. We can only speak of the Dionysian insofar as we are speaking subjects, that is, products of the veil of illusion. Indeed, the terms Dionysus and Apollo, being allegorical, illustrate the vacuity of language itself even more clearly than other, ordinary words, since they obviously do not quite mean what they are—as figures of speech, they always indicate something else, something elsewhere, missing from themselves. *Dionysus* in this sense is not immediately a danger so much as simply a name, assigned by Apollo, for the absence of Apollo. Thus, it would seem, we need not even concern ourselves with matters of danger and protection: if we are able to perceive and recognize such a thing as the Dionysian principle, as such and under that name, then we are in fact dwelling amongst the illusions woven by Apollo. The one principle cannot exist without the other; we either have both, or we have none—and are not even ourselves.

There is, however, at least one possible way in which Dionysus represents more than merely the Apollinian name for the primal absence of Apollo—that is, one way in which Dionysus is a *positive* principle. This is true insofar as there is a positive desire for the primal unity—indeed, a powerful drive, the obedience to which produces an element of pleasure. Even as we have a great desire to be and to develop ourselves, and to know ourselves, to maintain and to enlarge the empire of our individual subjectivity, we have at least as strong a desire to lose ourselves, to become part of something larger in which we are nothing, or, in Nietzsche's image, a drop in the ocean. This is the urge not only to listen attentively to music, but to clap hands, to dance, to embody and thus to *become* the music, and to become one with all the others who simultaneously express its rhythms with uncanny unity.

Thus, although the Dionysian principle may not be *perceived* and *recognized* in its essence, since those processes would require the Apollinian subject and its veil of illusion, this does not mean that one cannot have some *experience* of the Dionysian, firsthand, in certain realms that are not in language, nor that one cannot in fact register a yearning for the Dionysian or an imaginary, Apollinian, representation of the Dionysian from within the realm of normal, linguistic subjectivity. These Dionysian moments, so to speak, are the only occasions we have to transcend the doubts that language imposes upon us, doubts as to whether we understand each other and are understood, doubts that seem to sentence us to a tragic solitude that we feel continually at the core of our experience. The drive to be relieved of this solitude and of everything else that comes with it—alienating social codes of value and standards of behavior, pressures, and demands—finds eloquent testimony everywhere, from the crowds that flock to rock concerts to the groups of men and women laborers singing wistful work songs as they toil. The pleasure of rhythm transcends all boundaries—class, nationality, and race—and even, in the feeling of the subject of poetry in his or her ecstasy, the boundary between the living and the dead seems to fade.

Hence Dionysus is always represented as beautiful and seductive, always, of course, in association with the intoxicant wine over which he presides. One the one hand, Dionysus appears in ancient literature as dangerous because he demands utter surrender and abandonment to his power, derangement, annihilation of the social self.[9] Yet on the other hand, Dionysus is attractive, delightful, and quite irresistible, resembling no other god so much as Eros.

In using the term *drive,* I am consciously invoking comparison

---

9. Nowhere is this more obvious, of course, than in Euripides' *The Bacchae*. Yet according to Nietzsche, this dramatization of the conflict between rationalism and the cult of Dionysus is something of a special case, a sort of return of the repressed after the Athenian turn toward scientific rationalism symbolized most clearly by Socrates' banishment of poets from the republic in Plato's *Republic*. The images of Dionysus presented in Ovid's *Metamorphoses,* although written much later, were based on Greek legendary sources and perhaps might be used to help corroborate the salient features of the god's figure in Euripides' late play.

with modern psychoanalysis. But, in contrast to Freud's system of
two drives, here we have both the drives of Eros and of death combined
into one. The death drive for Freud (*Beyond the Pleasure Principle* [(1920)
1961]) is a drive to return to the origin of life in inorganic matter,
a virtual metaphor for Nietzsche's drive to return to the primal unity
out of which we were constituted as subjects. The drive to Eros, by
contrast, is the urge to join with others and to become a part of
something larger than oneself—which we have seen also as an attribute
of the attraction to the primal unity. So, whereas Freud's dualism
places psychic life between two conflicting drives, Nietzsche places
the world under a different dualism, that between, on the one hand,
the single drive that anticipates a combination of elements of Freud's
two, and, on the other hand, the symbolic representation of the drive,
which simultaneously expresses and obscures it, and which, indeed,
constitutes it as such, insofar as neither drive nor representation would
exist without the other.

Although the drive to Dionysian unity, which is also a drive to
the annihilation of the subject, cannot be described and is inaccessible
to us *as subjects* in the realm of language, the ecstatic Dionysian state
is accessible to experience through such rhythmic activities as music,
dance, and poetry, and, in a more complex way, through the imper-
sonation of an epiphanic version of Dionysus in tragedy, with its play
of representation and rhythms and its catastrophic plot. These two
different modes of access form an interesting dichotomous pair, one
that corresponds to the binary opposition in Jakobsonian theory
between the metaphoric and metonymic principles in language, that
is, between selection and combination, comparison and contiguity.

The metaphoric nature of lyric poetry accords with Nietzsche's
theory of the origin of lyric poetry in the raw energy of music:

> The Dionysian musician is, without any images, himself pure
> primordial pain and its primordial re-echoing. The lyric genius is
> conscious of a world of images and symbols—growing out of his
> state of mystical self-abnegation and oneness.... [T]he images of
> the *lyrist* are nothing but *his very* self and, as it were, only different
> projections [*Objektivationen*] of himself, so he, as the moving center
> of this world, may say "I": of course, this self is not the same
> as that of the waking, empirically real man, but the only truly
> existent and eternal self resting at the basis of things, through

whose images the lyric genius sees this very basis. ([1874] 1967,
50; emphasis added by translator)

If the images that we find in a lyric poem are actually projections of
the poetic self—in the special sense, not of an ordinary identity but
rather as an infinite Dionysian larger self—then these images are also
equivalent to each other. They all stand in metaphorical relation to
the Dionysian reality that none of them can actually embody, since
that reality is distinctively devoid of imagery. This notion corresponds
nicely to Jakobson's principle of equivalence, the thought process of
metaphor, as the basic rule that governs poetic language at every level,
from sound patterns to images to themes.

By contrast, in tragedy, according to Nietzsche, the audience is
brought in contact with Dionysus by means of viewing and hearing
the powerful god physically impersonated, in disguise, on stage as
the tragic character himself, suffering and offering wisdom in the
midst of the tragic catastrophe. The association between audience and
Dionysus here is not one of equivalence but one of contiguity: the
controlling principle is that of metonymy. If we take, for example,
Agamemnon in the first play of Aeschylus's *Oresteia,* we can see how
Agamemnon's own death is simultaneously the fulfillment of his fate
as prophesied by Cassandra and the consequence of his own actions
in abandoning his throne and sacrificing his and Clytemnestra's daugh-
ter. Agamemnon makes the god (fate) that makes him. In his own
death, Agamemnon represents the annihilation of the subject at the
point of that Dionysian recognition. The illusion of his subjective
agency is graphically symbolized by the robe in which Clytemnestra
envelops him before killing him: the web of illusion that, until the
last minute, preserves Agamemnon as a subject, even in the very act
of his reversion to the primal unity symbolized by death.[10]

---

10. This is by no means intended to be a thoroughly convincing reading of the
Agamemnon. Rather, it is my own attempt to sketch a possible application of
Nietzsche's theory to the interpretation of a tragic text. Nietzsche's own reading of
the *Alcestis* is, to my mind, hardly any more convincing. I supply my own reading
of a different tragedy here simply in order to go through the exercise of seeing
how the theory might work apart from Nietzsche's own words. Actually, I find
Nietzsche's theory rather weak when it comes to tragedy, even though tragedy is
obviously his primary focus, along with its various implications for moral philosophy.

Another contrast to the lyric's metaphoric approach to Dionysian music is found in epic. Here, Nietzsche argues, the imagery that serves to represent the Dionysian energy serves as well to repress it completely. The reader or hearer of epic, like the narrative voice itself, has fallen completely in love with the dream images of epic and has little sense of there being a terrible and sublime reality motivating them, disguised by them. It is as if we have a series of metaphors of Dionysian energy, none of which is actually thought of as a metaphor—the referent is repressed. Yet at the same time, the literal surface of the text does not have the same emotional effect as would the events it tells of, if these actually were happening. So the distance or removal created by metaphor is preserved, while the possibility of decoding the metaphor and arriving at the Dionysian is foreclosed. Hence the characteristic contemplativeness of Homer, the frequent interruption of emotionally charged scenes with extended similes that diffuse the tension, the beauty with which (according to Nietzsche) even the most horribly violent scenes impress us. Also, we might add, hence the meter of epos is not foregrounded, as are the meters of lyric.

To return to the lyric's metaphoric approach to the Dionysian state, we must note that the implications of this way of reading lyric poetry can become quite striking if we go beyond Nietzsche's own sketchy comments, especially as they relate to the question of subjects named in a poem. In concentrating on the ancient Greek poet Archilochus, the earliest recorded Greek lyrist, Nietzsche seems to assume the presence of only one express subject, the lyric "I." This assumption is at least partly in direct response to his contemporaries' attempts to characterize the difference between epic and lyric poetry as an opposition between objective and subjective expressions respectively, which particularly limits their conception of lyric poetry to a mere reflection of the popular high Romantic idea of an outpouring of subjective emotions or of "emotions recollected in tranquility." In other words, Nietzsche's main point is that the self that speaks in lyric poetry is not the poet's personal self but a larger, transsubjective being, which manifests itself more directly in music, but which can

---

By contrast, the theory of the lyric, which he presents near the beginning of *The Birth of Tragedy,* and the general structure of Apollo versus Dionysus, allow for considerably more interesting possibilities.

only find words in the indirect form of the poetic images that attempt to interpret that music. What Nietzsche does not seem to consider is the fact that plenty of poems, although they usually have only one speaker, have more than one grammatical subject. If in fact all the images in the poem are projections of the Dionysian self, then should this rule not apply as well to all the beings named in the poem, including the various characters or grammatical subjects? In that case, even if there are several people or objects in the poem that are expressly opposed to each other, on some deeper level they are all equivalent to each other in representing the Dionysian energy itself. This notion proceeds from Nietzsche's initial premise that Dionysus represents the condition of being prior to and without the principle of individuation. Of course, all of these projections are only accessible to us insofar as they are images, mediated by the work of Apollo. To recognize them as such, and to trace their connection to the original Dionysian energy, would be the work of interpretation.

How can this idea work in an actual reading of a poem? In particular, how can we think of diverse subjects in a poem, even those opposed to each other, as somehow equivalent, arising from the same undifferentiated energy—without reducing every aspect of the poem to mere nonsense? Is there any way, furthermore, for such a method of reading to leave a place for the poem's specific historical and social contexts?

Let us attempt to read an ancient poem to see how the subjects can be at once identified with each other and understood as mere illusions covering the naked power of rhythm. We choose a well-known poem of Sappho, the most celebrated lyric poet of antiquity; if Nietzsche's theory can work at all, it should help us to produce an interesting reading in this case.

φαίνεταί μοι κῆνος ἴσος θέοισιν
ἔμμεν' ὤνηρ, ὄττις ἐνάντιός τοι
ἰσδάνει καὶ πλάσιον ἆδυ φωνεί-
σας ὑπακούει

καί γελαίσας ἰμέροεν, τό μ' ἦ μὰν
καρδίαν ἐν στήθεσιν ἐπτόαισεν·
ὡς γὰρ ἔς σ' ἴδω βρόχε', ὥς με φώναι-
σ' οὐδ' ἒν ἔτ' εἴκει,

ἀλλ' ἄκαν μὲν γλῶσσα †ἔαγε†, λέπτον
δ' αὔτικα χρῷ πῦρ ὑπαδεδρόμηκεν,
ὀππάτεσσι δ' οὐδ' ἒν ὄρημμ', ἐπιρρόμ-
βεισι δ' ἄκουαι,

κὰδ δέ μ' ἴδρως ψῦχρος ἔχει, τρόμος δὲ
παῖσαν ἄγρει, χλωροτέρα δὲ ποίας
ἔμμι, τεθνάκην δ' ὀλίγω 'πιδεύης
φαίνομ' ἔμ' αὔτ[α.

ἀλλὰ πὰν τόλματον, ἐπεὶ †καὶ πένητα†

(Campbell 1967, 44)

[He seems as fortunate as the gods to me, the man who sits
    opposite you and listens nearby to your sweet voice
and lovely laughter. Truly that sets my heart trembling in my
    breast. For when I look at you for a moment, then it is no
    longer possible for me to speak;
my tongue has snapped, at once a subtle fire has stolen beneath my
    flesh, I see nothing with my eyes, my ears hum,
sweat pours from me, a trembling seizes me all over, I am greener
    than grass, and it seems to me that I am little short of dying.
But all can be endured, since ... even a poor man ... [11]]

At first glance, there are three characters, or personages, named
or suggested in this poem, corresponding neatly to the three singular
persons of grammar: the speaker, in first person, who is a woman;
the addressee, second person, who is another woman and with whom
the speaker is in love; and a third party, named in third person, who
is a man, and whom we could imagine also to be in love with the
addressee, or at least involved in some sort of erotic flirtation with
her. The triangle thus has the beloved at its apex and the speaker
and her male competitor at opposite ends of its base. This opposition
between the competitor and the speaker (to follow the poem's order)

---

11. This translation by Campbell (1982, 79–81) is literal, but, under the constraints
of English, it perforce must fail to get across the fact that the first-person subject
speaking in the poem is marked as feminine in Greek. The subject and the object
of desire are both women; the hypothetical intermediary figure sitting next to or
across from the beloved woman—insofar as he might exist at all—is a man.

seems crucial and is underscored by many subordinate contrasts: man versus woman, calm versus disturbed, simply sitting versus suffering a physical crisis, listening versus looking, sustained contact versus a single brief glimpse, enjoying self-control versus out of control, and having godlike power versus being possessed by an outside force.

This is how the poem may appear at first glance to the general modern English reader. But classicist John Winkler is surely right in pointing out, first of all, that "the man" of the first two lines of the poem is an indefinite expression (κῆνος ὤνηρ ὄττις), much better translated as something like "whatever man who" or "that man whoever" (178–80). This phrase furthermore is a common formula opening a speech of praise, and Winkler particularly compares this poem with Odysseus's praise speech to Nausicaa in *Odyssey* 6.158– 61. So there really are only two characters who can be thought of as present on the scene. Nevertheless, however formulaic, this rhetorical device clearly relies on the structure of contrast between a hypothetical other, who is male, and the "real" speaker, who is female.

But there is irony in this contrast. The speaker claims that she cannot look steadily at the beloved, cannot enjoy her sustained company, because one glimpse is enough to deprive the speaker of her normal senses and of her powers of speech. Yet the poem describes in great detail those very reactions—in other words, the poem quite eloquently speaks the loss of speech. Furthermore, if the speaker is not to be imagined as before the beloved, then where is she? Winkler compares this poem to Odysseus's speech, in which he exclaims that a "holy dread" grips him as he gazes at Nausicaa (*Odyssey* 6.61). But clearly in this situation, Odysseus is not so fallen under dread as to be unable to speak. The point is that, while on the one hand, the speaker is experiencing her reaction to the beloved as a loss of control, reason, and speech, on the other hand, the speaker is really just like the hypothetical other, the man, the Odysseus-like one, insofar as she dwells in her contact with the beloved and coolly observes— even enjoys—the "sweet speech" of her own body, her own reactions. As a lover out of control, the speaker is mortal—she comes close to death. But as the observer and recorder of her own reactions, in relation to that mortal self, the speaker is also like a god.

Like what god, to be precise? The god who, for Nietzsche, presides over the rendering of intense, turbulent, sublime experience into beautiful images and words that can be contemplated and enjoyed is, of course, Apollo. Thus both the hypothetical other and the present speaker are in some sense Apollinian—while the speaker is simulta-neously the one who suffers the sublime crisis itself, which places her in the sphere of Dionysus. The hypothetical other, moreover, is in the position of the reader relative to the poem, who is able to enjoy the poem's "sweet speech and lovely laughter." And in this sense, both the speaker as observer and the reader are what Nietzsche would con-sider appropriate for Homeric epic. This makes sense in view of the possibility of a strong allusion to the *Odyssey* suggested by Winkler.

At least in one way, then, the speaker and the hypothetical other, despite their rhetorical opposition, are actually to be identified. What about the beloved? It is to her "sweet speech and lovely laughter" that the lucky man can listen without coming close to death. I have already suggested that the speaker *must* be on the scene with the beloved in order for her speech to make sense, and that the speech is therefore self-contradictory. In this sense, too, the speaker is like her opposite. But she does not explicitly listen to the beloved's speech. Rather, we listen—not to her beloved, but to ours. For us, the beloved is the poem itself, whose speech is sweet to us, and whose voice laughs in the sense that it contains a self-contradiction that, in the tradition of the praise speech, is a kind of courteous feint, a facetious play that opens up the possibility of seduction.

But at the same time as the poem is for us a delightful "sweet speech," it is also terribly serious, and we feel the tension between these two ways of reading the same utterance. The beloved can then be read as an allegory for the poem itself, while the two different ways of reading the poem are allegorized as the speaker-as-lover and her opposite, the rhetorical "he" as well as the speaker-as-observer. But the *telling* of the poem is obviously the poem, too—the speaker's speech, her opposite's pleasurable listening. In other words, all three grammatical subjects can be thought of as metaphors for different aspects of the same thing, which is—the poem itself.

Although we have noted the Apollinian qualities of the speaker and the rhetorical "he," we must also observe that this fading of distinctions between the speaker, her rhetorical opposite (the hypo-thetical other), the beloved, and the reader is Dionysian in the sense that it negates the principle of individuation and makes us all part of the same larger subject. That subject is simultaneously listening to and uttering the sweet speech of the beloved, simultaneously suffering the throes of uncontrollable passion and enjoying the loveliness of their expression. Thus, even though the images are under the domain of Apollo, these same images lead us into a process whereby the distinctions upon which they are based fall away, and we, as individual readers, come "close to [the] death" of our individual subjectivity.

It must be said, however, that for Nietzsche even this process wherein subjectivity fades away is not quite directly Dionysian. Nietzsche presents the relations among the kinds of ancient poetry, epic, lyric, and tragic, as forming a progressive series whereby Greek society attempted through art to approach Dionysus more and more directly. Whereas the Homeric narrator and reader are foreclosed in the pleasure of dream imagery, the lyric "I" and the lyric reader have some sense of something beyond—but they do not, according to Nietzsche, arrive at that something. The lyric is infused with a sense of the unattainable or inexpressible, as we can see, perhaps, in Sappho 31, where the beloved is sublimely unapproachable for the speaker. By contrast, for Nietzsche, tragedy brings Dionysus on stage in something more closely approximating his full presence.

Nietzsche's sense of the limitations of lyric may be traced, in part, to his leaving out of discussion the matter of the poem's own rhythmical nature. While on the one hand he speaks of the images in poetry as dream representations of Dionysian music, on the other hand, once given that recognition, Nietzsche never seems to return to the idea of music in any literal sense—such as the obvious musical quality of ancient Greek lyric meters (quite aside from the fact that the poems were probably put to music and sung). In other words, Nietzsche's whole approach to poetry is somewhat constrained by his fixation on content and his neglect of form. Accordingly, in the foregoing Nietzschean reading of Sappho 31, I did not take the step of suggesting that the beloved is an allegory for the musical power of the poem itself, under whose spell not only the speaker but the reader has always already fallen.

But this step would not be inconsistent with the general tenor of Nietzsche's theory of poetry. Insofar as the meaningful surface of the text is the Apollinian veil of illusion that both represents and disguises the Dionysian musical energy that, to begin with, gives rise to the poem's making, the poem could be thought of as a record of its own genesis, from Dionysian musical energy to Apollinian imagery. And the process could be reversed in reading, so that the imagery *means* what it represents and hides—musical energy, the primal unity, the undoing of discrete individuation. In Nietzsche's genetic theory of poetry—his theory of how poetry comes to be—we find a second argument for this book's theory of poetry as allegory of rhythm. The first argument we saw in the previous chapter, in an extension of Jakobson's concept of poetry as metaphoric and governed by the principle of individuation. That argument was reader oriented, based upon how the poem's parallelisms would appear to the reader and structure his or her responses. Nietzsche's argument, and this slight extension of it into a theory of poetry as allegory of rhythm, is writer oriented, based upon the possibility of reversing the chain of descent from the play of imagery in poetry to the "spirit of music" that gave it birth.

Nietzsche's theoretical apparatus, wherein the image content of a poem is conceived as a dream representation of its sublime musical nature, is a powerful tool in understanding poetry and has far-reaching implications, many of which may be worked out beyond the confines of Nietzsche's own development. Nietzsche's theory helps to bring out the element of unrepresentability in poetry—an early version of the paradox inherent in poetry as telling rhythm—since the lyric indicates the unreality of its dream images without giving voice to the Dionysian reality that lies behind them. (By contrast, I suggest that that Dionysian reality cannot be given voice but is manifest in the poem's form rather than its meaning.)

Furthermore, the notion of the Apollinian illusion that both hides and points toward a Dionysian reality is an interesting inversion of traditional Platonic metaphysics.[12] For whereas in the mainstream

---

12. That Nietzsche is an inversion of Plato summarizes Heidegger's reading of Nietzsche. For Heidegger, however, this inversion is also a replication of the ongoing tradition of Western metaphysics, which denies Being and focuses attention on beings. My own reading of Nietzsche is similar in that, as just mentioned, Nietzsche confuses the categories of Apollo and Dionysos somewhat by presenting them as moral types alongside their purely allegorical meanings (image/rhythm), and by using the word *music* metaphorically throughout this moral discussion. For Heidegger's Being I might propose *rhythm,* since my point is that rhythm is an experience of the physical universe that is at least in some aspect not mediated by the codes, conventions, and prejudices of society that are intimately bound up with language and symbols. But when Heidegger himself reads poetry, as in "Language and the Poem" (1971b; on Trakl) and even in "Language" (1971a; also on Trakl, but better), he does not clearly focus attention on the material "being" (rhythm) of any poem any more

reading of Plato, the things we can perceive are mere illusions that emanate from a higher, less physical reality, in Nietzsche, the images and ideas of a poem, however abstract and transcendental, are mere illusions that cover and also represent a truth that is essentially physical: the rhythm of bodily being. While Plato's reading goes upward, so to speak, Nietzsche's comes downward. Furthermore, whereas Plato, in the *Republic*, has Socrates consider the "simple narration" (ἀπλῆ διήγησις—392d ff.) in first person to be the only acceptably "truthful" poetry, for Nietzsche, the first-person singer of lyric poetry is a manifestation—a mimesis of sorts—of the primal unity over which Dionysos presides, outside and beyond any "I" or self. Of course, these two things can in fact be seen as very close, depending on what we mean by truth. If we think of truth in Nietzschean terms as the primal unity over which all individuals are covering illusions, then Nietzsche could easily use Plato's own terms. Both of them, in a sense, suggest that mimesis is the representation of something beyond the self; but, whereas for Plato, truth is entirely beyond the world of the senses, for a Nietzschean point of view, I believe (allowing for Nietzsche's surprising and perhaps confused relative placement of rhythm and music), the truth is accessible through the senses in nonlinguistic, nonimagistic experiences such as rhythm and music.[13]

This distinction is especially important if we consider the place of Nietzsche's theory of poetry in the context of his general critique of Christianity, whose metaphysics is essentially neo-Platonic. Sublimity in Nietzsche is to be found not in the next world but in this; it is not ordinarily visible, not because it is essentially not physical, but precisely because we are constructed as metaphysical subjects and therefore are blind to it. Poetry at least leads us in the direction of undoing that metaphysical subjectivity and opening the way to the sublimity of the physical world.

In the following chapters, I shall explore some theories that seem to develop out of Nietzsche's basic structure and that elaborate it. I

---

than does Nietzsche, and he thus tends to reduce poetry to philosophy despite his own protestations to the contrary. On Heidegger's reading of Nietzsche, see Lacoue-Labarthe's essay "L'Oblitération" in *Le Sujet de la philosophie* (1979, 111–84).

13. For more on Plato and the problem of mimesis and truth relative to Nietzsche, see Lacoue-Labarthe's "Typography," especially the third section, "The Unstable" (1989, 96–138).

shall attempt to show along the way how these developments can contribute to a theory of poetry such as the one which I present in chapter 13.

A few comments may be appropriate at this point to explain further my exclusion of Martin Heidegger and Paul de Man from consideration within the Nietzschean tradition and as contributing influences in my theory. As I mentioned in chapter 1, although both thinkers showed a keen interest in poetry and both responded in some way to Nietzsche, neither of them shows any interest in rhythm in poetry and neither can be fit squarely into the Nietzschean tradition.

Heidegger shares with Nietzsche the sense that representation, and language if conceived as representation, is illusory—for Heidegger, representation obscures Being and thus truth. But whereas, for Nietzsche, the Dionysian—which he associates with the "spirit of music" and which I associate with rhythm—offers a kind of reality beyond the illusions of language, for Heidegger, there is no such recourse to the nonlinguistic: truth can be found by paying attention to how "language speaks." Thus in Heidegger's essays on poetry, such as "Language" (1971a), "Language and the Poem" (1971b), and "What Are Poets For?" (1971d), no special attention is devoted to rhythm, and there is no way of integrating the fact of rhythm into the discussion as the chief point of difference between poetry and prose. There is also the question of interpretive method as a corollary of the theory of what poetry is. For Nietzsche, it makes sense to understand the images of poetry as an allegory of poetry's own rhythm (or of its effect), since poetry issues out of the relation between Apollinian representation and Dionysian rhythm. Heidegger, too, seems to read a poem allegorically, at least in the case of the Georg Trakl poem, "A Winter Evening," in the essay "Language." Here, the poem provides Heidegger with a series of metaphors of the workings of language itself. Indeed, I am hard-pressed not to find in these metaphors a *representation* of the workings of language, despite Heidegger's efforts to get beyond language as representation. In short, for me, rhythm is crucial to a successful theory of poetry; and in leaving rhythm out, Heidegger's thinking on poetry does not seem to me as fruitful for my purposes as are those theories that maintain the tradition of Nietzsche's Apollo-Dionysos relation.[14]

---

14. Heidegger is a notoriously difficult thinker. I make no claims here to a

Another thinker with a lifelong concern for poetry who responds to Nietzsche is Paul de Man. In de Man's deconstructive view, Nietzsche's "text is held together by the pseudo-polarity of the Apollo/Dionysos dialectic that allows for a well-ordered teleology, because the ontological cards have been stacked from the beginning. . . . Truth, Presence, Being are all on Dionysos's side, and history can only occur as the birth and rebirth of a father in whose absence no son could ever exist" (1979, 83). That is, Nietzsche tells a story of the origin ("birth") of tragedy and all poetry in which the end of the story is the same as the beginning, since Nietzsche himself must be telling the truth about this history. To put it another way, *The Birth of Tragedy* presents us with the paradox of criticizing scientific discourse as illusory but engaging in scientific discourse to do so. For de Man, this larger deconstruction of the "genetic structure of literary history . . . leaves a residue of meaning that can, in its turn, be translated into a statement . . . about the limitations of textual authority" (1979, 99). That is, a careful reading such as his of Nietzsche's text reveals how *all* texts find themselves unable to base their claims for telling the truth on any stable ground outside of the text.

De Man's reading of the "pseudo-polarity of the Apollo/Dionysos dialectic" seems to me exceedingly reductive.[15] As I have attempted to show in this chapter, Nietzsche engages in two different kinds of argument in *The Birth of Tragedy,* one of which is liable to de Man's critique, and the other not. In Nietzsche's moral argument, Dionysos and Apollo are virtually types of actual people, and hence he promotes the former hierarchically over the latter. But in his theory of poetics, Dionysos and Apollo are only allegorical representations (thus admittedly Apollinian) for principles that are mutually determining effects of each other. The Dionysian in this sense is truth but not presence, since it is precisely the *absence* of the principle of individuation—the Apollinian—that gives it meaning as the Dionysian. In this sense, the relation between the Dionysian and the Apollinian are, as it were, already deconstructed. Indeed, deconstruction itself is not so much a

---

thoroughgoing understanding of Heidegger, and I anticipate that, were one to read his work closely enough, it is possible that my particular observations could be countered. A deeper exploration of his ideas about poetry are beyond my present scope.

15. For a very effective critique of de Man's argument by a different approach, see Corngold 1983.

critique of Nietzsche's pseudopolarity as rather a way in which recent criticism has come full circle to Nietzsche's profound insight.

In keeping with de Man's critique of Nietzsche, de Man tends to read poems as instances of the text undoing itself. Typically, the poem begins its work by inviting us to forget the fact that it is nothing more than a text and that language has only an arbitrary and conventional relationship with the world to which it purports to refer. The language of poetry conjures us with its factitious magic to feel as if its signs and the physical world were one. But the very process of attentive reading, such as de Man's own, leads us to the revelation of poetic language's failure to consummate its magic. Thus we are left with a stern, salutary lesson as to the illusory seductions of texts, a lesson that might be applied fruitfully to such texts as ideology that purport not to be literary texts at all but that are just as factitious (1984, 11).

My own theory, coming out of the Nietzschean tradition, coincides with de Man's in the idea that poetry reveals the limits of language. In Nietzschean terms, this is how the veil of Apollinian images in the poem allows the reader to intimate the workings of something beyond—its own undoing—the Dionysian primal unity, which is also an unknowable void. But de Man's reading can only go in a negative—here one might well say nihilistic—direction. Since he has no interest in physical rhythm and does not (at least not avowedly) preserve the Dionysos/Apollo structure, de Man does not account for what calls language forth to begin with. Hence, although de Man's arguments have persuasive force, it is hard to see how anyone sufficiently schooled in de Man might find any pleasure in poetry unless he or she had already felt tempted by poetry's seductions in a way that would overpower any theoretical discourse. By contrast, I see poetry as offering an ecstatic release from the limitations of any finite utterance and its culturally determined values in the face of the physical experience of rhythm—without, however, abandoning the work of representation upon which, after all, our very access to that ecstatic release depends. Thus poetry simultaneously challenges language and calls language forth, revealing the illusory play of language and knowledge and yet reveling in that play. It is de Man's very departure from Nietzsche's basic theoretical structure that accounts, in large part, for the disappearance of the pleasure of poetry from his theory. The pleasure of poetry is, of course, precisely what I hope to rediscover.

9

Psychoanalytic Revisions of Nietzsche: Freud and Lacan

The previous chapter argued that Nietzsche's theory of poetry can help answer some of the basic questions we have posed, chiefly with regard to the relation between poetic form, or rhythm, and meaning. But those who followed and borrowed from Nietzsche help to demonstrate the far-reaching implications of the relation between bodily rhythm and verbal meaning. One area of modern thought squarely within the Nietzschean tradition is psychoanalysis, which further elaborates the relation between the two sides of poetry, while at the same time making clear some of his implications beyond the reading of poetry.

Nietzsche's theory of poetry suggests that the structure of the experience of poetry stands as something of a parable of mental life in general, and that poetry thus reveals basic facts and qualities of subjectivity. The relation between, on one hand, the Dionysian absence of a principle of individuation, and, on the other hand, the Apollinian veil of illusion—between, respectively, the primal unity toward which rhythm leads us and the imagery and language that enable us, as subjects, to know what poetry means—this relation reveals to us the instability at the core of our subjectivity. At the same time, we are restored by our momentary lapse into the freedom of being deconstituted as subjects, or perhaps by our fleeting half-awareness that such a lapse could occur. These more fundamental notions of the relation between subjectivity and physical reality, and the construction of the subject, are primary elements of Nietzsche's legacy to later thought. These are particularly the notions developed in Freud and later psychoanalytic thinkers; and these notions have the most bearing on a postmodern theory of poetry, which will seek to connect the experience of poetry with the conception of the subject as constructed, socially contingent, and in some way factitious.

In particular, the idea, first clearly articulated in Nietzsche, that the images in poems are dream images that translate into the Apollinian veil of illusion the primary Dionysian energy is further developed in Freud's theory of how actual dreams work, especially nocturnal dreams. Since Freud explicitly connects literature to the process of daydreaming, he indicates a clear relevance of his theory to the question of how poetry works. But Freud's theoretical writings on dreams and on the unconscious and the drives provide the basis for a much more sophisticated model for poetry than does his essay on literature and daydreaming. Many discussions of Freud's contribution to literary theory begin—and too often end—with Freud's essay, "The Relation of the Poet [*Dichter*—also simply creative writer] to Day-Dreaming" ([1908] 1963c). But this essay forms only one piece of an intricate jigsaw puzzle that accumulates throughout Freud's development. By gathering together sundry ideas from Freud's texts, I shall show that Freud comes very close to the theory of poetry as allegory of the sublime power of rhythm.

The contribution of psychoanalytic theory to a new theory of poetry is not exhausted with Freud, however. Lacan's elaboration of the relation between subject and body, or between what he calls the "symbolic register" and the "real," will inform the notion of the body as source of sublime experience in the theory developed here. This chapter will thus explore the notion of the real in Lacan following a review of some of Freud's basic concepts.

The explicit purpose of Freud's essay ([1908] 1963c) is to explain how creative writers are able to come up with their material, to propose a theory of inspiration. Freud points out that the process of creative writing is virtually the same as the process of daydreaming, in which everyone engages. Daydreams, or fantasies, in turn, are susceptible to interpretation by means of the same devices as are dreams in Freud's *The Interpretation of Dreams*. At the core of daydreams as well as imaginative writings is a hero:

> There is one very marked characteristic in the productions of these writers which must strike us all: they all have a hero who is the centre of interest, for whom the author tries to win our sympathy

by every possible means, and whom he places under the protection of a special providence.... It seems to me, however, that this significant mark of invulnerability very clearly betrays—His Majesty the Ego, the hero of all day-dreams and all novels. ([1908] 1963c, 40)[1]

Freud's purpose is understanding literary *production* rather than literary reception or the text itself. Nevertheless, if our sympathy is won over to the hero "by every possible means," then the reader finds some pleasure in *identifying* with the hero (or heroine) and thus experiencing the euphoria of his (or her) invulnerability as an assurance to his or her ego. Given this inference as a theory of reading, we are still far away from our concerns with poetry. For Freud's comment focuses entirely on the paraphrasable *content*—the plot turns that aggrandize the hero. And the effect will be felt in relation to the ego, which is, of course, an individual social and verbal agent—rather far removed from the Nietzschean picture of the Dionysian primal unity found in rhythm.

At the very end of his essay, Freud makes comments that are more specifically relevant to the nature and structure of poetry. For he brings up the question, by now a familiar challenge to biographical readings, of why other people should take pleasure in one person's personal daydreams and ego self-aggrandizement. Freud supplies two answers. The first is in line with the inference on identification just suggested: "The writer softens the egotistical character of the day-dream by changes and disguises" (43) and thereby, presumably, boosts the universality of the hero(ine) and facilitates the reader's identification with him or her. In addition, however, the writer

bribes us by the offer of a purely formal, that is, aesthetic, pleasure in the presentation of his phantasies. The increment of pleasure which is offered us in order to release yet greater pleasure arising from deeper sources in the mind is called an "incitement premium" or technically, "fore-pleasure." I am of opinion that all the aesthetic

---

1. I have deliberately chosen to quote from Freud using the popular individual volumes of his works, rather than the Standard Edition, because the former are much more likely to be at the reader's easy reach.

pleasure we gain from the works of imaginative writers is of the
same type as this "fore-pleasure," and that the true enjoyment of
literature proceeds from the release of tensions in our minds.
Perhaps much that brings about this result consists in the writer's
putting us into a position in which we can enjoy our own day-
dreams without reproach or shame. (43)

In poetry, as Anthony Easthope suggests, this forepleasure would be
found specifically in the rhythm and other sound effects of form (1989,
20; see also 1983, 31–34, which refers primarily to Freud [1905] 1989).

The structure of the poetic artifact that Freud suggests here is
one in which the truth, which originates as the writer's personal,
egoistic fantasy, is clothed, so to speak, in an alluring but deceptive
garb, the ornament of verse. In other words, here we have the classical
rhetorical model of poetry of the Renaissance, sometimes also referred
to as the "sugared pill": the pleasures of verse enable us to tolerate
the bitter truth. Only here, the bitter truth is the alienation of
enduring—or enjoying—someone else's ego-fantasy.

The problem with this structure should be clear: the relation
between verse rhythm and meaning is really left out of theory. There
is no particular reason a writer would choose verse rhythm over any
other type of rhetorical ornament, such as tropes or figures such as peri-
odic sentences. Thus we cannot explain the difference between prose
and poetry, and we can only regard the choice of verse rhythm among
other pleasurable devices as an accident. Finally, it is not clear why or
how the pleasure of formal features such as verse rhythm should rub off
on the fantasy that constitutes the content. Why should one regard the
latter as pleasurable simply because the former is?

Although it is certainly important that rhythm be associated
directly with the pleasure principle, it is not in the reduction of this
pleasure to a mere seductive forepleasure that this early Freud essay
makes a substantial contribution to a theory of poetry. Rather, it is
in the association of writing with daydreams and thus of the inter-
pretation of writing, including poetry, with the interpretation of
dreams. For the interpretation of dreams involves the discovery of the
relation between images that have come to consciousness and other
functions, wishes, that remain unconscious. Here, we have a structure
that resembles that between the Apollinian veil of images and the
Dionysian energy: the images simultaneously manifest this unconscious

energy and bar it from the conscious world, where by breaking out it could destroy the possibility of consciousness itself.

The Interpretation of Dreams ([1900] 1965) makes clear both the place of Freud's early thought within the Nietzschean tradition and the divergence from Nietzsche. A dream is a representation in images of an unconscious wish. But the unconscious wish itself takes the form of a *verbal* construct, which could then be rediscovered in the process of psychoanalysis. This verbal construct, which lurks somewhere in the unconscious, Freud calls variously the dream thought or the latent content of the dream, as opposed to the images, the manifest content (or simply dream content), that the dreamer experiences and some of which he or she can recall. The reconstruction of this verbal wish formula is then a satisfactory resolution of the mystery of the dream.

> The dream-thoughts and the dream-content are presented to us like two versions of the same subject-matter in two different languages. Or, more properly, the dream-content seems like a transcript of the dream-thoughts into another mode of expression, whose characters and syntactic laws it is our business to discover by comparing the original and the translation. The dream-thoughts are immediately comprehensible, as soon as we have learnt them. The dream-content, on the other hand, is expressed as it were in a pictographic script, the characters of which have to be transposed individually into the language of the dream-thoughts. . . . Suppose I have a picture-puzzle, a rebus. . . . [O]bviously we can only form a proper judgement of the rebus if we . . . try to replace each separate element by a syllable or word that can be represented by that element in some way or other. . . . A dream is a picture-puzzle of this sort. ([1900] 1965, 311–12)

The dream images represent the wish but simultaneously distort its expression so as to enable it to pass the censorship imposed by consciousness. Without this distortion, interpretation would not be necessary; but without it, the dreamer would probably be unable to remain asleep, either because his or her wishes would be too shocking, or because they would impel physical action that would prevent sleep.

As in Nietzsche's model of poetry, images simultaneously represent and distort, or suppress from consciousness, a secret force. But whereas in Nietzsche that force is secret precisely because it could not be perceived otherwise—it would obviate the possibility of an individual perceiving subject—in Freud, that secret can in principle be known and should be known as part of the therapeutic process. For Nietzsche, since the verbal (qua communication) is always symbolic, any verbal formula would have to be considered part of the Apollinian web of illusions in which we live our everyday lives, and not as the ultimate secret.

But for Freud, too, the verbal formula of the wish that lies behind dreams and daytime fantasies is not the ultimate secret—that is, not eventually. Years later—first in his *Three Essays on the Theory of Sexuality* ([1905] 1975), then in "Instincts and Their Vicissitudes" ([1912] 1963a), and most of all in "The Unconscious" ([1915] 1963e) and "Repression" ([1915] 1963d)—Freud develops the notion of unconscious *drives*. This word can be used to translate *Triebe* in German, which unfortunately was misleadingly translated in the English Standard Edition by word *instincts*. From this point onward in Freud's thought, there is a marked distinction between *ideas* (*Vorstellungen* or *Vorstellungsrepräsentanzen*) and drives. The drives, like Nietzsche's Dionysian sublime, are not directly accessible to consciousness. Ideas, however, can take verbal or imaginary forms and can thus be expressed as dream thoughts.[2] The drives are intimately associated with the body—as, for us, will be the drive to rhythm:

> By an "instinct" [*Trieb*] is provisionally to be understood the psychical representative of an endosomatic, continuously flowing source of stimulation, as contrasted with a "stimulus," which is set up by *single* excitations coming from *without*. *The concept of instinct is thus one of those lying on the frontier between the mental and the physical* [emphasis added to this sentence]. The simplest and

---

2. On the whole matter of the drives and their (non)representability, see Laplanche and Pontalis 1973 on "Instinct (or Drive)," 214–16.

In Freud's late *Outline of Psychoanalysis* (1940, 22–28), not all dreams issue from ideas that in turn represent unrepresentable drives; there are dreams of the id (the seat of the drives) and dreams of the ego (responding to tensions closer to consciousness). But, as I discuss further in this chapter, *all* mental life has its ultimate source in the drives, as Freud clearly states both in *Beyond the Pleasure Principle* and in *The Ego and the Id*.

likeliest assumption as to the nature of instincts would seem to be that in itself an instinct is without quality, and, so far as mental life is concerned, is only to be regarded as a measure of the demand made upon the mind for work. What distinguishes the instincts from one another and endows them with specific qualities is their relation to their somatic sources and to their aims. The source of an instinct is a process of excitation occurring in an organ and the immediate aim of the instinct lies in the removal of this organic stimulus. ([1905] 1975, 34)

As Freud later specifies in "The Unconscious," these drives, which may be thought of as bodily pressures exerting themselves upon the mind or as sources of an indefinite mental energy coming from the body (Laplanche and Pontalis 1973, 214–16), can never make their direct appearance in consciousness.

An instinct can never be an object of consciousness—only the idea (*Vorstellung*) that *represents the instinct*. Even in the unconscious, moreover, it can only be represented by the idea. If the instinct did not attach itself to an idea or manifest itself as an affective state, we could know nothing about it. Though we do speak of an unconscious or a repressed instinctual impulse, this is a looseness of phraseology which is quite harmless. We can only mean an instinctual impulse the ideational presentation (*Vorstellungsrepräsentanz*) of which is unconscious, for nothing else comes into consideration. ([1915] 1963e, 126; emphasis added; see also [1912] 1963a, 87)

Ideas are connected to drives insofar as the drives occupy or invest ("cathect") particular objects, memories, or impressions, and then an energy of feeling, or affect, is often attached to those ideas as well. Affect is very much like the drives in being an indefinite energy of emotion, but there are different affects, and affects do come to the surface of conscious experience as emotions. They have no verbal content, while ideas usually do.

In this context, it is interesting to note that Schopenhauer, who was a very important influence on both Nietzsche and Freud, used the word *Vorstellung* in the title of his book, *The World as Will and Representation*, to mean "representation." Here is a point of contact with Freud (as well as Nietzsche). For Freud's "ideas" (*Vorstellungen*) are *representations* of the drives, signs attached to the force that they signify but that they also repress, covering them, as Nietzsche's Apollo does the energy of Dionysos, in a veil of illusions. And for Schopenhauer as for Freud, a certain kind of knowledge of the representations among which we live enables us to see beyond these illusions. But whereas for Schopenhauer the goal of this insight is an attitude of resignation, for Freud, the goal is more paradoxical. On the one hand, psychoanalysis renders unconscious thoughts conscious; on the other hand, the core of unconscious mental life, the drives, can never come to consciousness. They are entirely unrepresentable.

We may speak, then, of two major phases in Freud's thinking about the relation between outward representations, such as dream images and waking thoughts and actions, and their internal sources. At first, the latter are unconscious verbal thoughts or wishes, which can be brought to consciousness. Later, even these thoughts are in turn representations of other, darker forces: the entirely unrepresentable drives. Interestingly, both of these phases may be derived from elements in the Jewish mystical tradition, or Cabala. Corresponding with the first is the idea that an individual human being may be thought of as a Torah—a holy scripture—available for and even inviting interpretation by the same methods rabbis use in teasing out the more arcane meanings of the Torah proper (Bakan 1975, 246–70). This analogy is set up in reverse within the central mystical text, the *Zohar,* where the manifest content (so to speak) of the written Torah is an outer garment clothing the truth of the Torah, which interpretation may lay bare (Bakan 1975, 247). Corresponding to the second phase is the notion that the Torah itself is the outward clothing of the *Shechinah,* the divine presence—itself mystical, ineffable, unrepresentable. From the *Zohar* again:

> The created Torah is a vestment to the Shekinah, and if man had not been created, the Shekinah would have been without a vestment like a beggar. Hence when a man sins it is as though he strips the Shekinah of her vestments, and that is why he is punished; and when he carries out the precepts of the Law, it is as though he clothes the Shekinah in her vestments. (quoted in Bakan 1975, 274)

The association of Freud's thought with that of Schopenhauer, on the one hand, and perhaps with Cabala, on the other, ties it doubly with mystical traditions—respectively Indian and Jewish. And the definitive core of mysticism, as I would define it, is the paradoxical effort to give voice to the ineffable, to represent the unrepresentable. Here, in short, we see the connection between Freud's theories and the reading of poetry as allegory of the sublime—that is, as a representation of the unrepresentable effect of the physical rhythm of poetry, and an attendant acknowledgment of the impossibility of the task. I should only add that the passage from the *Zohar* quoted above clearly puts the ineffable *Shechinah,* or divine presence, in the place of the *body,* relative to its verbal clothing, the Law or written Torah. Here, as in the theory of poetry as allegory of the sublime, the (unconstructed) body is at the core.

To summarize—and, somewhat artificially, to form a more or less coherent system out of these elements of Freud's thought—we may represent the movement of energy from the drives to dreams and other conscious experiences as a series of transformational steps, like reactions in chemistry:

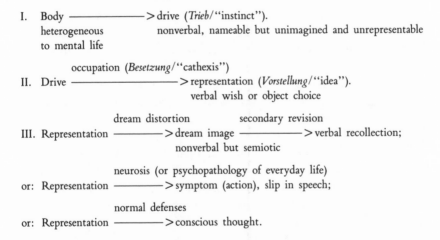

I. Body ——————> drive (*Trieb*/"instinct").
    heterogeneous   nonverbal, nameable but unimagined and unrepresentable
    to mental life

            occupation (*Besetzung*/"cathexis")
II. Drive ————————> representation (*Vorstellung*/"idea").
                        verbal wish or object choice

            dream distortion   secondary revision
III. Representation ————> dream image ————> verbal recollection;
                        nonverbal but semiotic

            neurosis (or psychopathology of everyday life)
or: Representation ————> symptom (action), slip in speech;

            normal defenses
or: Representation ————> conscious thought.

Later still, Freud organized the drives somewhat by classing them into two categories—the erotic drives, and the newly introduced death drive—in *Beyond the Pleasure Principle* ([1920] 1961). The new topology, introduced in *The Ego and the Id* in 1923, placed these drives at the bottom, as it were, of the id. Freud used the term *es*—German for "it" and translated as the Latin word for "it," *id*—which he borrowed from Georg Groddeck, who

himself no doubt followed the example of Nietzsche, who habitu-
ally used this grammatical term for whatever in our nature is imper-
sonal and, so to speak, subject to natural law. ([1923] 1962, 13n3)

The parallel here between the id and the Dionysian is striking: both
Nietzsche and Freud indicate the *transpersonal* or *impersonal* nature of
this force, which is not contained within the individuated subject. In
both cases, it is the unknowable ultimate truth.

Interestingly, even after Freud introduces the dualism of Eros and
death in *Beyond the Pleasure Principle*, he replicates the structure of
representative and unrepresentable among the drives in *The Ego and
the Id*. The fundamental, "displaceable and neutral energy" that drives
mental life in its vicissitudes "proceeds from the narcissistic store of
libido . . . it is desexualized Eros" ([1923] 1962, 34). By contrast, "the
death instincts are by their nature *mute* and . . . the clamour of life
proceeds for the most part from Eros" (36; emphasis added). Thus
even at the level of the fundamental, unrepresentable drives, one, Eros,
is in effect standing in a representative relation to the other, death.
At the same time, the function of Eros par excellence, the orgasm
or sexual release, is an instance of the working of the death drive,
since it involves a return of the organism to a previous condition and
a net reduction in vital tension (31, 37). The very vitality of Eros
might then be thought of as a temporary repression of the drive
toward death, which is the very source of energy that pushes erotic
urges toward release.

This replication of the structure, representative/unrepresentable
or known/unknowable is something of a hallmark in the career of
Freud. In Freud's earlier thinking, the mind can be divided up into
the system Pcpt-Cs (perception consciousness), perhaps including the
Pcs (preconscious), on the one hand, and the system Ucs (unconscious),
on the other. The former faculties are accessible to consciousness, the
latter not. Images are found in consciousness; unconscious ideas, mem-
ories, wishes, and desires are hidden. Conscious thoughts and images
represent these unconscious processes. But these unconscious processes
can be brought to consciousness by the analyst, in the forms of verbal
wishes.

But if these functions can be brought to consciousness, then, at
least in theory, the unconscious could eventually be emptied out of
content—and yet it is precisely the movement of impulses from uncon-

sciousness to consciousness that constitutes mental life. The conquest of the unconscious by consciousness would bring the whole system to a crashing halt. Later, the boundary of the unknowable would be redrawn so as to preserve it from analysis. The drives were found in the wholly unconscious id, *along with* ideas that represent them. In addition, a large portion of the ego itself was now unconscious. And later still, Freud *names* the drives as Eros and death, and thus seems to bring them closer to the conquering force of conscious knowledge. But as if to compensate for this conquest, he makes one of these drives, death, in some fundamental way intrinsically unknowable or "mute."

We may see this shift of the boundary and replication of the structure knowable/unknowable as a natural result of an irresolvable conflict, an ongoing dialectic, driving psychoanalysis. On the one hand, there is the hypothesis of an unconscious source of energy that sustains conscious psychic life, rather as Schopenhauer's will forms the substrate of the world as representation. On the other hand, psychoanalysis as a science cannot resign itself to leaving anything unknown. Finally, the only truly unknowable force is death itself— a fitting image for that about which nothing further can be said.

We have a structure in Freud that is now, in toto, analogous to the model I am presenting for poetry: images represent—and simultaneously repress—the bodily energy that is paradoxically unrepresentable. But whereas Freud's theory cannot give up the possibility of knowledge, in the theory of poetry as allegory of rhythm these images of poetry can be seen, as it were, to confess the impossibility of their task of representation. That is the very energy that these representations have to offer us, as they attempt to address the bodily rhythms that simultaneously make their call to us.

Freud's ideas bring us near the theory of the allegory of rhythm in the ways I have outlined. There are other developments in psychoanalysis since Freud, especially by his structuralist descendant Jacques Lacan, which contribute considerably to the Nietzschean tradition and thus to the elaboration of the present theory of poetry.

The notion that for the normal, social subject, the Dionysian primal unity only exists insofar as it can be inferred "retrospectively" from the position of Apollinian subjectivity (and Apollinian illusion) corresponds closely to another psychoanalytic concept: Lacan's register of the real, in relation to the other registers of the subject's being, the imaginary and the symbolic. The real subject only exists as an unrepresentable lack in the very center of one's being, an absence whose presence (so to speak) only makes itself felt indirectly through the workings of desire and symbolic representation, whose unmediated core is utterly inaccessible, and whose existence thus can only be inferred from the position we normally occupy, a position of subjectivity constructed in the imaginary and the symbolic.

According to Lacan, the construction of the subject (as the subject of perception and speech and of social interactions) begins at an early age—around six months—at the mirror stage. At this developmental stage, the child first has a clear view of his or her own image in the mirror, or, perhaps, the body of another child, or even the body of the mother, and draws a one-to-one correspondence between the parts of his or her own body and those of the image. It is at this point that the child acquires the first sense of his or her own bodily coherency as a discrete being—in the realm of the imaginary, in a way dependent upon the experience of a coherent image or gestalt. Yet this occurs at a point at which the child's physical development and motor control fall far short of the perfection of his or her projected image—the child can barely stand, and movements are somewhat chaotic as compared with the coherency of the image. Thus the image is an initial object of desire—and yet at the same time a threat to the supremacy of the subject gazing at it. This competition between two different sorts of self sets up an initial aggressive tendency that continues for the rest of the person's life, as the feelings first encountered with the image, feelings of love and hate, desire and destructiveness, are directed toward other children, adults, and even inanimate objects, which represent "part objects" of the original bodily *imago*. The life of the human subject as we know it, therefore, begins with a splitting, a profound alienation at its very core.[3]

The aggressivity introduced by the imaginary would make any substantial intersubjectivity, let alone society, impossible. But at a slightly later stage, the child is introduced to language, which brings with it a multiplicity of replaceable objects and a different mode of mediation,

---

3. This discussion is based on Lacan's famous essay, "Le Stade du miroir comme formateur de la fonction du Je" ([1949] 1966c). I also found very helpful Eve Bannet's chapter on Lacan (1989, 12–48), and Jameson 1988a. See also Lemaire 1977; and Jacqueline Rose's introduction to Mitchell and Rose 1982.

making social relations and exchange possible—as well as laws, prohibitions, conformity, and yet another, even more all-encompassing mode of alienation.

One might be tempted at this point to conclude that, since the results of the mirror stage and later the acquisition of language are nothing but internal division, aggression, and alienation, the goal of psychoanalytic treatment should be somehow to reverse this process by returning the subject to the real. But this would be impossible, and such a project involves a misunderstanding of the very nature of Lacan's registers. Since the world of language is in fact the symbolic order, and since the coherence of the ego (which, after the introduction of the symbolic order, is the subject of speech and thought) depends upon the imaginary presence of the mirror image, without these structures imposed upon the subject, the person would hardly be human—hardly a person at all. (Indeed, defects in the introduction of the imaginary or the symbolic are a Lacanian way of explaining psychoses such as childhood autism and schizophrenia.) But even further, one cannot properly speak of a real outside of the context of the imaginary and the symbolic. As we have already noted, the relation between the real on the one hand and the imaginary and symbolic on the other is closely analogous to the relation between the Dionysian and the Apollinian: the very naming of the real is only possible from the position of "the other," that is, the complex, conflicted, and alienating structure of the imaginary and the symbolic. Insofar as the real subject, the subject-as-lack, can be thought of as a space or a bubble of nothingness in the center of the constructed personality, that bubble only exists *because* there is so much alien material—the eternal conflict of the imaginary and the eternal chain of signifiers in the symbolic order—set up all around it like a perpetually swirling and shifting layer of soapy water.[4]

---

4. Things get even more complicated because Lacan fairly consistently slips from talking about the real (as the unspeakable) to talking about the Freudian id, which, as the unconscious, is for Lacan "structured like a language" and therefore the very locus of the subject's internal construction from outside by the alienating symbolic order, the subject's "being spoken." Furthermore, Freud's id encompasses an analogous ambiguity to begin with. On the one hand, the id is the seat of the drives, which are essentially unrepresentable in their unmediated nature. Yet on the other hand, the id contains the unconscious "representations" (*Vorstellungen* or

Yet is there nevertheless, in Lacan, a drive to return to the real—even though the real is only inferred, and is therefore something of a fiction created in imaginary and symbolic life in order to refer to its own annihilation? Certainly, there is no such explicit drive as such. Indeed, Lacan and his commentators have very few words to spare on the real in general, as compared with Lacan's increasing obsession with the symbolic order. Yet without such a drive, which might in turn be represented as either an individual or a collective utopian fantasy, how else might we explain the purpose of analysis? For in Lacanian analysis, the whole goal of practice seems to be to bring the patient to the point where his or her own subject-as-lack, his or her reality, so to speak, can somehow mark its place. The real subject cannot speak, of course, but the patient in analysis can be brought to the point where he or she is somehow aware of the illusory nature of all desires, fantasies, projections, defenses, and compulsions.

Thus neither on a political nor a personal level can the real be the object of a utopian nostalgia, as Frederic Jameson points out (1988, 112). Indeed, while the goal of analysis is the point where the analysand marks his or her place as a subject-as-lack (i.e., as a nothingness), Lacan is hardly explicit about what the advantage is of coming to such a point. Still, one can compare this self-realization of sorts, a comparison that Lacan himself seems to invite from time to time (and that Jameson pursues), to the discovery of one's authentic being in Sartrean existentialism. That is, the real in Lacan must provide a certain freedom from the thoroughgoing determinism of the symbolic and from the never-ending strife of the imaginary—even if, as Eve Bannet (1989) suggests, this freedom is no more than the freedom to

---

Vorstellungsrepräsentanz) of wishes (also unconscious) which make their appearance in conscious life through dreams, fantasies, jokes, works of art, mistakes in speech, accidents, and so on. Perhaps nowhere is the Lacanian version of this slippage more striking than where Lacan quotes Freud's maxim, "Wo es war, soll Ich werden" (1973, 43–51), apparently using *es* and its French translation, *ça*, to refer to the real, the subject-as-lack. (Lacan translates *Wo es war* as "là où c'était" and the sentence variously, in one instance as "là où c'était, . . . *le sujet doit advenir*" [45].) In Freud, by contrast, *es* clearly refers to (or is translated in English as) the *id*, a somewhat more positive concept—hence the tradition in Anglo-American ego psychology to think of this dictum as proposing the goal of analysis as the bringing to consciousness (*ich*/ego) of unconscious wishes (*es*/id) in order to make them accessible to language and reason.

destroy. At any rate, this freedom clearly has a potentially political as well as a personal dimension, as could be seen in the popularity of Lacanian theory among participants in the May 1968 uprisings in Paris.

There must be, then, a kind of drive to return to the real, even though Lacan does not articulate it as such. The drive to return to the real is the drive to be free, and it also helps account for the purpose and goal of psychoanalysis. To return to our comparison between the Lacanian real and the Nietzschean primal unity (or Dionysian), one can trace the analogy through the negation of illusion, which is also a negation of language, to the negation of the subject and the subject/object dichotomy, and even as far as the hypothesis of some kind of drive to return to this primal state. This latter can be inferred in Nietzsche and Lacan, respectively, from the existence of poetry and from the goals of psychoanalysis. There are surely other similarities as well, but there are also some interesting differences. In both Lacan and Nietzsche, the real has a utopian dimension, but in different ways. Whereas for Lacan, what might be attractive about the real is a moment of freedom (however limited its ultimate benefits), for Nietzsche, the Dionysian state is truly a state of unalienation. And whereas for Lacan, the real is ultimately individual, indeed solitary, since it is an escape from everything social (i.e., the symbolic order), for Nietzsche, it is language that alienates us from our fellow beings, and the music of Dionysus that brings us back to a primal sense of communion. While Nietzsche's concept is clearly more Romantic, it also seems much closer to Freud's otherwise bizarre (and quite modern) notion of a death drive that amounts to our desire to return to the state of nonindividuated inorganic matter whence we had once arisen. This is true, as noted earlier, insofar as Nietzsche's drive to Dionysus has elements of both Freud's erotic and death drives, since both are subsumed under the image of the fusion of the primal unity.

Both Freud and Lacan certainly read Nietzsche, however reluctant the former was to admit it (see Assoun 1980). Therefore, what we seem to have is a developing tradition in Western thought that can be traced from Nietzsche—although, as noted earlier, it certainly does not start with him, having roots in Schopenhauer and Kant before him and ultimately in Buddhism and other very ancient non-Western traditions. (Of course, ancient Greek tradition has the god Dionysus

himself arrive late from his homelands in Asia.) What we see appearing
again and again is the general outline of a structure in which everything
we think and everything we know in the ordinary social world, the
world of language, distills into representations some nonlinguistic
reality that is itself utterly unrepresentable, that "resists symbolization
absolutely." Thus there are, in effect, two realities for us. One reality
is the world as we make sense out of it (and as we, ourselves, are
made a part of that sense) through the workings of society and
language. The other reality is brute, unconstructed, asocial, and non-
sensical. We know nothing about this latter reality—by definition,
since our knowledge is an aspect of our sense making—except for
the fact that it is there, since we know that we are making sense
out of *something* that does not already offer that sense to begin with.
A further insight is offered only very allusively and vaguely by
Nietzsche: the notion that the social, sensible reality always bears
signs to us that there is something behind their web of illusions that
defies them, that language and systems of social meaning always reveal
their own failure to represent the unrepresentable reality and therefore
fail fully to fulfill their very purpose—to make sense. This self-betrayal
is suggested in one of Nietzsche's powerful cadences:

> In the Dionysian dithyramb man is incited to the greatest exaltation
> of all his symbolic faculties; something never before experienced
> struggles for utterance—the annihilation of the veil of *māyā*, one-
> ness as the soul of the race and of nature itself. . . . [S]o the dithy-
> rambic votary of Dionysus is understood only by his peers. With
> what astonishment must the Apollinian Greek have beheld him!
> With an astonishment that was all the greater the more it was
> mingled with the shuddering suspicion that all this was actually
> not so very alien to him after all, in fact, that it was only his
> Apollinian consciousness which, like a veil, hid this Dionysian
> world from his vision. ([1872] 1968, 40–41)[5]

---

5. We should not be mislead by Nietzsche's use of the word *symbol* in this
passage into thinking that Nietzsche conceives of the Dionysian as essentially
symbolic, that is, as representing some other reality. On the contrary, Nietzsche
here describes the impulse of the Dionysian dithyramb as making extraordinary
demands upon one's symbolic faculties to represent its truth: "something never
before experienced struggles for utterance" (*etwas Nieempfundenes drängt sich zur
Äuserung* [1984, 33]). The general confusion of terms in evidence here is akin to

The "shuddering suspicion" that some unacknowledged truth is "not so very alien to [one] after all" is a neat definition of the uncanny (*das Unheimliche*) in Freud. In the Freudian view, dreams, works of art, jokes, quirks of behavior, and even the largest governing principles of social behavior such as religion, law, and courtesy, all betray to the well-initiated perceiver the fact that they simultaneously mask and represent a repressed truth; and the structural imperfections in both the masking and the representation are what enable the analytic investigator to discover the existence of the hidden and unrepresentable drives. This basic set of assumptions continues to hold, of course, in Lacan.

Since Lacan, a number of other theorists, principally French, have turned the focus of psychoanalytic thinking more particularly on the phenomenon of rhythm and its relation to the subject—how, in particular, rhythm challenges or disrupts the subject as constructed within the symbolic order. Accordingly, these theorists have been concerned with a combined psychoanalytic and philosophical approach to the subject that holds some promise for us as a contribution to a theory of poetry.

These writers include Nicolas Abraham in the fifties and sixties, Kristeva in the seventies, and in the eighties Philippe Lacoue-Labarthe. Abraham writes as a psychoanalyst about the phenomena of rhythm and temporality; although some of his concepts seem close to Lacan's, he does not use Lacan's vocabulary, and his own approach, though structuralist, seems closer to the mainstream of Freudian thought as it is known in the United States, Britain, and Germany. Kristeva's concepts of the body and the symbolic order are very close to Lacan. Lacoue-Labarthe refers explicitly to Lacan as well as to Theodor Reik; yet there are also points of contact between his thinking and that of Nicholas Abraham, to whom we turn next.

---

that provoked by the notion of "Apollinian music" as opposed to the Dionysian—and indeed, in this same passage, the former is actually defined as rhythm! Nevertheless, it makes the best sense to see this confusion of terms as resulting from a somewhat unsystematic hypostatizing of the allegorical figures, Apollo and Dionysus, with which Nietzsche is working, so that each figure, in turn, seems to have attributes appropriate to the other. In addition, Nietzsche shifts rather freely between a principally analytical discourse, which is more systematic and straightforwardly allegorical, and a more moral discourse, in which the allegorical figures become personality types. A helpful general comment on Nietzsche's philosophical methods is Walter Kaufmann's review article (1967).

10

Nicolas Abraham; With an Excursus on Rap

The previous two chapters have traced a Nietzschean tradition that leads toward the approach to poetry advocated in this book, at the heart of which is the idea of a relation between the represented and the unrepresentable, the verbal utterance and the sublimity of physical rhythm. Although they do not specifically discuss rhythm, the psychoanalysis Freud and Lacan contribute to this tradition is a powerful elaboration of the way in which the relation between the represented and the unknowable or unrepresentable characterizes the human subject itself, and thus the relation between discourse and the body. Several psychoanalytic and philosophic writers following Freud and Lacan focus more directly on the relation between rhythm and the sublime body and on its implications for poetry. The first of these chronologically, from the early 1960s, is the French psychoanalyst Nicolas Abraham.

Abraham is important to the Nietzschean tradition in part because he is the first within it specifically to advance a theory of rhythm in poetry. As I hope to show, however, Abraham also exposes both the strengths and the weaknesses of using unmodified psychoanalytic concepts in making up a viable theory of poetry. For what I have suggested as Freud's conflict between the mystic and the scientist—one who honors a preserve of the unknowable, and one who must assume that all things can ultimately be known—remains in Abraham's psychoanalytic theory of poetry. The result is that rhythm, while at first appearing as an energy of which the verbal surface of the poem is an allegorical representation, turns out to be recuperable as a meaningful sign itself for a particular quality of emotion. Hence we slip into the rhetorical approach to poetry at the very moment when we seem to have gotten free of it.

In order to show how much of the basic psychoanalytic structure of Abraham will work for the reading of poetry, I shall, with all due respect, attempt a correction of Abraham by presenting my own reading of another poem to balance his. Abraham reads an allegory of rhythm as affect in a famous poem by Goethe, "The Sorcerer's Apprentice." I read a postmodern analogue of the Goethe poem that in broad outline touches on a similar theme: the subject's being overwhelmed by a force that seemed to promise more power for him, but that grew beyond his control. My postmodern answer to Abraham's reading of Goethe will be a reading of a rap, Tone Lōc's "The Funky Cold Medina." These two readings side by side will point up the similarities and the differences between the psychoanalytic developments in the Nietzschean tradition and the theory of poetry as allegory of the sublime. At the same time, this will be a demonstration of the ability of the latter theory to find meaning and depth in popular as well as literary poetry and, to some degree, to account for the former's popularity.

Abraham's *Rythmes* is a posthumous collection of three essays, representing three sequential attempts over more than a decade to define and analyze the phenomenon of rhythm, especially as manifested in poetry, from a psychoanalytic point of view. As Abraham explains in his third and most successful essay, "Pour une esthétique psychanalytique: le temps, le rythme et l'inconscient" (1985, 109–37; orig. 1962), psychoanalysis offers a promising way to approach this question, since it is concerned with the genesis of mental phenomena.[1] In order to explain our ability to detect and create rhythms and to discern imperfections in rhythm with ease, philosophy must resort either to the assumption of a priori mental faculties or to mere phenomenological description, which describes but does not explain or predict (114). While Abraham's ensuing psychoanalytic theory takes on a decided resemblance to a phenomenological narrative description—following the responses to rhythm of an ideal subject, who is in fact the imaginary projection of the writer—Abraham seeks to get beyond the

---

1. A translation is Abraham 1986. I have preferred to provide my own translations here, however.

limits of mere observation (and disguised autobiography) by associating rhythmic phenomena with general concepts of psychic development fairly well established in psychoanalysis.

Abraham's striking achievement is in developing a psychoanalytic method of reading without resorting to a psychoanalysis of the *author* for which the work is a mere symptom of the author's psychic life and conflicts—before such psychoanalysis of the *text itself* had become popular practice, at a time when psychoanalytic readings were still largely biographical and were therefore insulated from the influences of formalism, structuralism, and even the New Criticism. Abraham views the text of the poem as representing its own intrinsic psychic faculties, its own ego, superego, and id. Abraham and Lacan have in common a structuralist bias in their very conception of psychoanalysis, with the result that the text as a system of signs, rather than the personality of the author, remains in focus. This is obviously useful to us in the case of poetry, since a move away from the text and toward the author is in all likelihood a move away from the rhythm of poetry and toward a narrative that takes its place, the narrative of the author's biography or autobiography.

In line with the Nietzschean theoretical tradition outlined here, Abraham sees the essence of the poem as its rhythm, of which the verbal meanings and images are an allegorical representation (or series of allegories) similar to the manifest content of a dream in Freud. Unlike Nietzsche, however, Abraham views the rhythm itself not as a drive, an unrepresentable energy, a sublime force, or a manifestation of the primal unity; rather, in a more specifically Freudian vein, rhythm for Abraham is an expression of affect, prior to and beyond its expression in words or ideas. Sorting out the difference between affect and drive in Freud himself, and therefore in writings after Freud, is by no means a simple matter. For our purposes, the chief difference seems to lie precisely in the question of subjectivity: affects are subjective; drives are not. The affect is an emotional energy that the subject feels and experiences as his or her own, whereas the drives— a point that Lacan particularly underscores—are experienced, through the mediations of affects and representations, as coming "from elsewhere."[2] Thus affect is already a function of a constituted subject and

---

2. In Freud, affects as well as ideas (*Vorstellungen,* representations) are attached

expresses itself, usually, as a specific emotion—whereas the drives are impersonal, work before the subject is constituted as such, and are more indefinite energies. These working definitions may be useful to bear in mind when considering Abraham's treatment of rhythm as a manifestation of affect.

Abraham characterizes rhythm by using an abstract paradigm, such as a series of sixteen trochees (stress syllabic, not pure quantitative). Abraham analyzes this structure strictly in the terms generally used by modern music theorists—that is, in terms of tension and release, expectation and satisfaction. (Later, he associates this natural alternation with the infant's first impulses in sucking from its mother's breast.) Within the first two trochees, the second has something of the same function in relation to the first that the second *syllable* has in relation to the first—an easing of tension, a kind of cadence. Then the following two trochees, numbers three and four, serve the same function in relation to the first two—and so forth, until we reach sixteen. Each time we hear (or read and imagine hearing) a complete set of trochaic feet composed of a number of feet that is a power of two (two, four, eight, sixteen), we feel in retrospect the symmetry of rise and fall that divides the series we have just heard into two neat halves. We feel as if we heard what we might well have expected to hear; a desire or expectation is projected into the immediate past, and we enjoy its satisfaction. In addition, as soon as we begin to exceed the close of any particular unit—say, when we notice that the rhythmic series is indeed going on after the second trochee—then our expectations are raised that another, larger symmetry will be completed. If we hear three trochees in a row, in other words, we expect a fourth, so that we would have a symmetry of two and two, within which each set of two comprises a smaller rise and fall. If we hear five trochees in a row, we expect to hear a total of eight, comprising four rising and four falling, each four of which of course contains a smaller rise and fall, and so forth. The longer the unit we have just completed, the stronger our cumulative expectations become that the entire unit will be repeated to provide the larger symmetry, enabling us to think of

---

to the drives in the process of cathexis—that is, the "occupation" (*Besetzung*) of an object or the image thereof by energy from the drives. See Freud [1912] 1963a, [1915] 1963e, [1915] 1963d; Laplanche and Pontalis 1973, "Affect" (13–14), "Cathexis" (62–65), "Ideational Representative" (203–5), and "Instinct" (or Drive)" (214–17).

what we have just heard as the rise before the fall. Abraham notes that this effect reaches a point of diminishing return after sixteen units: the next even structure would require thirty-two trochees, which is probably too long to hold the listener's sustained attention; and sixty-four is certainly too long, unless some extraordinary devices are contrived to reinforce the pattern, such as elaborate rhyme schemes.

Abraham now places this process of hierarchical levels of relative tension and release into the psychoanalytic context by associating it with two different phenomena. First, running through all three essays as a common thread is a concept of rhythm as something that induces a dream state. Because the regular rhythm continually satisfies the expectations it arouses in the listener, it creates a feeling of perfect control, of mastery, of the omnipotence of the subject—a feeling Freud generally associates with the infantile concept of reality, in which there is hardly a difference between dreams and waking facts. The ego is safe, the world will give it what it expects, so it is in a position to dream of its own wishes. Within this state, of course, the power of the wish (the term Abraham uses, rather than id) still cannot be allowed its physical enactment: the superego must assert a constraint upon the wish by forcing it to be no more than a dream. Even though the rhythm seems to have lulled the superego to sleep— that is, the superego in its capacity as internal reminder of the reality principle, the superego's other guard, the one who protects us from our own tendency to enact our wishes in reality, remains vigilant.[3] It seems as if Abraham even sees rhythm itself as a kind of enactment of the push-pull between unconscious wish and superego within the dreamworld of the ego's imaginary omnipotence; but the main function of rhythm is to induce the ego into such a state that the wishes can be played out in the form of dreams.

Abraham furthermore traces rhythm to the basic physical experiences of desire and satisfaction, and here he naturally associates this natural alternation with the infant's first impulses in sucking from its mother's breast. At the same time, however, the effect of protracted satisfaction created by the hierarchical organization of rhythm into ever

---

3. Abraham has the superego in charge of the reality principle. In Freud, the reality principle is a function of the ego—but the superego is, in fact, a specialized portion of the ego.

longer units corresponds to the superego's infinite deferral of satisfac-
tion, which again has the net result of turning the focus of the ego
from reality to fantasy—a fantasy that will, of course, reflect not only
its wish but its current situation of deferred satisfaction as well.

How Abraham makes use of this particular psychoanalytic model
of rhythm, and of the dual structure of rhythm and dream or affect
and representation, is clear in his suggestive reading of Goethe's
poem, "The Sorcerer's Apprentice" (*Der Zauberlehrling*), a dramatic
monologue.

In "The Sorcerer's Apprentice," the meter begins with even
numbers of trochees, falling easily into the rise-and-fall patterns
described above:

> Hat der alte Hexenmeister
> Sich doch einmal wegbegeben.
> Und nun sollen seine Geister
> Auch nach meinem Willen leben.

> [The old Master-Sorcerer
> has gone away for once, at last.
> And now his spirits are quite sure
> to do my bidding just as his.]

Here and in the next stanza, Abraham draws our attention to the
fact that the rhymes alternate rather than following in simple couplets.
The perfect evenness of the rhythm created by the various hierarchical
levels of the same rise-and-fall pattern should cause us to expect simple
couplets as the immediate fulfillment of expectations. The fact that
this fulfillment comes less expectedly at a delayed point suggests, for
Abraham, a certain "calcul surnois" (1985, 125), a sly plan lurking
beneath the innocent dream state suggested by the meter alone. The
poem's content tells us, of course, that the apprentice does have such
a sly plan to steal his master's magic formula—but then, later, it turns
out that the magic world into which the apprentice thus enters has
its own "calcul surnois," which will take him by surprise, even though
it is quite logical in retrospect.

After these first four lines, the pattern shifts to three trochees
per line, and then, with the spell, two trochees:[4]

---

4. I avoid the term *trochaic trimeter* because it, like many of the traditional terms

Seine Wort' und Werke
Merkt' ich und den Brauch,
Und mit Geistesstärke
Tu' ich Wunder auch.
"Walle, Walle,
Manche Strecke,
Daß zum Zwecke
Wasser fließe
Und mit reichem
Vollem Schwalle
Zu dem Bade
Sich ergieße."

[All his words and works
I noted and the method,
and with this spirit-power
shall I make magic, too.
"Flow, flow,
many reaches,
that to the goal
would water stream
and in a heavy
full flood
into the bath
would pour itself."]

Here, Abraham notes, the odd number of realized beats in the apprentice's boast just before he utters the spell denies the hearer the sense of completeness brought about by the fully realized tetrameter lines in the beginning. This transition signals the passage "from the universe of magic without surprise of the first quatrain to the management

---

for meter in European languages, is misleading. In this case, the term suggests that the meter is structured in fundamental sets of three, whereas in fact, it is quite clear that the fundamental line is still a four-beat line, against which we understand that three of the beats are realized and the fourth is counted in silence. The notion of a silence built into such lines is discussed, along with a much better method of metrical analysis, in Attridge; and the former principle will also come into play in our reading of some Emily Dickinson poems later. The two-beat lines of the spell in this case are probably to be read simply as the equivalent of the original four-beat line, broken in half; there are no silent beats to be inferred here.

of a world that offers no resistance" (125). In other words, the full tetrameters create the affect of the omnipotent ego, a condition that makes possible the magic of dreams. The incomplete tetrameters threaten the possibility that dreams will become reality: not every beat is realized in the form of words that describe dream images. Anxiety mounts.

Abraham does not comment on the further reduction to two-beat lines, but it would make sense to see this as a return to the mood of omnipotence created by the tetrameters, only this time the speaker seems to be trying to take more aggressive, conscious control over that very process. This further accession to power only increases our expectation that the force that holds wishes in check and keeps them in the realm of dreams and out of reality—that is, the superego— will make its forceful return.

The general plot, of course, bears out our expectations. The apprentice himself (i.e., the ego) reveals his own anticipation of the return of the superego by forgetting the second half of his spell, the means to stop the water from coming when the bath is quite full. When, after watery disaster has struck, the humbled apprentice calls his master in desperation, the sorcerer's arrival and assertion of his power over the spirits only serves to reinstate the ego's original position as dreamer and thus to preserve it from the dangers of its attempt to bring its wish into reality. And at this moment, when the balance between ego and superego is reestablished and the difference between dreams and reality is clearly demarcated, the poem naturally ends.

There are several attractive advantages to Abraham's method, as the foregoing reading shows. Abraham succeeds first of all in including the poem's rhythm in an interpretation of its meaning without reducing the rhythm to a mere rhetorical effect used to get the content across. Instead, following the tradition of Nietzsche, the images of the poem are thought of as dream images that represent allegorically the same forces that we can feel being carried through in the rhythm in a realm that is somewhere between the physical and the mental—that is, the affective. Abraham's description of the effect of rhythm as lulling the superego to sleep in order to liberate the free play of the ego's dream-making omnipotence corresponds well with everyday experiences of repetitive sounds or feelings. For Abraham, both meter and content are different modes of expression of the same essential affect, the subconscious wish—which is, in effect, the wish of all wishes, the wish that wishes be true. This idea gives the reading a remarkable coherence and unity without reducing the poem to the critic's own prose paraphrase. Although the example of the specific poem seems to work only too well, one can imagine at least the possibility that the theory would not constrain all poems to mean the same thing, that there would still be an area of free play in the specific interplay between psychic conflict, of affect, and dream representation.

The limitations of Abraham's theory are more or less the points on which psychoanalysis in general may be criticized. The tendency of psychoanalytic theory to be ahistorical and thus apolitical probably need not apply here, since there is room for historical and political context in each poem's specific relation between the dream images and the affect that they represent. Nevertheless, there is something reductive about the concept of affect itself, as an instance of the internal conflict among the text's four psychic agencies, the ego (or "I"), the wish, the superego, and reality. The essence of the poem is its dreamwork, not the drive that it is supposed simultaneously to represent and to repress, since that drive, or wish, is always ultimately the same: to be omnipotent, to have one's wishes be real, or, as in Abraham's reading of Poe's "The Raven," to fill the emptiness of one's subjectivity and thus to make one's desire a reality. Although Abraham is fairly consistent in maintaining the sense that the images are allegorically representing the affective energy of the rhythm, there is a certain sense that even the rhythm is still *representing* something— that is, the conflict among the internal psychic agencies, which only psychoanalysis has the privilege to *name* in a relatively objective and direct manner. Finally, the pursuit of omnipotence for the self stands in marked contrast with the Nietzschean loss of self through the transpersonal experience of rhythm—a loss of self that promises to be radically liberating and to make poetry a powerful, potentially mystical, experience.

While this element in Nietzsche's theory is discarded, Abraham's tendency to allow affect to slip away into symbol continues in the tradition of an unusually neo-Platonic statement in Nietzsche:

> Language can never adequately render the cosmic *symbolism* of music, because music stands in a *symbolic* relation to the primordial

> contradiction and primordial pain in the heart of the primal unity, and therefore *symbolizes* a sphere which is beyond and prior to all phenomena. Rather, all phenomena, compared with it, are merely *symbols*. ([1874] 1967, 55; emphasis added)

Thus music is not really a thing-in-itself, but a mere symbol of something else, something that Nietzsche, in philosophical prose, is privileged to name. Herein lies the contradiction at the heart of Nietzsche's *The Birth of Tragedy*, of course, whereby Nietzsche's most hostile criticism is hurled against the Socratic replacement of poetry with science, but yet Nietzsche's own discourse is in the scientific mode originated by Socrates. As a result of Nietzsche's tendency at moments like this to reduce practically everything into a symbol for a relatively abstract principle, he can see lyric as doomed to nothing but failure:

> Hence *language,* as the organ and symbol of phenomena, can never by any means disclose the innermost heart of music; language, in its attempt to imitate it, can only be in superficial contact with music; while all the eloquence of lyric poetry cannot bring the deepest significance of the latter one step nearer to us. (55–56)

The limitations inherent in Abraham's theory are roughly the same as those placed upon Nietzsche's theory by this passage: lyric poetry ultimately loses its interest for us because even its nonlinguistic elements are mere representations of something else, something that is perhaps better approached, or at least approached in a more clearheaded manner, by some other mode of discourse.

The reduction of rhythm to a mere sign of something else is only an occasional theme in Nietzsche, who otherwise seems to recommend the opposite, especially in his opening discussions of Dionysus as an abstract principle. But this reduction is more in keeping with the general tenor of psychoanalysis, which proposes for itself the task of addressing the irrational, in effect by bringing it under the domain of reason. The result is that in psychoanalysis, to a greater or lesser degree, we become prisoners of our own understanding— indeed, of our selves. Everywhere we go, we are trapped within our own symbolic systems, our own meanings, our own reason. And while the "talking cure" promises to make these meanings and systems more fluid, to undo their neurotic rigidity, we always seem to be stuck inside their boundaries—so that, while psychotherapy offers us the freedom to change, the question of whence that very freedom arises remains a mystery.

Freud and Lacan have ways of getting around this problem. We have seen how, in Lacan, at the very core of the subject itself there is a lack, a preserve of the unknowable and a resistance to reason. In Freud, we see a more dynamic conflict between his own will to reason and his need to preserve a space for the unknown. Thus the structure known/unknown is repeated in many different places in Freudian psychology: the ego is known, as compared with the id, but the ego is largely unconscious, and the id contains representations, which are available to knowledge, as well as drives, which are not. In dealing with poetry, however, we need to establish more clearly the relation between the known and the unknown, the readable and the unreadable, or reading itself threatens to become altogether impossible. And, as I have argued in the earlier chapters of this book, the place of rhythm in the reading of poetry will have to be such that it cannot simply become either another sign or an aid in the expressiveness of signs; for if rhythm is thus reduced to rhetoric, poetry will lose its specificity in relation to prose and will have little or no reason to be, specifically, poetry.

It is possible to retain at once the promising aspects of this theoretical tradition *and* the continued value of poetry itself if we make a single important modification. This would be, instead of thinking of poetic rhythm as a sign representing something, to accept it as a function that is *doing* something—something, moreover, that we can only describe inadequately, for which our discursive description is at least as inadequate as the dream images of poetry itself, if not more so. In other words, we can get out of the bind of mere representation by thinking of rhythm as reality itself—a reality that is peculiar in its insistence, its intrusion upon our mediating linguistic systems, its raw power.

Read this way, Goethe's *Der Zauberlehrling* is one poem in a sort of genre of both high-culture and popular poetry addressing the power of its own rhythm, or more generally the rhythm of poetry, and registering anxiety over the fact that this power, once discovered, cannot be controlled. The sublime power of rhythm may be figured in infinite, historically and culturally specific ways; it may be eroticized as a seductive force, it may be politicized as a tyranny—or its opposite, a revolutionary uprising. And just as infinite, and as historically and culturally encoded, are the interpretations of its uncontrollability, its tendency to evade the very cultural codes that attempt to channel it precisely by naming it or putting it into images.

A ready example of this genre is a rap that was popular in the United States for an unusually sustained period—that is, a few months. One could as easily choose many other raps or other popular (or highbrow) poetic forms to demonstrate a version of this genre, texts that may be better composed and are sure to be less repugnantly homophobic. Still, "Funky Cold Medina" by Tone Lōc offers a remarkably clear demonstration of the playing out of the discovery of rhythm's power and the anxiety over the impossibility of its being controlled. As such, it presents a happy coincidence, a popular, postmodern parallel to Goethe's masterful poem.

> I'm coolin' at a bar
> and I'm looking for some action,
> but like Mick Jagger said
> I can't get no satisfaction.
>
> The girls are all around,
> but none of them want to get with me.
> My threads are fresh and I'm lookin' def.
> Yo, what's up wid' ol' L. O. C.?
>
> The girls were sharp and shocking
> at the other end of the bar
> having drinks with some no-name chump
> when they know that I'm a star.
>
> So I got up and strolled over
> to the other side of the cantina.
> I asked the guy "Why you so fly?"
> He said "Funky Cold Medina."
>
> This brother told me a secret
> on how to get more chicks:
> put a little Medina in your glass
> and the girls will come real quick.
>
> It's better than any alcohol
> or aphrodisiac:

a couple of sips of this love-potion
and she'll be on your lap.

So I gave some to my dog
when he began to beg,
and then he licked his bowl and then he looked at me
and did the *wild thing* on my leg.

He used to scratch and bite me;
before, he was much, much meaner.
But now all the poodles run to my house
for the Funky Cold Medina.

[You know what I'm saying? I've got every dog in my
   neighborhood breaking down my door! I've got Spuds McKenzie,
   Alex from Stroh's—they won't leave my dog alone with that
   Medina, pal.][5]

I went up to this girl.
She said, "Hi, my name is Sheena."
I thought she was good to go with a little
Funky Cold Medina.

She said, "I'd like a drink."
I said "O.k., I'll go get it!"
And then a couple of sips, she go and lick them lips,
and I knew that she was with it.

So I took her to my crib,
and everything went well as planned,
but when she got undressed it was a big ol' mess:
Sheena was a man.

So I threw off bounds—I don't fool around
with no Oscar Meyer Wiener!
You must be sure that the girl is pure
for the Funky Cold Medina.

[You know? Ain't no playin' with a man. This is the 80's and I'm
   down with the ladies, you know?]

---

5. The rapper's spoken commentaries, which are noticeably nonmetrical, are
represented here in square brackets.

Back in the saddle,
looking for a little affection,
I took a shot as a contestant on
The Love Connection.

The audience voted,
and, you know, they picked a winner:
I took my date to the Hilton for
Medina and some dinner.

She had a few drinks,
so I'm thinking, soon, what I'll be getting—
instead she started talking about
plans for a wedding.

So wait! Slow down, love,
not so fast! I'll be seeing you!
That's why I found you don't play around
with the Funky Cold Medina.

[You know what I'm saying? That Medina's a monster, y'all!]

(Tone Lōc 1989)

"Funky Cold Medina" is a narrative poem that can be divided into an initial introduction and three anecdotes following it to illustrate a point. The introduction, set in a bar, represents the male speaker comically as full of himself and yet unsuccessful in finding women who might be interested in him sexually. Happily, a man behind the counter has the perfect remedy: an aphrodisiac. Interestingly, he first seems to say that the potion must go in the *speaker*'s glass; this idea is not borne out later, however. We should also note that the remedy is said to be, not an aphrodisiac, but *better* than any aphrodisiac. This should give us pause as to its symbolic significance.

The following three episodes demonstrate at once the power of the Funky Cold Medina and the speaker's pathetic inability to control its awesome results. First, for some inexplicable reason, the speaker yields to the temptation of giving it to his (male) dog—and immediately becomes the focus of his dog's sexual advances. Next, as one might expect, the whole neighborhood's dogs are flocking to his home without cease. Here, we might note that the other dogs named seem also to be male, suggesting, from the speaker's point of view, an utter chaos of sexual desire.

In the second episode, the speaker is more successful in seducing a woman, but when she undresses at the speaker's home, this woman turns out to be a man. This gives rise to a series of rather flimsy homophobic ad-libs (prose in brackets) on the part of the speaker/rapper, which make sense as an expression of his effort to cling to his social norms in the face of the uncontrollable power of the Funky Cold Medina. For example, "This is the 80's and I'm down with the ladies" treats homosexuality as a fad that has rightly disappeared in response to the advent of AIDS in the last decade. This neoconservative sentiment clashes tellingly with other elements of the rap's tone. Finally, in the third episode, the speaker succeeds in finding a date who is a woman, but, so effectively has the aphrodisiac worked on this woman, she has on her mind, not sex, but—marriage. Thus the speaker's initial goal, which seems rather simple to start with, must go unrealized in the midst of an ever-expanding vortex of possibilities.

It is not difficult to see how "Funky Cold Medina" can be read as an allegory of the uncontrollable power of the rhythm of rap music. The conception of that dance rhythm as seductive lies behind the boasting, at once about sex and musicianship, that forms the stock and trade of rap and that arises out of street traditions much older than the contemporary rap form. Here we have Dionysus in his erotic aspect: the music propels us to sex, but most of all it moves us to dance. But these impulses of the body—rhythm, sex, dance—these are at once simpler and much more intricate, more infinite, than any socially constructed code of analysis, behavior, or decorum. The energy that rap unleashes can go in any direction, and this prospect may well lead the rapper not only to arrogance but also to anxiety. The impossibility of controlling the power of rap music is perhaps never less clearly admitted than in the trials and persecutions against The 2 Live Crew for their relatively less sophisticated, or at least less verbal, "Nasty as They Wanna Be." The power of rap rhythms may seem particularly menacing in its immediate social and historical context, in the eyes and ears of the white middle class, insofar as it represents a power upon which young black men, whose exclusion from power and wealth has been aggravated through the eighties in the United States, may successfully capitalize.

So the power of rap is figured as an aphrodisiac that is *not* quite an aphrodisiac, but better, more powerful. The potion is "cold"—uninvolved with its victims, impersonal, or rather transpersonal. Its power is contagious, so its objects are ubiquitous and come in all varieties, sexes, and species. But the power is also felt most keenly by the subject who produces the rhythm, or, perhaps to put it more accurately, *through whom* the rhythm is produced. Hence the representations of that power are oddly, comically narcissistic: he is first instructed to put the potion *in his own glass*. Even the homosexuality that runs as an undercurrent through the poem may be seen as an extension of this self-involvement. The revelation that the first successful date is actually a man is the more shocking, in that case, precisely because it is uncanny: the speaker should have known it all along; the speaker has, indeed, produced the scene himself. When the speaker succeeds in discovering the wholly other, the second date, then naturally her fantasies are different from his. But at this point, the social control connoted by the idea of marriage enters into the speaker's dreamworld, and so, naturally, the poem soon comes to an end. Here we can see another parallel with Goethe's *Der Zauberlehrling* in Abraham's reading, where the return of the superego shatters the dreamworld and brings the poem to its close. But in our present reading, what is broken up is not only a dream, but a dream representation of a real force, a sublime materiality. The introduction of the repressive social code works not so much to disenchant the world of dreams as to return us to the state in which the sublime power of reality is hidden from us, the normal state of prose.

"Funky Cold Medina" ends quickly, but not without a warning. Yet the warning is hard not to take comically, and one does indeed reflect back upon the whole narrative as an elaborate joke. Everyone knows that aphrodisiacs don't really work. Dogs mounting their owners' knees or gathering in groups, transvestites seducing unsuspecting straight young men, and unknown dates proposing marriage— none of these are truly extraordinary events. Indeed, in retrospect, it is striking how ordinary—even natural—they all are. In sum, we must regard the Funky Cold Medina as ambiguous in its efficacy: perhaps it is an aphrodisiac, or perhaps it is just an excuse for the speaker to tell a story. But this ambiguity coheres with the ambiguous tone of the speaker's whole narrative: is he boasting or is he complaining? When he calls himself a "star," is it sincere or ironic? The important point is that these ambiguities do not undermine the power of the rap's rhythm at all: they merely express the inadequacy of the rap's allegory to represent that power fully. A free-floating, somewhat

self-effacing irony is thus a most effective strategy for at once naming
the power of rhythm and admitting that the name is but a name and
falls short of its referent.

The rhythm of "Funky Cold Medina" can fairly easily be
understood as a sign itself. Like all raps, this one is in tetrameter,
but the second and fourth lines generally realize only three of the
four beats, bringing this rap squarely in line with the ballad tradition.
Occasional internal rhyme in the second and fourth lines of the
stanzas further associates it with a subgenre of ballad to which
Coleridge's "Rime of the Ancient Mariner" belongs. These metrical
features surely generate usually unconscious but nevertheless persuasive
generic expectations.

Nevertheless, it is by considering the same rhythm under its
aspect not as a sign for the meanings associated with a generic
tradition, but as a physical effect, an appeal to the body, that we can
successfully steer clear of the limitations imposed by the psychoanalytic
model presented by Nicolas Abraham. In so doing, we do not follow
the letter so much as the spirit of Nietzsche's theory of the lyric in
reasserting the primacy of rhythm, its ability to bring us beyond the
endless play of mere signs, and its power to define the strategies we
use to name it and to tame it in the name of reason.

Julia Kristeva: Body and Symbol

While Abraham's use of psychoanalysis to read poetry has the effect of bringing rhythm within the purview of its rational explanations, some two decades later Julia Kristeva turns to psychoanalysis in order to account for rhythmic forces at work prior to the very advent of rational thought in the individual subject. In so doing, Kristeva opposes the tendency of psychoanalysts—and Lacan in particular— to slip into speaking about the symbolic order (and thus the rationalizable, if not the rational) every time they mean to be speaking about the unconscious and the irrational (see Barzilai 1991). For Kristeva, prerational, rhythmic forces continue to work throughout life, after the advent of subjectivity within the individual, as a kind of unconscious substrate, both supporting and disrupting the activity of reason. In Kristeva's *Revolution in Poetic Language* (1984), this notion of the interaction between the rhythmic and the rational is framed within a literary theory. But her book is also much more: an argument against the modern philosophical tradition of Hegel and phenomenology (and even structural anthropology); a psychoanalytic theory of the development of the subject that makes use of Freud and Lacan but also goes beyond them; a theory of language and of the genesis of the linguistic subject; a theory of the nature and origin of poetry or "poetic language," including how it differs from other modes of discourse; and a theory of *early modern* (late nineteenth-century avant-garde) poetry and the significance of its formal and rhetorical departures from tradition. As such, and replete with learned references to Hegel, Husserl, Heidegger, and Frege among philosophers, to Hjelmslev, Chomsky, and various other modern linguists, to Freud and Lacan and to post-Lacanians, and to modern French feminist thought, *Revolution* is notoriously intimidating and hard to read.[1] Kristeva explains a great deal—perhaps even too much—leaving the commentator at something of a loss as to what to consider most important. But her basic theoretical structures still participate, in their own fashion, in the tradition of Nietzsche. And while the theory of poetry as telling rhythm—the allegorical interpretation of poetry as paradoxically representing its own unrepresentable rhythmic power—is relatively a simpler structure than Kristeva's, her purposes are different. Kristeva's theory focuses not on methods of reading but on the nature and genesis of language in general and literary texts in particular. Given that focus, Kristeva argues forcefully for an understanding of poetry that places rhythm and the nonsensical, rather than theme or content, front and center.

Although I am considering Kristeva within the context of theory of poetry, Kristeva's sense of poetic language is not limited to verse. In this regard, Kristeva continues the tradition begun by Aristotle and developed in modern times by the formalists of calling poetic any literary language in either prose or verse. It is assumed that there are observable features of the language itself, and not just its

---

1. See, for example, the recent exchange of articles between Calvin Bedient (1990, 1991) and Toril Moi (1991). *Révolution du langage poétique* is Kristeva's dissertation for the French *doctorat d'état*. As such, frankly, it is written in what we Americans call dissertationese.

Moi also gives a helpful and very readable, if brief, exposition of Kristeva's theories in chapter 8 of her *Sexual/Textual Politics* (1985, 150–73). A more thorough treatment of Kristeva is the volume by John Lechte (1990). Also interesting and helpful is chapter 7, on Kristeva, in Coward and Ellis 1977, 122–52. This last is especially helpful in giving a quick overview of Husserlian phenomenology and Lacanian psychoanalysis insofar as they are important contexts for understanding Kristeva.

Moi, Lechte, and Coward and Ellis are all sympathetic presentations of Kristeva's theory. Significantly, none of them, however, focuses on Kristeva as a theorist of *poetry*. Moi is concerned primarily with Kristeva's contribution to feminism via her exploration of the subject and its potential for revolutionary self-transformation. Lechte presents Kristeva as a theorist of the avant-garde, especially within the context of Marxism, which (in its orthodoxy) has tended to ignore or attack the avant-garde and to deny it any revolutionary potential. Coward and Ellis present Kristeva primarily as a theorist of the subject, and thus, like Moi, emphasize the revolutionary potential of the continually contested and remade subject-in-process, especially within a post-Marxist context.

social context or use, that distinguish the literariness of a literary text. In fact, beneath its daunting surface, and aside from a very elaborate psychoanalytic apparatus with equally elaborate post-Marxist social implications, Kristeva's general concept of the literary text has much in common with the now-familiar formalist notion of literary language as an instance of language turning its focus in upon itself and especially—as in Jakobson's "poetic function"—upon its *material* substance. At the same time, however, Kristeva shares with some formalist writing a certain equivocation between generally literary language and actual poetry, between text and poem, an equivocation heightened by Kristeva's emphasis on the rhythmic elements of poetic language.

Somewhat in line with some of the concerns of the formalists, *Revolution in Poetic Language* can be thought of as an attempt to answer (among others) the question of what poetic language does, for the individual who writes it or reads it and for the society in which it appears. But Kristeva's answer appears to be rather different from the formalist notion of defamiliarization.[2] In order to answer the question, Kristeva turns toward more basic questions about the relation between the subject of language and the language he or she speaks. For Kristeva, the subject is never a static entity. It produces itself in the language it speaks. Thus the relation between the subject and language is a complex and politically crucial dialectical process. Far from the subject simply being the producer or consumer of language to serve as communication, Kristeva's subject alters language a bit by speaking it, and then language alters the subject in turn. Because the subject of language is so dynamic, when language focuses on itself enough to bring to the surface elements of its own conflictual and dialectical origins—as literary language does—then it participates in a process of historical change both for the individual subject and

---

2. In fact, even in this regard, Kristeva is not so far different from the formalists as she might seem. Defamiliarization is a way of making experience—both of the world represented in literature and of the language in which it is represented—fresh and new, so that then one can perceive with restored vigor the realities of the world and, by implication, the fact that those realities are only a set from among many other possibilities. This opening out or freeing up of one's mind that comes from turning away from mere language as communication is the basis of Kristeva's revolutionary conception of literature.

for the society in general. This is the revolutionary potential of literary language, according to Kristeva.

For Kristeva, the subject is not a simple, coherent, unitary subject, there, like God, from the start. This well-established notion of the subject, Kristeva points out, is the model developed by Descartes and passed down through the philosophical tradition of Kant, Hegel, and the phenomenologists. The problem with this model of the subject is that, while it is used to explain everything else—perception, judgment, language, action, law, art, politics—there is no explanation for *it*. How did the subject get there? If, as the Cartesian subject, I can say, "I think, therefore I am," how did I get around to start thinking? What was I before I started thinking—or at least started knowing that I was thinking? What do I become when I am not thinking about the fact that I am thinking? Do I still exist then?

These questions are more germane to the issue of literariness than one might at first suppose. It is very difficult for us to conceive of anything like thought that would have nothing to do with language. In fact, our tendency today, under the influences of structuralism and poststructuralism, is increasingly to consider thought entirely inseparable from the symbolic processes of which language is the most obvious and most intricately developed instance. But if the Cartesian subject is the subject of language, then how can we ever speak of the subject's *acquiring* language? This happens, obviously, when a child is learning to speak, understand, read, and write—and also when an adult learns a foreign language. It also happens when someone reads or writes a poem, insofar as something new in language is then becoming part of the subject's cumulative experience. Literariness is generally thought of as a distinctiveness from other uses of language, and there is a certain newness about the experience of a work of art. This freshness cannot be explained if we think of the subject who makes and who enjoys the artwork as always already there, eternally the same in every aspect and fixed from the beginning.

If, moreover, one wished to maintain, as Kristeva does, that art and literature play a major role in social change, it would make best sense to think of these cultural practices as having such an historical effect precisely because they change the way people think, speak, and look at the world—in other words, they change the subject. This in turn would only make sense if the subject is thought of not as a fixed entity but as a dynamic participant in a process that involves change and conflict everywhere. Hence, for Kristeva, the subject is a *sujet en procès:* at once a "subject in process" and a "subject on trial," always being called into question by the very forces that brought it into being.

Hegel and the phenomenologists, especially Husserl, do concern themselves with how the subject changes over time. That is the predominant question guiding dialectical reasoning. But in none of these philosophers does the subject have a definable origin. The subject is assumed to exist, and philosophy studies the consequences of its existence in the realms of perception, knowledge, truth, and so forth. In order to find some theoretical framework within which to ask the fundamental question of the subject's coming into being, Kristeva turns to psychoanalysis—especially to the writings of Freud, Melanie Klein, and Lacan, who are concerned both with the development of the subject and its relation to language. Kristeva's theory may then be seen as a new chapter in this ongoing psychoanalytic project—a chapter that highlights the importance of literary language in the individual and social history of the subject.

For Kristeva, as for Lacan, the being who exists before a coherent linguistic subject is organized is, on the one hand, a kind of nothingness or chaos, but also, on the other hand, a very dynamic state. Lacan may call this state of being, as it is faintly recollected by the later, constructed subject, by the name "the real"; but Kristeva distinguishes it from the real and resists Lacan's tendency to subordinate it to the symbolic order—both in his concept of mental life and in the focus of his theory (Barzilai 1991, 296). According to Kristeva, beginning near birth, as part of the process of growth, the indefinable and unimaginable continuum of the infant's sensations becomes broken up somehow into divisions. These divisions are neither stable nor permanent; on the contrary, constantly changing, they are part of the dynamic chaos of the presubject. One might think of what life would be like in this state (rather like imagining life on the surface of the sun!) as a kind of *space*—ever changing, moving, with no defined boundaries, but having some possibility of being filled with something, like a blackboard upon which one could now mark some momentary divisions with a chalk, yet one would always be erasing the lines simultaneously. (Think of the popular American child's toy known as the Etch-a-Sketch.) It would be inappropriate to say that at this point the child is thinking, and thus we cannot speak of a subject at all. Kristeva's metaphor for this state of affairs is precisely *space*, for which she uses the ancient Greek word, *chora*. This word has additional resonances because of its use in Plato's *Timaeus* in an exposition of Socrates' theory of the origin of the universe. The chora there is the original space in which the demiurge forms the universe—which is also compared, not surprisingly, to the space of the womb.[3]

For Kristeva, this space, the chora, is not only characterized by a kind of free motion of somewhat distinct forces; it is more specifically the field for the free play of various and conflicting drives. More particularly again, we should recall the dualism of drives in Freud, which, after his pivotal *Beyond the Pleasure Principle* ([1920] 1961), were established as the forces of love and death—the drive to become one with other beings and to put things together, and the drive to return to the prior state of being, the state of inanimate matter. In the infant, the drives may be thought of as diametrically opposed forces, expressed, for example, in the urge to suck the mother's breast and

---

3. A study of poetry and theories of poetry or related matters over time reveals, repeated as a kind of motif, the metaphor of an empty vessel or container whose outer surface is decorated with markings. To name just a few, ancient and modern: the Platonic chora, which may be connected to the idea of Socrates being a midwife for the truth; the "ivy cup" in Theocritus *Idyll* 1; Donne's "The Canonization," Gray's "Elegy in a Country Churchyard," and, most of all, Keats's "Ode on a Grecian Urn," all three of which are discussed in Cleanth Brooks's *The Well Wrought Urn* (1947); Heidegger's essay, "The Thing" ([1951] 1971d); and Kristeva. In Keats, as in Kristeva, the vessel is feminine ("unravished bride of Quietness"), a kind of womb. The association of jars or other vessels with the woman's body can be traced back at least as far as archaic Greek culture; see duBois (1988).

Noland 1991 rightly stresses how Kristeva characterizes the chora as maternal and as part of or connected to the mother's body. Nevertheless, Noland also observes how in a somewhat later text, *Stabat Mater* (1977), Kristeva seems to call into question the simplicity of "the mother" as a purely biological, physical entity. "What Kristeva confirms in 'Stabat Mater' is not the existence of a maternal language, but rather the *desire* to believe that there was one. Accordingly, poetry does not actualize a homogeneous maternal chora, but rather, expresses a nostalgia for its ontic possibility" (139–40). If indeed the semiotic chora turns out to be, in Kristeva's thinking, a phantom generated by desire, which in turn is a product of the imposition of the symbolic order, then there never is any material base upon which prelinguistic play develops, but only a retrospective fantasy thereof, once language is acquired. It is frankly hard to see how we are not simply going around in circles.

to spit it out or bite it, to take in and to reject, as described by Melanie Klein. An important part of Freudian theory is the idea that, in the unconscious, conflicting drives cannot be resolved or decided—they simply must coexist. This is because there is no such thing as "no" in the unconscious; since nothing can be negated, even contradictory forces must dwell together in constant struggle. Kristeva then proposes that these opposing forces are transformed from pure conflict into a kind of rhythmic pulsation by the moderating, stabilizing influence of the chora. The weight of a pendulum works similarly: the pendulum resolves the conflicting forces of leftward and rightward swinging into an alternation from left to right, by virtue of its weight. In electronics, a capacitor performs a similar function within an oscillator circuit, accumulating electrical charge until a certain point, at which it is released, only to start over again, with the charges reversed and the eventual flow going in the opposite direction.

The chora is then characterized by shifting divisions among discrete units of energy and sensation and by rhythmic alternations. To return to my analogy with the blackboard, because the chora is a space for a kind of marking, Kristeva refers to the activity therein as *semiotic,* to distinguish it from the activity of the more fully constructed subject, which is *symbolic.* One might regard the use of the word *semiotic* as unfortunate, since, in view of the whole modern science of semiotics, one thinks of the word as having to do precisely with the operation of symbols or signs and their meanings. But Kristeva's French distinguishes between *le sémiotique,* which has the special meaning under discussion here, and *la sémiotique,* which is the more general study of the sign. Moreover, Kristeva emphasizes the difference in etymological meanings between the two terms. True, *semiotic* derives from a Greek word used to mean "sign"; but the emphasis is on the *marking* or *scratching* of a sign on material. By contrast, *symbol* literally calls up the image of "throwing together" the sign next to its meaning, the signifier thrown down next to its signified. So the emphasis here is on the relation between the two components of the sign and thus the working of symbolic representation rather than the mark-making characteristics of the signifier. The infantile stage before the accession to the symbolic stage is thus, for Kristeva, a period of the free play of sounds and gestures. These sounds and gestures will eventually become used as signs, but for now, they are simply distinctive expressions relative to each other, forming rhythmic alternations. One need only think of those commonplaces of baby talk, "gagaga" and "googoogoo," the infant's clapping hands and kicking feet. "Dada" and "mama" are mere sound play before they come to mean father and mother.[4]

The repetitive tendency of this infantile sound play also follows the Freudian principles of the primary process in dreams, displacement and condensation. In displacement, one sound is equivalent to another in some way and therefore can replace it. In condensation, a single sound can represent or condense within it many different impulses. For Kristeva, these two opposing principles give rise, after the acquisition of language, to the two basic principles of language and figurative expression, selection and combination, or metaphor and metonymy.[5]

---

4. Kristeva later on suggests that sounds such as "mama" and "papa" have a kind of spontaneous personal meaning for the infant uttering them before they are even words in any proper sense. That is, each sound the infant utters expresses some sort of drive or instinctive function—for example, *m* in "mama" arises from oral drives to take in (the breast), to introject; *p* in "papa" arises from anal-aggressive drives (to spit out, etc.). Kristeva then claims that poetic language allows such direct expressions of drives in sounds to break through the surface of communicative, symbolic language. This theory certainly provokes thought; but why what is true of poetic language is not just as true of every linguistic utterance, since all language is made of sounds or gestures, is unclear. Probably the formalist notion of poetic language being by nature focused on its material being and not on its communicative value (see also Frege [1892] 1980) helps to account for her privileging of that special subset of all utterances. But one of Jakobson's most emphatic points in "Linguistics and Poetics" (1960) is precisely how common phrases like "Jack and Jill" or "I like Ike" demonstrate the workings of the poetic function in everyday communication.

5. Selection and combination give rise, respectively, to metaphor and metonymy according to Jakobson (see chap. 7 above). Kristeva then carries over from Lacan ("L'Instance de la lettre" [(1957) 1966b]) the neat identification of the Freudian terms *condensation* and *displacement* with the rhetorical tropes, respectively, metaphor and metonymy. Lacan in turn derives this identification from Jakobson 1971, but Jakobson himself suggests, somewhat more logically, that both displacement and condensation are like metonymy, while *substitution* and *symbolism* are like metaphor. It might be better to consider the Freudian binary pair as another set of axes that would cross those of metaphor and metonymy. (This gives us four dimensions, which can't be drawn or visualized, but that is mere inconvenience.) *All* metaphors and all metonymies—that is, all tropes—are in fact displacements: they displace the original term and use another term instead. Words rich in significant associations,

Eventually, the mentally healthy (i.e., not psychotic) child develops a more coherent social self, a subject that accords with the Cartesian concept, and that, for Lacan as well as for Kristeva, is by definition a linguistic subject, one who can string conventionally defined words together into meaningful sentences that can have a truth-value. The child acquires this self gradually, and chiefly by means of two stages proposed by Lacan. The first is the mirror stage, in which the child develops a (usually visual) image of his or her own bodily unity in contradistinction to everything outside that unity—a boundary surrounding a coherent entity. A few years later, the child enters the Oedipus complex, at which point he or she is introduced to the function of symbols themselves by means of the symbolic importance of the father's phallus and the fantasy of castration—the play of absence and presence that leads to the idea of manipulating things that stand for other things that are absent.

Kristeva thinks of this developmental process as the child's taking of a *position* in relation to the world of other people and objects, and thus calls it the *thetic* phase, since *thesis* in Greek means "a setting, placing, arranging;... a being placed, position, situation" (Liddell and Scott). The subject who manipulates symbols may be thought of, as in most poststructuralist theory, as a position within a weblike system of symbols and values; and as in poststructuralism generally, so in Kristeva, the social and the symbolic are basically the same thing (1984, 72). As the subject comes into being and takes its position in the sociosymbolic order, it also becomes implicated in the values and beliefs, the prejudices and habits of mind, of the society.

---

such as the serious puns prevalent in Renaissance literature, show condensation; they may or may not also be tropes such as metaphors or metonymies. A given trope may be more "displaced" than another trope, if the term being used is more remote either in likeness or in connectedness to the term suppressed (i.e., the referent). A catachresis might be thought of as a trope whose quantity of displacement exceeds some threshold that could be defined by further research. Some allegories seem flat because their metaphors have very little condensation; others, such as *The Faerie Queene*, condense a great deal on many levels.

For an excellent critique of Lacan's and Jakobson's efforts to connect Freud's terms with rhetorical tropes, see Lyotard 1991b. This essay itself, in its discussion of the Freudian dream, bears some remarkable points of contact with the present theory of poetry, as well as some divergences; a closer reading of it is beyond my present scope.

But these initiatory processes, the mirror stage and the Oedipus complex, do not simply befall the child from somewhere outside. The capacity of the chora to make momentary divisions and breaks predisposes the developing child to make a permanent break between himself or herself and the outside world, among discrete objects that he or she perceives, and between things and the symbols that represent them.[6] Yet Kristeva describes the thetic as itself a breaking away from or breaking up of the original, chaotic and continuous chora, a violent shattering of semiotic play and of the cloudy unity with the mother. Thus, paradoxically, the chora's very characteristics lead to its own fragmentation. (In Lacan, too, the acquisition of the social "I" is a thoroughly alienating process that brings with it a desire always to return to the indefinable, wordless wholeness that had been there before its advent.) While it serves as the very image of coherency, the social, linguistic subject is made precisely by breaking the vessel of its origin, the chora.

But the paradox goes further, and the chora, although rent, does not go away. For the overriding principle at work in the chora is a kind of negativity that Kristeva calls rejection (*rejet*)[7], and that rejection now works against the thetic just as it has worked against the chora itself to begin with. Kristeva takes great pains to compare this negativity both to the philosophical, especially Hegelian, concept of negativity and to the psychoanalytic concept of negation, and then to distinguish her term from both. One of Kristeva's most abstract (and abstruse) concepts, rejection is a sort of force that breaks things up and thrusts things away or out. The rejection at work in the chora to begin with is what makes possible the periodicity of the semiotic—instead of everything being totally mixed up in a state that is truly formless and void, the chora already separates out different elements and estab-

---

6. This break is *permanent* insofar as the subject continually reaffirms or re-experiences it; if it fails to do so, the result is a slippage into psychosis—one cannot simply return to infancy. But Kristeva always represents functions of the subject, such as the thetic break, as ongoing, dynamic processes rather than fixed states or unalterable features. The subject is continuously, repetitively undergoing the thetic phase, while simultaneously experiencing its own undoing under the power of the semiotic chora.

7. Lechte and Kristeva's translator, Margaret Waller, translate *rejet* as "rejection"; Coward and Ellis prefer "expulsion."

lishes enough stability in each one so that a rhythm will result. (The awkwardness of my language here imitates Kristeva's and responds to the difficulty of talking about what life would be like if one were not a subject with "a life" as such—without falling into familiar but misleadingly subjective metaphors.)

Unlike Hegelian negativity, rejection does not lead to a totalizing negation of the negation—there is no resolving synthesis, even momentarily—although, in other ways, the idea that one's life is propelled onward along its path by a series of conflicts, one succeeding the other, carries over to Kristeva from the Hegelian-Marxist tradition. The concept of negation in psychoanalysis (Freud [1925] 1963f) "Negation" avoids such totalization, since there negation is really the sign of repression and thus of the continued presence, under the surface, of something positive. If the patient tells the analyst, "I don't hate you," one can assume that the patient *does* hate the analyst and is revealing simultaneously both hatred and the need to hide it from consciousness.

But unlike this psychoanalytic negation, Kristeva's rejection does not involve repression, strictly speaking. To begin with, most of what is going on in the Kristevan model of the developing subject is unconscious to begin with, and Kristeva follows Freud's notion that there is no such thing as "no" in the unconscious—nothing can be repressed, nothing can be annihilated. Forces in the Freudian unconscious are often in conflict, pitted against one another, but those conflicts occur precisely because everything is affirmed, nothing is made to disappear. Freudian repression is not a function of the drives in relation to each other, but rather a function of the relation between unconscious drives and conscious processes.[8] Rejection, unlike repression, is itself a function of one of the drives: the death drive, which gives us, in Freud, both the urge to expel, separate, and disintegrate and the compulsion to repeat and thereby create a rhythm. Death is also the urge to return to the earlier state—ultimately, the state of inanimate being. Rejection thus involves breaking up and casting out, but not doing away with anything.

The force of rejection breaks up the chora to provide a discrete

---

8. This is true, even though repression itself, according to Freud, is unconscious. This fact makes repression a very complicated and troublesome concept in Freud, despite its obvious centrality. See his essay on "Repression" ([1915] 1963d).

"position" for the thetic subject. But it then breaks up that thetic subject as well, allowing a subtle influx of chaotic, rhythmic energy from the semiotic to make itself felt in and through the subject's symbolic operations, in a manner reminiscent of Freud's "return of the repressed."[9] Perhaps we may turn back to Jakobson's observations of the working of the poetic principle in everyday language for examples of what Kristeva means: the urge to say "Jack and Jill" rather than "Jill and Jack," the popularity of the slogan "I like Ike," and, for that matter, that of the alliterative and rhythmic "no new taxes" or the propaganda label "freedom fighters" all demonstrate the operation of euphonic, rhythmic wordplay lurking underneath the surface of mere communication. Verbs like *ululate* and *lucubrate,* whose Latin etymologies are opaque to speakers of English, have serious meanings but can create humorous effects merely because of their playful sounds. And the poetic (or literary) text, for Kristeva as for Jakobson, focuses special attention upon this nonsensical play of signifiers. It is a kind of compromise (but not a resolution) between the semiotic and the symbolic.

Without this compromise, there would be two alternative directions in which the chora could go. On the one hand, the chora could continually break up the thetic so that a subject position is never clearly established. The result is psychosis. On the other hand, without the compromise made possible by poetry, the chora could be so hemmed in and controlled that only the symbolic order and its established social values would prevail. Thus there would be no change, no history, and perhaps the whole system itself would fall apart, because there would be no life impulse to sustain it.

For Kristeva, the ceremonial act of communal sacrifice typifies this triumph of the symbolic. Here, the sacrificial object—an animal, as in Old Testament Judaism, or a young god, as in Christianity— is slaughtered in order to mark the transition from material things to symbols, "killing substance to make it signify" (1984, 75). In this

---

9. Since the chora, with its breaking up and its repetitiveness, is informed by the death drive, and the thetic, breaking up the chora, is also a product of the death drive, poetic language is a case of the death drive working against the death drive. This gives us a collapsing of Freud's dualism into a monism of death. Compared to other problems in Kristeva's logic, however, this one is minor.

way, sacrifice is a "counterpart to the thetic moment instituting symbolism" (74).[10]

> This violent act puts an end to previous (semiotic, presymbolic) violence, and, by focusing violence on a victim, displaces it onto the symbolic order *at the very moment* this order is being founded. Sacrifice sets up the symbol and the symbolic order at the same time, and this "first" symbol, the victim of a murder, merely represents the structural violence of language's irruption as the murder of soma, the transformation of the body, the captation of drives. (75)

But Kristeva also points out that a recitation of poetry is often included within the ceremony of sacrifice, before the actual slaughter. A familiar example is, of course, the recitation and later the dramatic enactment of a choral ode to the god Dionysus before the slaughter of a goat (τράγος), which, as Nietzsche points out, gives us the origin of tragedy. Poetry in this instance serves as a counterbalance to the violence of the sacrifice, allowing a controlled expression to the semiotic impulses that would otherwise be completely repressed by the symbolic order. Although it may seem that poetry actually contributes to the regime of the symbolic in such instances, because the poem, presumably, expresses the symbolic significance of the sacrificial event, Kristeva probably works on the assumption that everyone would already know the significance of the sacrifice, and other, nonpoetic verbal formulas might serve the purpose of making it explicit, if necessary. For Kristeva, the sacrifice itself is symbolic and is the basis of a contract within the society whereby the meanings of symbols in general are ratified. The poem, then, provides something in excess of this institution of the symbolic: it grants the semiotic a return from its banishment, but only within a disguise that makes it safe.

As in Nietzsche, then, poetry (or literature, or artistic practices) has the individual and social function of *preserving* individual sanity and social order precisely by permitting some free play to the original,

---

10. The chora is not exactly "substance" the way the victim's body is, but it *is* material and bodily—it is an aspect of the life of the body.

nonsensical chaos, within a structure that maintains symbolic sense as well. On the one hand, poetry assaults and challenges the social status quo, the normal, conventional system of symbols and their values. On the other hand, poetry safeguards that same system from being completely exploded by the forces that it represses or rejects.

The idea that artistic practices have, on the social or political level, at once a challenging and a stabilizing role, that the work of art is simultaneously innovative and conservative, is neither limited to Kristeva nor to Nietzsche before her; it is almost a commonplace today. In American New Historicist readings of Shakespeare, for example, one comes time and again to the conclusion that Shakespearean drama has equal and opposite political significance, both as a potentially revolutionary challenge to, and as a conservative voice upholding, the (royal, Church of England) status quo. Likewise, Leonard B. Meyer observes offhandedly that comedy "tends to be politically conservative" (1983, 521n5), since the comic resolution always involves the restoration of order after a disturbance. Might one not say the same for tragedy, which eliminates the disturbing element by means of the sacrificial nemesis? And isn't melodrama, too, a reassurance of the stability of the prevailing order, in which a better condition can be achieved through earnest effort and faith in that very order? Fredric Jameson observes a pattern of challenge and recovery in popular movies such as *The Godfather* (1979). It turns out, in fact, that, if we are looking to define the political significance of *any* work of art, we shall inevitably see, with almost tiresome predictability, the same delicate balance of revolution and repression, disturbance and recovery, challenge and conservation.

Nor need one resort to so complex a psychoanalytic apparatus as Kristeva's in order to explain why this must be the case. Literature is made of language, which is always already there before the text comes into being and before the reader reads it. In order for the text to be apprehended as such—that is, as something made of language—it must recall the already existing codes, even if it then alters them somewhat within its own workings. But those very alterations, the revolutionary elements of a literary work, have no meaning and therefore no effect whatsoever unless they are seen against a firmly established context of language as it already exists and is shared by the community of readers. What is true on the level of mere words and sentences is also true for higher-order forms of organization such as genres: every work simultaneously evokes a genre, with its generic expectations, and frustrates those expectations slightly by fulfilling the genre in a new way. What is true of all literature is true a fortiori of verse, whose rhythms recall traditions and their associations at the same time that the realization of those traditions must be new. If the realization of language, genre, and verse structure are not somehow innovative, then, once again, the text will lapse into meaninglessness; its interplay with the linguistic intertexts will be imperceptible. Thus every poem must be simultaneously novel and conservative.

Kristeva does not describe the revolutionary properties of the literary text in terms of its thematic meaning, however, and in this way, she avoids a mere restatement of its double, contradictory social effect. Instead, she appeals to the notion, well known from Roland Barthes's writings, of *jouissance*. It is not so much that literary texts *say* something new or even that they say something in a new way, but rather that they cause the workings of communication in language to come a bit unhinged, allowing the reader to experience the elating, arresting, and even disturbing freedom of the play of sounds that underlies language but also undermines it. For better clarification of the concept of *jouissance*, I turn to a passage from Barthes's *Le Plaisir du texte*, which contrasts that term with the apparently tamer *plaisir* (pleasure):

> The text of pleasure: the one that contents, fulfills, gives euphoria; the one that comes from the culture, doesn't break with it, is tied to a *comfortable* practice of reading. The text of bliss [*jouissance*]: the one that puts one at a loss, the one that discomforts (perhaps even to a certain boredom), causes the reader's historical, cultural, and psychological foundations to totter, along with the consistency of his tastes, his values, and his memories; it puts his relation to language in crisis. (1973, 25–26; my translation)

We should not turn back from Barthes to Kristeva without first noting that the apparent contrast upon which this passage rests is in fact undermined by the rest of Barthes's essay. If on the one hand the "text of pleasure" is different from the "text of bliss," on the other hand, *both* kinds of reading are aspects of the pleasure of the text. There obviously is pleasure in bliss—otherwise, why seek it?—

and pleasure, hopefully, leads to bliss after a certain point. In Barthes, these terms are playfully evanescent and not a rigidly binary pair of the classically structuralist sort.

But for Kristeva, the contrast is marked and is analogous to her structural contrast between the utterly heterogeneous semiotic and symbolic functions. In a text, the aspect of language that communicates meaning is symbolic. Sound effects such as rhymes (especially internal or accidental), local alliteration, assonance, and other sorts of repetitions of particular phonemes or sound figures bear witness to the breaking through of semiotic processes into the symbolic surface. These evidences of the semiotic can then be analyzed and considered as such. Kristeva uses several examples from Mallarmé and Lautréamont, demonstrating different minute facets of her theory in each case. For our purposes, her treatment of Mallarmé's "Prose (pour des Esseintes)" is of particular interest because that is the only text included that follows a clear metrical pattern and thus the only one that virtually anyone will agree is a poem.

In the first quatrain, Kristeva notes, there is a preponderance of voiced and unvoiced labial stops compounded with *r* sounds (e.g., *rb*, *tr*, etc.) (1984, 241–46):

> Hyperbole! de ma mémoire
> Triomphalement ne sais-tu
> Te lever, aujourd'hui grimoire
> Dans un livre de fer vêtu.
>
> > (Mallarmé 1966, 68)

> [Hyperbole! from my memory can't you rise triumphantly,
> today mumbo-jumbo in an iron-clad book?]

Following Mallarmé's own lead, Kristeva concentrates on these sounds, but with a difference. The nineteenth-century poet had freely associated various ideas and images with various sounds, in a well-known essay called *Les Mots anglais. P,* for example, is associated in Mallarmé's mind with "the very plain meaning [*intention*] of piling up, of acquired wealth, or of stagnation" (quoted in Kristeva 1984, 242). But Kristeva adds a developmental, psychoanalytic dimension to this free-associative cataloging of sounds. "The phallic aggressive drive /tR/, /dR/, /f/, etc. and anal /gR/ . . . is opposed to the oral incorporating drive (suction) of . . . /m/" (242).

Whereas Mallarmé's obviously idiosyncratic and playful associations would seem to undermine both too serious a reading of his essay and the possibility of attributing to him a coherent and fully formed theory of sounds and meanings, Kristeva's use of psychoanalysis borders on the claim that the sounds of words have natural relations to their meanings that we find in Plato's *Cratylus*. Now, there is some reason today for linguists to believe that there is some actual relation between the development in children of the articulation of certain phonemes and their use for certain sounds, most obviously the *m* in *mama* and other words for *mother* and the stops (*p, d, t,* etc.) in words for *father* such as *papa* and *dada* (see Jakobson [1960] 1971b). But it is also clear that other forces at work in language, such as historical sound changes and derivational rules, supersede these quasi-biological principles very quickly.

What might be left of the quasi-biological could be precisely what Kristeva is getting at in Mallarmé's "Prose" as the semiotic. But what does one do with this observation? The specificity with which she assigns psychoanalytic drives to particular phonemes seems to lead us in the direction of an actual coherent *code* or interpretive framework—and yet that is precisely what Kristeva avoids.

We are thus still left with the question of reading: how do repetitions or patterns of certain phonemes bear upon our reading of the text? If we assign psychoanalytic meanings to the phonemes, are we not then, in effect, conscripting them for use as representations— that is, as signs? And what relation should these signs have to the overt meaning—such as it is, which is difficult enough to arrive at— in Mallarmé's very symbolic and allegorical poem?[11] We are back to the same question, in different guise, with which we were faced earlier

---

11. For an excellent reading of this poem, see Fowlie 1962, 192–209. See also Cohn 1965, 240–60 (whom Kristeva cites), whose free-associative interest in repeated sound motifs falls short of Cratylism, but whose reading, at the same time, is nowhere as coherent or as useful as Fowlie's. Let us admit that, after all, one would like to know what the poem is all about.

Critics seem generally to agree that Mallarmé was virtually obsessed with the thorough intentionality of his texts. *Un Coup de dés jamais n'abolira le hasard,* far from celebrating the throw of the dice, places every aspect of the text, including the physical placement of the words on the page, under the author's individual control, and thus frees the poet from the tyranny of chance (see Beaucourt 1973, 7536.) Insofar as everything is intentional, it follows that every aspect of the text is consciously meaningful.

under terms of the relation between form and theme. Do the sound effects support the apparent meaning? Do they subvert it? Or does the thematic content, as I have ventured to suppose earlier, actually allegorize in images and ideas, not so much the specific psychoanalytic drives or other associations of particular sounds, as the mere fact of the materiality of those sounds, the force of something attractive and compelling that has no intrinsic *meaning* whatsoever?

The problem of reading is the first of three weaknesses that, in conclusion, I should like to note about Kristeva's theory. In addition, there are, secondly, a prevarication or equivocation regarding the relation between the conscious and the unconscious status of features of the text and, thirdly, the insistence on excluding from the semiotic the most obvious and most effective rhythmic principle in most poetry, audible meter. I shall take up each problem in turn, beginning by going back to the first, the matter of reading and finding meaning.

On Kristeva's behalf, one might say that her purpose is not to make the meaning of the text accessible. Quite on the contrary, meaning is subject to the already existing social structure of codes and values, informed by the oppressive patriarchal ideology implicit in the post-Lacanian feminist use of the term symbolic order. Sound patterns are there precisely to resist meaning, and, when it comes to the text, Kristeva's task is in the main merely to point such patterns out to us, who have been blind and deaf to them because of our very pursuit of socially recuperable meaning. But if this is the case, and if the point is to see the irruption of the semiotic into the symbolic order, then it really should make no difference what the text actually says, as long as it makes some kind of sense and is also full of irrational sound patterns.

But then, how do we account for the presence of meaning at all? Is it entirely trivial? Why can't the same effect be created if we have a newspaper column rewritten to have an excess of alliteration?[12] In the case of a notoriously rich and difficult poet like Mallarmé, where the very difficulty seems to stimulate us to solve its interpretive riddles, it is hard to escape the feeling that the introduction of an extra dimension (the semiotic) that has to do with any literary text

---

12. This is aside from the point, noted earlier, that newspaper columns *are* full of conscious and unconscious sound and syntactic patterns, in accordance with Jakobson's observations.

but nothing to do with the specific poem's content simply makes an already complicated situation hopelessly more complicated. In this case, Kristeva's theory does not seem to serve one of the most basic functions of theories in general, as expressed in Ockham's razor: the solution should be simpler and easier to understand than the original problem.[13]

As we have already seen, Kristeva's binary opposition of semiotic and symbolic is in fact her inheritance from the Nietzschean tradition. But Kristeva chooses to abandon Nietzsche's allegorical approach to the relation between images and rhythm. As a result, we are left with no way to talk about images and meaning without making rhythm appear subordinate to these things. Since Kristeva is avoiding the demotion of rhythm to a mere rhetorical device, she must leave meaning out altogether. An unaccountable exception to this abandonment of meaning, however, is when she brings meaning back in unexpectedly, through the back door of psychoanalytic associations between phonemes and drives—where it has nothing to do with the ordinary, symbolic meaning of the poem as a linguistic utterance. This odd recuperation of meaning leads me to my second criticism.

The second weakness in Kristeva's theory follows on the question of what to make of evident forms of nonsymbolic patterning, such as the repeated r sounds in the first quatrain of "Prose." Kristeva's point seems to be that there is a legible and audible record, in the text, of the irruption of semiotic impulses across the symbolic surface. But in the course of demonstrating that these sound patterns originate in unconscious drives, do they not then become, in fact, conscious? Especially insofar as Kristeva relies on Mallarmé's own free-associative comments about the meanings of sounds (comments that, by the way, are certainly intended to have much more limited application than Kristeva would allow), Kristeva's argument actually urges us to think of sound patterns as a part of the poet's conscious artistry, like any other intentional feature.[14]

---

13. Here and there, a few readings of poems have benefitted from Kristeva's *Revolution in Poetic Language*—such as Enterline 1987 and Hayes 1989, both of which are about not early modern texts but, respectively, a Marvell lyric and a thirteenth-century Middle High German song. In both of these very interesting readings, ironically, Kristeva's principles are conceived purely in psychoanalytic terms and are found in the *thematic content* of the poems, not in any formal features.

14. This point has already been made, in another way and in more neatly political

Why, for that matter, should we presume, conversely, that the images or ideas in the poem are conscious? Why must we conceive of the symbolic order as so perfectly coherent and flat that all symbols have equally patent meanings and intentions? The tradition of psychoanalytic reading has, rather, gone in the other direction. Images and ideas, in Freud as in Nietzsche, are placed between the unconscious world of drives and desires and the conscious world of perceptions and the limits imposed by reality. Fantasies are crystalizations of the voice of the unconscious speaking to us.[15] The theory presented in this book, poetry as allegory of the sublime, follows the Nietzschean tradition precisely in this regard. In this way, we can speak about the unconscious or unknowable forces driving the poetic utterance without, in the very process of speaking, obliterating the difference between those forces and the language we are already calling conscious or knowable to reason.

Finally, although both Kristeva's theory and the theory of poetry as allegory of the sublime seem to share an assumption of the preeminent importance of rhythm in poetry, Kristeva actually seems to exclude from her consideration of rhythm what would seem to be its most obvious manifestation, meter. This exclusion is not adequately justified. In fact, it is never really clear why a book on poetic language that stresses the subversive power of semiotic rhythms would not even spend any substantial time on the audible rhythms of meter. In what way is Mallarmé's *Un Coup de dès,* upon which she rests much of

---

terms, in Joan Brandt's excellent "The Theory and Practice of a 'Revolutionary' Text: Denis Roche's 'Le mécrit'" (1984). Starting by placing Roche within the political-historical context of the French *Tel Quel* group of the sixties and seventies, she reads his last published text, a prose poem of sorts, as a sort of manifesto of, more or less, the same politics of disruption and irruption as revolution as we find in Kristeva's theory. Brandt then demonstrates that such a reading only shows that, if we know what Roche's poem means and tells its audience of political insiders, the text is speaking just as flatly and univocally as any "traditional," canonical poetic text. Brandt refers to Kristeva's earlier published Σημειωτικὴ; what she says of Roche in this context is true of Kristeva's *Revolution,* which is very much a part of the same post-Maoist project.

15. This is of course a basic principle throughout Freud's writings from *The Interpretation of Dreams* on; but relative to literature, see, for example, his "The Relation of the Poet to Day-Dreaming" ([1908] 1963e) and chapter 9 above.

her argument, more musical or more rhythmic than, say, a lyric of
Ronsard? Perhaps Kristeva wishes to maintain the broadness of the
term poetic language to include any literary text, whether in verse
or in prose. But in her reading of Mallarmé's "Prose," which is,
despite its ironic title, in verse, Kristeva seems to take the position
that the frequently but irregularly appearing r sounds in the first
stanza are somehow a more significant and more unconsciously power-
ful rhythm than the much more obvious, and by habit more thoroughly
naturalized, regularities of syllable, rhyme, and (perhaps) beat. Doubt-
less, Kristeva would regard such a familiar metrical form as too
thoroughly co-opted by the symbolic order, because of its weight of
tradition, to serve as an example of the semiotic. But this is to pretend
that there is never any material basis whatsoever for sound patterns
that are championed by tradition—as if, in listening to a waltz or
ragtime, one can hear absolutely nothing but the tired fact that waltzes
and rags are traditional and have symbolic meanings. It is also to
pretend that alliteration has *no* traditional basis and has *never* been
institutionalized as part of good rhetoric, both of which propositions
are plainly false.

More importantly, Kristeva has among her various purposes an
explanation of the evolution of poetry in the modern age toward
free verse and the pivotal role of writers like Mallarmé for poetry
and Lautréamont for the novel. The revolution in poetic language
thus takes on, as one of its meanings, the shift in literary prac-
tices at about the turn of the nineteenth century. Kristeva offers a
theory that valorizes this shift as an assertion of the semiotic, while
meter, somehow or other, is apparently lumped in with the elements
that had gotten to be nothing more than fetishes of the symbolic
order:

> Poetry emerged alongside sacrifice as the expenditure of the
> thesis establishing the socio-symbolic order and as the bringing
> into play of the vehemence of drives through the positing of
> language. But starting with the Renaissance and the brief Roman-
> tic celebration of the sacrifices made in the French Revolution,
> poetry had become mere rhetoric, linguistic formalism, a fetishi-
> zation, a surrogate for the thetic. The established bourgeois regime
> had been consuming this kind of poetry since the Restoration and

especially during the Second Empire, which began in 1852, reducing it to a decorative uselessness that challenged none of the subjects of its time. (1984, 83)

This is revisionary literary history, to put it mildly. In connection with meter, it ignores the fact that Hugo, one of the most influential poets of the Second Empire's more conservative phase, had altered meter to include rhymes that sound alike but are spelled differently and variously placed caesuras in the alexandrine. Meanwhile, the majority of Mallarmé's output in poetry is in traditional strict meters— and the same is true for the rest of his and later generations of French poets. The decorative poetry of which Kristeva speaks here probably includes standard Romantics like Lamartine. But any line or stanza of Lamartine will inevitably be as informed with sound play as its counterpart in Mallarmé.

Nevertheless, there has certainly been a noticeable shift in the modern period in the practice of published poets, not only in French but in English, Spanish, German, and many other languages, away from traditional, audible and palpable, regular rhythms, and toward free verse. Usually this shift has been presented *by its practitioners* and by editors and sympathetic critics as a revolution of general import and as a liberation. But throughout literary history, poets are perennially, at once, both avowedly rebelling against and less obviously conserving the poetic traditions from which they learned their craft. In recent years, critics have attempted to explain the rise of free verse in the modern age through a partisan history, according to which traditional meters *had* to be abandoned—it was the only reasonable choice for a poet of this century. Inevitably, meters are represented as lifeless symbols of stuffy bourgeois conformism, and musicality is always, oddly, discovered in sounds that are repeated but have no regularity and little of what we actually expect when we listen to music most of the time.[16]

---

16. Todorov (1987) is an example. Steele (1990) also seems to tell a sympathetic history of free verse, but it is much more careful and subtle than Kristeva's, and his conclusion provides a salutary and well-considered critical view of the meaning of free verse today. Before both of these and Kristeva, however, Octavio Paz had argued a similar but more limited and hence more persuasive point (1972). For Paz, there had long been a problem with French meter to begin with: since French does

There are other less deterministic and less partisan explanations for the rise of free verse and the abandonment of meter in much printed poetry. Modernist experiments included the stripping away of many basic artistic principles—tonality in music, representation in painting, musical accompaniment in dance, even dialogue in drama— with the apparent goal simply of discovering what minimal elements it takes to make a work of art. As such, these innovations make statements and help us to learn about ourselves and our expectations of art, but they cannot be made forever without becoming their own oppressive system of conventions—only now, as opposed to the conventions against which they had rebelled, these innovations cannot even claim a basis in intuition or popular culture as the conventions before them could do—such as the ballad or the nursery rhyme. Earlier in this book, I also suggested that the abandonment of meter in poetry can be associated with the pressures of the information age to reduce everything to ideas or statements (even the statement that there is no statement); as such, the institutionalization of free verse is not a resistance but a concession to developments in capitalist production. At any rate, the point to keep in mind is that strict verse

---

not have a strong stress pattern, its meters are organized according to number of syllables per line (thus making rhyme a necessity to help us distinguish the ends of lines as units), but this structure is inherently unstable, not having an audible enough regular rhythm to begin with. Hence the shift away from traditional meters in French meant the abandonment of constraints that really were artificial (because inaudible). The notion of such a liberation then caught on with Anglo-American poets like Pound, even though English poetry had no such instability. Historically, the French alexandrine (for example) arose to begin with out of a medieval Christian Latin version of the classical Latin iambic trimeter, simplified to have only the paradigmatic twelve syllables. Here, the musical beat is clear, even though words in the earlier part of lines do not have to conform in stress contour to the beat (this clash or counterpoint in the beginnings of lines is common and unproblematic in classical Latin verse). Phonological changes in French, such as the weakening of the mute *e*, result in a further distortion of the rhythm of the line, so that the way French language works in the seventeenth-century alexandrine is already rather far from the way it works in everyday speech (Deloffre 1984, 23–30; Elwert 1965, 18–27). Again, no comparable change comes about in English or German. But working against Paz's theory, which is generally compelling, is the fact that free verse in modern French poetry is not any more rhythmically regular or musical to the ear, using normal prose pronunciation, than is the classical alexandrine of the seventeenth century.

continues to be used in many a published poem and in popular practices such as song and rap, from which written poetic traditions trace their origin in the past and perennially draw renewed energy.

How, in short, do we understand Kristeva's privileging of free verse in a book whose focus is on the physical rhythms of poetic language? This problem leads us, finally, to Kristeva's very title. Is the revolution a social revolution provoked or encouraged (or even achieved) *by* poetic language, or is revolution simply an internal characteristic of the history of literary works, or is revolution some even more abstract, metaphysical quality about literature? Conceived most narrowly, Kristeva's theory seems to say simply that two late nineteenth-century avant-garde French writers, Mallarmé and Lautréamont, achieved a revolution (in literature? in society?—the latter would seem doubtful!) by means of the introduction of nonmetrical but rhythmic structures and of disruptions of normal syntax, style, and logic. More broadly, Kristeva may be saying that all literary texts are somehow revolutionary, that the mere act of composing literature is revolutionary. Dare one go even further? One of the lessons of poststructuralism has been to undermine the clear opposition between literary and nonliterary discourse—we are all texts ourselves, *il n'y a pas hors de texte*—and thus everything is always revolutionary! Clearly, the word *revolution* suffers some weakening of meaning here. This weakening is analogous to the loss of meaning in the word *poetry* as soon as we put aside, as theory has done since antiquity, any distinction between prose and verse and claim that the meter of verse is a mere trivial ornament of some poetic works. And at this time, when few read poetry for pleasure, this theoretical stance is very unlikely to help make a case for poetry's continued viability, when prose can do just as well or better.

Despite these many problems, Kristeva makes some very important contributions to the theory of poetry. First among these is the attempt to integrate the psychoanalytic view of the text as the record of an interaction between conscious and unconscious forces with the analysis of literary language as performed by linguistics. Kristeva also continues the Nietzschean tradition by reasserting the importance of rhythm in poetry and its connection to the body. Ultimately, the problems we run into in her application of this approach can be traced to her tendency, mentioned in the beginning of this chapter, to explain too much, for example, both to explain the nature of all poetry and simultaneously to explain—and champion—the rise of free verse.

But more crucially for us, Kristeva abandons Nietzsche's insight into the allegorical relation between poetic images and the non-imaginary, nonsymbolic power of rhythm. This is the very aspect of the Nietzschean theory that I shall seek to develop more fully in the theory of poetry as telling rhythm. Before I pursue a more thorough presentation of this theory, however, I shall examine one more present-day theory that comes close to it in its concern for rhythm, music, and images in poetry: the recent work of Philippe Lacoue-Labarthe.

12

Philippe Lacoue-Labarthe:
The Subject as Rhythm

Thou, silent form, doest tease us out of thought
As doth eternity.

—John Keats, "Ode on a Grecian Urn"

French philosopher Philippe Lacoue-Labarthe will be the last figure of the Nietzschean tradition whom we shall examine before turning to a more detailed exposition of the theory of poetry as telling rhythm. During the seventies and eighties, Philippe Lacoue-Labarthe, like Julia Kristeva, turned his attention to the relations between rhythm and thought that have bearing upon both poetry and philosophy. This is evident in Lacoue-Labarthe's essays collected under the title *Le Sujet de la philosophie* (*The Subject of Philosophy,* the first volume of the French *Typographies* [1979]). Like Kristeva, Lacoue-Labarthe follows the Nietzschean tradition in a certain core thought: the musical or rhythmic is a state of being outside of and prior to the social, verbal, thinking subject, while the latter is a kind of construct that simultaneously represents (in images and in symbols) and represses its musical other, which is also its origin. Unlike Kristeva, but like Nietzsche, Lacoue-Labarthe does not inquire into the origin of rhythm itself; he accepts it as more or less a biological given. Lacoue-Labarthe *is* interested—as are nearly all writers within the Nietzschean tradition traced here—in the way in which this preverbal, prerational, presubjective rhythmic force makes itself felt within language, the rational, and the experience of the subject of thought and social life. Whereas for Kristeva the key point is that the rhythmic chora irrupts into the symbolic order and puts it into question, Lacoue-Labarthe goes beyond this relation between rhythm and subject. While Lacoue-Labarthe shares with Kristeva the idea that rhythm undermines the solidity of the subject, he also suggests that rhythm simultaneously provokes a reaction—a repressive effort continually to reinforce the subject. Meanwhile, however, one of the ways in which the subject strengthens itself is by contemplating itself philosophically, which leads it inevitably to a consciousness of its own limits and what is beyond them—that is, rhythm. Rhythm leads to thought, but thought leads back to rhythm.

Lacoue-Labarthe's work is not explicitly about poetry, but about philosophy. Rhythm destabilizes philosophy and provokes more philosophy as a reaction, but philosophical contemplation tends to lead toward an awareness of the rhythm that lies beyond it. Like Kristeva, Lacoue-Labarthe does not follow through on Nietzsche's idea that the relation between music (Dionysus, rhythm) and representation (Apollo, images and thoughts) is allegorical—that images and thoughts allegorically represent the unrepresentable effect of music and rhythm. But Lacoue-Labarthe's analysis of the relation between rhythm and thought has all the elements necessary to see this relation as allegorical in the case of poetry.

Lacoue-Labarthe's revelation of how thought leads to rhythm and rhythm leads to thought supports the notion of a dual structure in poetry, since both of these ingredients work in poetry patently at the same time. In the final essay of the volume, "L'Écho du sujet," moreover, Lacoue-Labarthe explicitly discusses rhythm, and he suggests a way in which rhythm can be thought of as giving rise to the visible forms of images without being those images—shaping them without being them. This mutually generative relation between rhythm and image should lead logically to a return to the Nietzschean concept of the *representational* relation between the two. It also looks forward to the concept of an *allegorical* relation between rhythm and image, which would make it possible to read the images and ideas in poetry as allegories for the sublime power of the rhythm that they, as words, simultaneously embody. For if subjective thought is conceived, following Lacoue-Labarthe, as both an original product of the rhythm that shapes it and as a repressive reaction against the destabilizing effects of that same rhythm, then we could think of this repressive reaction in Freudian terms. That is, the repressive defense mechanism always *represents* or symbolizes, in some indirect way, the drive that it represses but that provokes it to begin with. The most useful example of this aspect of the Freudian defense mechanism is the dream image, for dreams are, in fact, defenses against the eruption of drives that would, if enacted, disturb the dreamer's sleep. The dream images thus serve to repress the drives, but they simultaneously *represent* them in such a way that the analyst can reveal the presence of the drive.

In order to follow more closely Lacoue-Labarthe's argument for the mutually generative relation between rhythm and thought— philosophy leads to rhythm, but rhythm both shapes and provokes philosophy—I shall trace his arguments in *Le Sujet de la philosophie* more or less in their own terms. Lacoue-Labarthe's focus is primarily not on poetry but on philosophy. But I shall draw out whenever possible the implications of this ideas for the theory of poetry. Lacoue-Labarthe is only beginning to receive serious attention from readers in the English-speaking world. As a consequence, I have decided to explore elements of his argument in some detail, even when they momentarily seem to have strayed from my central topic, poetry. My hope is that this analysis will be helpful in introducing Lacoue-Labarthe's thought in general. I ask the reader to have faith, however; even points that seem to be exclusively philosophical will lead to an important insight into poetry.

Lacoue-Labarthe arrives at the mutually generative relation between rhythm and poetry by wrestling with a fundamental problem in philosophy today: How is it possible to get outside of philosophy enough to speak about it—without falling right back into it? A philosopher can easily enough stand outside and discuss—analyze, criticize—another philosophy, but how can one do the same in relation to philosophy as a whole? For whenever one analyzes and criticizes any philosophy or even the very idea of philosophy, the results, we must admit, tend to look strikingly like more philosophy.

This question has become a fundamental problem in the context of poststructuralism, because of its emphasis on being caught in language and texts. Likewise, insofar as poststructuralist concerns are also social and political questions, even if they don't sound that way, the question of how one can get outside of philosophy to put it into perspective is a social and political question. For this question concerns the possibility of seeing clearly, and thus having the ability to change, the subject of philosophy. And in some sense, the subject of philosophy that gives Lacoue-Labarthe the title for his book is also the subject of the social order. If we want somehow to change the society, to make it better and more just, then this change will also have to involve how individual people think and how they participate in the social order. But how do we go about even thinking about that philosophical subject without replicating within our own thoughts the very fundamental problems that we are uncovering in it? After all, the same basic processes that constructed the philosophical subject we are analyzing has also constructed *us* as philosophical subjects. The difficulty of standing outside thought to think about it can be connected to the fact that, historically, major political revolutions have tended, despite their liberatory rhetoric, to give rise to hierarchical social orders that fundamentally replicate the regimes they replaced. A poststructuralist analysis of this frustrating tendency in revolutionary politics suggests that the concepts of society, governance, law, and so forth within the framers of the new society are already conditioned by the power structure prevalent within the deposed social order.

How, in short, can we criticize or change the way we think, if our ideas for change are products of the social system that has also produced the injustices we wish to remedy? Here, ultimately, is where poetry comes in. For Lacoue-Labarthe's answer, particularly in the concluding essay, "L'Écho du sujet," is that *rhythm* is a constructed social order. This notion provides support for the idea that poetry gives its readers something important and unique, something that can be usefully constrasted with philosophy as a whole and helps to complement theory and philosophy in important ways.

Thus Lacoue-Labarthe's questions about philosophy lead to yet more fundamental ones, which eventually take us on the way to poetry: What *is* the subject of philosophy? What, for that matter, is the subject itself? In Lacoue-Labarthe, even the abstractions of philosophy are a way of writing oneself, of writing autobiography—that is, a way of forming and putting up a social ego that is, in reality, the illusion of the self appearing in the mirror. In other words, philosophy is a written version of Lacan's mirror stage. And beyond that specular image is, as in Kristeva—a rhythm. But unlike Kristeva, Lacoue-Labarthe sees that rhythm not as an analyzable and theorizable process, but as something at work before the birth and after the death

of the subject (as we normally experience the subject).[1] The death of
the subject is its uncanny truth, which cannot be revealed in philosophy
and theory except indirectly. This indirect revelation is made insofar
as the gesture of autobiography denies the power of rhythm—for the
subject's very defense by means of denial reveals the fact that there
is something against which the subject is defending itself—that is,
rhythm. Insofar as rhythm not only remains after the death of the
subject but is a force beyond the individual subject, it constitutes a
threat to the subject's stability. But for Lacoue-Labarthe, the death of
the subject threatened by rhythm is not merely negative. Rather, it is
a moment of mystical affirmation. And at that affirmative moment,
where theory fails, rhythm begins to speak. Lacoue-Labarthe's use of
poetry and of quotations from poetry implies that poetry is a way in
which rhythm *can* speak. And although he does not develop any rig-
orous notion of the nature of poetry, the theory of poetry as an allegory
of the sublime power of rhythm would explain quite well the function
of poetry within Lacoue-Labarthe's scheme.

Throughout "L'Écho du sujet," Lacoue-Labarthe approaches the
question of how to get beyond philosophy, and his discussions revolve
mainly around texts of Nietzsche, Heidegger, and Freud. Nietzsche
has a privileged position in relation to this question because of his
continual concern with the criticism of the Western philosophical
tradition and his interest in kinds of writing that, since Plato, have
been considered insufficiently objective or authoritative to count as
real philosophy. Nietzsche's early work, *The Birth of Tragedy,* mounts
a strong polemic against Plato's exclusion of poets from the republic
and thus from truth; it thus vindicates poetry, music, the irrational,
and everything associated with the god Dionysos, against Plato and
the whole of Western philosophy. Lacoue-Labarthe is surely not the
first to notice the paradox of Nietzsche thus criticizing the authori-
tative, prosaic, philosophical mode of truth in a work itself written

---

1. Of course, Kristeva, too, sees rhythm (i.e., the chora) as bringing about the
death of the subject—or rather, putting the subject in a dynamic struggle as the
"subject-in-process" or "subject-on-trial." As we have seen, however, the death
drive is also involved in the very formation of the thetic subject, so that the
distinction between what is the social subject and what is not becomes unclear.
Kristeva, in the final analysis, seems to leave little room for us to think our way
out of the social subject.

in authoritative philosophical prose. But how could Nietzsche have avoided this paradox—of replicating in his own critique the very thing that he is criticizing?

Lacoue-Labarthe develops two different answers to this question. One answer looks toward the stylistic devices Nietzsche used in the bulk of his oeuvre after *The Birth of Tragedy*. The other answer looks outside philosophy and criticism altogether, toward poetry and music. To appreciate this second answer and its specific importance for Lacoue-Labarthe, we must first consider the first answer, having to do with style.

In "La Fable," the first essay in *Le Sujet de la philosophie*, Lacoue-Labarthe opens the question of how one can get out of philosophy to talk about it, and then focuses more specifically on what Nietzsche's alternatives might be. It might be thought that Nietzsche could write from a position sufficiently outside philosophy to criticize philosophy if he wrote in some more literary mode, such as in poetry or in fiction. But then, he would have lost the authority of truth he wished to keep in order for his criticism to be taken seriously. The problem is, as Lacoue-Labarthe notes, that philosophical *writing* is always already literary. Here, he is following a common recognition in poststructuralism that has prevailed at least since Derrida's essay "White Mythology" (1982). In this essay, Derrida demonstrates that Western philosophy is based upon certain metaphors such as the "light" of truth, which are, of course, literary figures. So the problem Nietzsche was facing has actually been a problem inherent in philosophy from the start. As soon as one notices that the philosophical work is a literary *text*, one sees the distinction between philosophy and literature fall away. But this deconstruction doesn't help much in the project of getting outside of philosophy so as to speak about it without replicating it. Here, literature is not the opposite of philosophy— philosophy is actually a kind of literature—so literature cannot provide a discourse qualitatively different from philosophy and based on substantially different assumptions.

In most of the works coming after *The Birth of Tragedy*, Nietzsche abandons sustained prose exposition for the brief, fragmentary aphorisms of *Beyond Good and Evil* and *Human, All Too Human*. In "Le Détour" (1979), Lacoue-Labarthe suggests that this stylistic defice is a way of avoiding both (*a*) the trap of *The Birth of Tragedy*'s paradox and (*b*) the trap of foreskaing any claim to truth by writing an avowed fiction (i.e., "literature"). During the same period in which he was writing *The Birth of Tragedy,* Nietzsche was doing research in classical rhetoric. (The notes for his courses on this subject were translated for the first time into French in 1971 in the same journal issue in which "Le Détour" first appeared.) For Nietzsche, according to Lacoue-Labarthe, rhetoric, that is, the *art* of the orator, provided a middle ground between philosophical exposition and literature and thus provided the model for Nietzsche's writing, as is most obvious in the aphoristic and highly oratorical *Thus Spake Zarathustra.*[2]

Interestingly, however, as Lacoue-Labarthe reveals in the next essay, "Nietzsche Apocryphe" (1979), this solution was anticipated by Plato himself. For although Plato has Socrates exile poets from the republic, and although in the *Phaedrus* Socrates decries the impossibility of truth's being expressed in oratory or any text whatsoever, Plato's own writing is itself a kind of literature. And especially in the dialogues, it is a literature that mixes together every literary genre delineated in the *Republic,* including especially comic drama and oratory. Nor, indeed, does Lacoue-Labarthe's recognition of Plato's literariness involve some new, poststructuralist redefinition of literature—it is based on Plato's student Aristotle. Far from being the truthful opposite of mere literary fiction, Plato's philosophical text is a culmination and summation of literary modes.

But if Plato includes literature in his philosophy at the same time he excludes poets from his republic, Nietzsche's (apparently unwitting) replication of Plato's approach to writing is a conscious and avowed effort to make philosophy more like literature. In this sense, Heidegger was right in his reading of Nietzsche, which is the focus of Lacoue-Labarthe's next essay, "L'Oblitération" (1979). That is, Nietzsche is as Heidegger suggests both a culmination and an end—a death—of the tradition of Western metaphysics.[3] But Heidegger's terms are quite different from those of Lacoue-Labarthe. For Heidegger, the Western

---

2. Lacoue-Labarthe reads without much questioning Nietzsche's identification of the aphorism as more oratorical and artistic than a sustained prose argument. Presumably, the connection between aphorism and oratory can be found in the fact that it is more memorizable and repeatable orally than a sustained argument would be; to some extent, it relies upon rhetorical figures such as repetition and antithesis, and on poetic features such as isorhythmic units and rhythmic cadences.

3. Heidegger's reading of Nietzsche is presented in his two-volume *Nietzsche.* For a convenient, if brief and necessarily reductive, summary of Heidegger's interpretation of Nietzsche as it is usually understood, see Boutot 1989, 75–76.

metaphysical tradition inaugurated by Plato has brought about the gradual and continuous effacement of Being from memory, until, in Nietzsche, Being has been completely forgotten, in favor of individual beings. Heidegger argues that, in order for us to recover Being in philosophy, we must now make philosophy more like poetry (or literature), which is the revelation of Being in language. Yet, as Lacoue-Labarthe points out, such a reading of Nietzsche reduces him and ignores the features of Nietzsche that "Nietzsche Apocryphe" makes clear.

Heidegger's obliteration is simultaneously a complete erasure and a blurring in such a way that a trace remains. One of the things that Heidegger obliterates or forgets (*oublie*) is precisely the literary quality of Nietzsche's texts (Lacoue-Labarthe 1979, 165–70). But then again, as we have just seen, this poetic quality has been there all along, as far back as Plato. Philosophy has always been literature (*écriture*), even if we have pretended that literature and philosophy were opposites. Philosophy's literariness has been constant; yet just as constant has been the gesture of obliteration. As Lacoue-Labarthe demonstrates, this double movement, which consists of obliterating prior philosophy and then *unconsciously* replicating philosophy, is an intrinsic element in the very impulse to do philosophy—or, indeed, to think. If we recall that philosophy has always been a kind of literature, we come back full circle to the idea that literary representation is always simultaneously an obliteration and a rediscovery of the truth.

Nor is the poetic quality of Nietzsche's philosophical prose the only thing that Heidegger obliterates to enable his own philosophical project to proceed. He must insist on being different from Hegel— while Hegel did philosophy, Heidegger now "thinks"; while Hegel raised questions from the past, Heidegger seeks the unthought behind thinking. Yet Heidegger seeks to discover this unthought by taking a "step backward" toward the pre-Socratics—that is, he raises questions from the past. And Heidegger's unthought itself, Being, is very hard to distinguish from Hegel's Absolute. In short, Heidegger takes great pains to distinguish himself from Hegel precisely because his ideas, especially in his early *Being and Time,* are hardly distinguishable from Hegel's.

Likewise, in his commentary on Nietzsche, Heidegger notices only certain aspects of Nietzsche's philosophy, so as to make Nietzsche the last metaphysician rather than the precursor to himself. What

Heidegger most wishes to avoid in Nietzsche, according to Lacoue-Labarthe, is the threat of madness—a loss of the subject. (One can see the importance of madness throughout Nietzsche's work, beginning with the god Dionysos, and also in his own life.) And yet Heidegger's own insistence on the priority of Being over the personal author—Being speaks through the writer for Heidegger—is just another loss of the subject. Here, too, obliteration plays the role of effacing a similarity in order to enable the newer writer, Heidegger, to proceed as if he were exploring as yet unknown territory.

First Nietzsche and then Heidegger might well have proclaimed, like Monty Python, "And now for something completely different!"—and yet what they have brought out onto the stage is actually the poetic (literary) prose that is *more of the same*. The solution Heidegger and Nietzsche before him have come up with in a tradition that looks back to Plato's philosophy is in fact a way of *replicating* the subject of philosophy, which is the subject of theory and of society. These philosophers have been engaged in a kind of repetition compulsion. As in Freud, the repetition compulsion has something to do with a kind of death drive; in the cases Lacoue-Labarthe analyzes, however, the death of the subject of thought is at stake. The fear of the kind of death of the thinking subject that Heidegger saw in the later Nietzsche's purported madness prompted Heidegger to obliterate Nietzsche's own project of going beyond metaphysics—so that then Heidegger himself could replicate this very going-beyond in the form of opening up the question of Being.

The theme of the compulsion to repeat is highlighted in Lacoue-Labarthe's second-to-last essay, "La Scène est primitive" (1979), which is about Freud in relation to Nietzsche. But here, one notes for the first time a decidedly positive sense in the discussion of repetition and the death drive, a turn toward the affirmative that prepares the way for the final essay. Just as Heidegger "thinks" for fear of losing the thinking subject—that is, for fear of madness, so both Nietzsche and Freud reveal the fundamental nature of tragedy as an apotropaic game of representation, which wards off the unrepresentable par excellence, death. But the death with which Nietzsche and Freud are concerned is not restricted to the death actually thematized in tragedy. The argument holds for all art, insofar as art is immortal and separated from the ebb and flow of life. And if it holds for all art, then, Lacoue-Labarthe argues, it also holds for all thought, all philosophy (since these are literary)—including psychoanalysis. In all of these, then, Lacoue-Labarthe takes Freud's binary opposition, death/libido, and assigns to them, respectively, the terms *Unrepresentable* and *Representation* (see my own discussion in chap. 9). While this system works for all sorts of art and thought, psychoanalysis is particularly good at showing the instability of the subject of philosophy, even the subject of psychoanalysis, since these are, in a sense, charms mumbled repeatedly in the face of something to which absolutely no words can be applied: death itself.

But even Freud's work shows signs that a recognition of this instability of the psychoanalytic subject raises serious anxieties. For one thing, Freud made no effort to publish the essay comparing psychoanalysis to theater that gives Lacoue-Labarthe his basic text. What may especially have aroused Freud's anxiety is a discussion of the difference between ancient and modern drama, in which Freud suggests that the latter appeals to a neurotic spectator because it displays conflicts between conscious and unconscious impulses. But does this mean that the whole audience is neurotic? If so, what does *neurotic* mean? Are we all in imminent danger of losing our ability to repress our drives—especially the death drive? And if so, how can thinking continue, since thinking is conscious and consciousness is founded on the repression of the drives? Lacoue-Labarthe thus finishes by showing a kinship between Freud's analytical work and the tragic dedication of the heroic soul whom Nietzsche champions: both expose themselves to the energy of the unrepresentable—death in Freud, Dionysos in Nietzsche—in order to elicit a greater vitality in representation, as a kind of ethical act.

All of the foregoing essays take on major figures of modern Western thought, Nietzsche, Heidegger, and Freud, and, basically, deconstruct them. Each time, a given term is set apart from philosophy—poetry, rhetoric, thought, and psychoanalysis—only to see how the distinction cannot be preserved. At the same time, however, a quite different opposition comes to the fore: one between language in general, call it philosophy, theory, thought, or whatever, and the *loss of the subject* in madness or death. As we have seen in chapter 8, the opposition between these two terms—say, between Apollo and Dionysos—is of a very different sort: neither a distinction between comparable terms nor a hierarchical system, the relation between these two items is, as it were, *already* deconstructed, because it is the relation between representation and the unrepresentable that calls representation into being. Neither makes any claim to presence or independence, and thus neither can have priority over the other. Lacoue-Labarthe himself makes this point indirectly, by mentioning that only Nietzsche's description of classical Greek tragedy as a reconciliation between Dionysos and Apollo would be worthy of deconstruction (1979, 212). But this notion itself emerges from what I have considered to be Nietzsche's slippage from a purely allegorical treatment of the two figures into an ethical treatment of them as types of actual behavior or approaches to life. As pure allegory, the terms are always already deconstructive and provide the basis for all the deconstructions Lacoue-Labarthe conducts in the rest of his book.

And it is also this Nietzschean system that provides Lacoue-Labarthe with his turn toward affirmation and that places Lacoue-Labarthe most clearly within the Nietzschean tradition. There really *is* something outside philosophy, something that ensures our freedom to change and to find a more just way of conducting our social and political life. But that thing is outside philosophy precisely because it itself is not representable; it calls philosophy, representation, into being.

This thing, call it Dionysos or death or the loss of the subject or madness, must truly and *necessarily* be unrepresentable—for if it were not, it would indeed wind up being part of philosophy. But if so, then is it simply nothing at all? Where does the subject go when it is lost? Is it simply an emptiness that ensures our freedom to change our philosophies? Or is there something there, despite its unrepresentability? Or bettter, is this *nothing* a merely negative absence, or is it an *affirmative nothingness?*

For Lacoue-Labarthe, the answer is certainly the latter. The unrepresentable is not "anything," but it *is* affirmative and imparts a kind of affirmative energy to all the toil of humanity it calls into action. To come closer to the relation between analytical thought and this Dionysian affirmative nothingness, Lacoue-Labarthe, in the final essay, "L'Écho du sujet" (1979), turns to a psychoanalytic writer's relation to the music that haunts him. That psychoanalyst, Theodor Reik, is not very popular today, perhaps in part because he tends toward autobiography rather than abstract theory—but for that very reason, he provides Lacoue-Labarthe with an excellent case of the *personal* experience of the relation between representation and the unrepresentable that he is pursuing.

The echo of the subject in Lacoue-Labarthe's title is at once a replication (echo) of the philosophical subject *and* something really different, depending on how we listen to the echo. For what interests Lacoue-Labarthe about Reik is that, on the one hand, he theorizes about the mind and about his own life, while on the other hand, he also confesses that he is haunted by certain melodies that come up at odd moments, whose ineluctable presence he does not understand. In not one but several of his writings, Reik begins a work of self-analysis by recounting a moment in which he hears strains of music, either in real life or in his mind: a piece of music by Max Bruch that recalls the melody of the Kol Nidre, a part of the Jewish Day of Atonement liturgy; the blasts of the shofar heard on that holiday; or the haunting memory of the final movement of Mahler's Second Symphony. Thus Reik provides particularly clear instances of the relation between haunting melodies coming from elsewhere and one's own analytical thoughts. Indeed, his very efforts to understand these musical epiph-anies stretch the resources of Reik's psychoanalytic theory to the limit and beyond.

Reik's efforts and their failure provide a striking analogue to poetry as presented in this book. Already, we can see that Reik's project involves the bewitching encounter between the verbal powers of theory and the nonverbal power of music. I proposed this very sort of encounter in chapter 3 as the principle behind poetry—poetry in the strong sense of the term as it has been used throughout this book. Reik's efforts also enable us to witness how, at the point where theory fails, poetry makes its entrance.

Lacoue-Labarthe (1979, 223; [1975] 1989b, 142) prefaces his con-sideration of Reik by recalling Nietzsche's assertion near the beginning of *Beyond Good and Evil:* "Gradually it has become clear to me what every great philosophy so far has been: namely, the personal confession of its author" (Nietzsche 1966, 13). Philosophy, or theory, is always autobiography, because it involves a kind of abstract writing of the self. By writing the self, Lacoue-Labarthe does not mean simply describing oneself in writing, which of course philosophy to some extent does as well. (Think, for example, of Hegel's lengthy and painstaking account in *Phenomenology of Spirit* of the progress of the for-itself toward absolute knowledge, which is simultaneously an account of the philosopher, himself, writing *Phenomenology of Spirit*.) Beyond this, there is the notion that the self is the product of a kind of continual self-composition. What am I? Anything I say in answer to this question is what I make of myself at that moment. It is a kind of autobiography that *makes* me what I say I am. To some degree, when I explain my opinion to someone else, I am simultaneously making that opinion coherent enough for myself to believe in it. This notion of self-writing is by now fairly familiar in poststructuralist thought.

But as Lacoue-Labarthe maintains at the outset, the exposure of the self as a matter of self-writing, and therefore the modern and postmodern critique of the subject, have only led paradoxically to "a certain acceleration" (*précipitation*—1979, 223) of answers to "the question of the subject"—leading in turn to a kind of "madness."

> This process has its effects probably throughout the entire realm of art (and why not science as well, something that should be examined) and most certainly is not foreign to the social and political configurations we live under. . . . And yet, though we may name it for economy's sake a process of the *decomposition* of the subject, everything happens as though it produced within itself a strengthening or *reinforcement* of the subject, even in the discourses that announce its dissolution, its shattering, its disappearance. ([1979] 1989a, 143)

I believe that Lacoue-Labarthe is subtly referring here to poststructuralism, the movement in philosophy and the human sciences in which he himself plays a substantial part. Poststructuralism is usually, or at least usually appears to be, a critique of the thinking that has come before—for example, a critique of philosophers such as Hegel. Even Lacoue-Labarthe's previous chapters in *Le Sujet de la philosophie* appear, more or less, as critiques of Nietzsche, Heidegger, and Freud. But it is by now clear that the critique of philosophy always leads to more philosophy—the critique *is* philosophy—in which the same blind spots are always inherited. The repetition compulsion brings on a mania of self-writing.

This mania is not only a headache for a few poststructuralist theorists. Lacoue-Labarthe strongly suggests that, as a principle at work in society, it is and has been very dangerous. For the mania to criticize and simultaneously to write oneself as the truth emerges out of a fundamental anxiety that Lacoue-Labarthe discusses in an essay whose title coins the term *typography* ([1975] 1989b).[4] Here, Lacoue-

---

4. This essay is available in the one-volume collection translated into English, *Typographies,* but not in the original French two-volume *Typographies.*

Labarthe demonstrates the working of this anxiety since Plato's exclu-
sion of poets from the republic, for fear that their representations in
art are secondary (as compared with reality) and therefore false. But
this exclusion masks a fundamental and unavoidable apprehension that
one is oneself always already fictional and secondary, that one's identity
is always already a self-writing, a fiction, an imitation. A telling
footnote in "Typography" recalls the violence with which people have
sought to dispel their anxiety by oppressing, obliterating, extermi-
nating the "other" who can be taken as a scapegoat for all falseness
and all secondariness—in European history, women and Jews ([1975]
1989b, 116). In order to appreciate Lacoue-Labarthe's point in the
context of American culture, one need only recall the frequency with
which racists have compared African-Americans with apes or other
primates, implying that they are mere imitations of real human beings,
aping the gestures of the white original. (A similar gesture is made
against gay men and lesbians.) Racists, anti-Semites, and sexists both
here and in Europe have tended to act violently against this perceived
"falseness" of the other at times when they themselves are under the
stresses of poverty and unemployment, and fear, without admitting
it, that they themselves may be to blame (rather than their economic
or political systems). Am I not real man enough, or a real enough
American, to be hired? Well, then, I'll make sure that I'm as real
as can be—by making someone else the *real* falsehood, and then by
violently sacrificing that scapegoat.

   An intellectual may wish to turn to theory to expose this problem
and then to resolve it, but, as we have seen, theory has tended to
replicate the self-writing it criticizes elsewhere. Here, we must recall
Lacoue-Labarthe's opening question in "La Fable": how does one get
outside of philosophy in order to talk about it? How can one talk
about the subject without *reinforcing* the subject and therefore, perhaps,
perpetuating the very social structures and habits of thought one
hopes to change in the name of justice or the redress of social ills?

   As an odd clue, Lacoue-Labarthe notes in "L'Écho du sujet" that
two people whose philosophies are very overtly also autobiographies,
Nietzsche and Rousseau, were also failed or would-be musicians. Music
seems to have the power to provoke autobiography, confession, theory.
Moreover, music, Lacoue-Labarthe points out, is quite different in
nature from theory and from self-writing. For these latter, as we
know from Derrida (especially from "White Mythology" [1982]),

rely and have always relied upon a *visual* system of metaphors—to know oneself is to *see* oneself. Likewise, in Lacan, the first rudimentary makings of the self emerge at the mirror state—as a visual image of the body's coherence in contradistinction to its surroundings and to other people—which is the onset of the "register of imaginary." By contrast, and although one often associates certain mental images with music, music itself is not visual or imaginary in the first instance.[5] Nor is it symbolic in the way that language, laws and customs, prejudices, and theory are. In describing Reik's efforts to understand the relationship between music and his own thought, which Lacoue-Labarthe thinks of as music's provocation of Reik's compulsion to write himself, he comments:

> It is as if Reik blurred all the divisions (often strict) to which Freud submits, and plunged into a sort of hole or gap between the "symbolic," if you will, and the imaginary—a hole that is not necessarily occupied by something like the "real" [even if it] be . . . consigned to impossibility. ([1979] 1989a, 153)

Perhaps the real is too completely devoid of any form (let alone content), and rhythm is, after all, orderly. But Reik's treatment of haunting melody interestingly parallels Lacan's treatment of the real in a way Lacoue-Labarthe does not seem to notice: both theorists slip continually and irresistably from confronting the untheorizable element under discussion (music, "real") into the more familiar ground of the self or the symbolic. The impossibility to which Lacoue-Labarthe refers is the very failure of theory that he finds at telling moments in Reik in order to point out the special relationship between music and theory: music (rhythm) elicits theory but is itself beyond theory and disrupts theory—and therefore it both elicits and disrupts self-writing.

Reik's self-analysis, which shows both the compulsion of self-writing and the failure of self-writing, begins with the recollection of an important incident in his life:

---

5. Music is also not, in the first instance, symbolic, although, through the use of titles, program notes, associations with ballet or other narrative arts, and musical quotations, it can acquire certain symbolic values. See Benveniste ([1951] 1966), who explains how language is properly "semiotic," while music is not.

On the evening of December 25, 1925, Freud telephoned Reik (then on holiday in the Austrian Alps) to inform him of the death of Karl Abraham—who, it should be emphasized, had been Reik's analyst (his instructor analyst) and his friend—and to ask him to deliver the funeral eulogy before the Vienna Psychoanalytic Society. This is where it starts. Reik, naturally, is shocked. He leaves his hotel to walk in the night, following a snowy path up into the forest. . . . During the walk, Reik catches himself humming a tune that he initially does not recognize, but soon identifies at the first return or repetition. It is the opening measures of the chorale that forms the final movement of Mahler's Second Symphony, a chorale constructed upon a poem by Klopstock that Bach had already used, and entitled *Aufersteh'n,* or "Resurrection" (from which comes the name of the symphony). ([1979] 1989a, 153–54)

Lacoue-Labarthe is interested both in Reik's efforts to understand the uncanny (*unheimlich* in the Freudian sense) insistence of the melody in Reik's mind at that moment and in the fact that Reik had to put aside the completion of this book for twenty-five years—suggesting a powerful inhibition. He is also interested in the obvious connection in this instance between Reik's being haunted by a melody and his impulse to analyze his feelings, to theorize and to confess.

In fact, Reik's self-analysis reveals some reasons for the inhibition that make good sense within the conceptual framework of psycho-analysis. The death of his teacher brings Reik closer to his own Oedipus complex in relation to this paternal figure. By an arcane series of free associations, Mahler is likewise placed into an Oedipal relation to his master, the composer and conductor Hans von Bühlow. The analogy Reik : Abraham : Mahler : von Bühlow is, in fact, further extended by a third term—with Freud on the side of the psychoanalysts as their *Urvater* and Beethoven (or Bach?) in the same position on the side of the composers. The music was thus voicing Reik's desire for Abraham's death, his exhilaration at the chance to take Abraham's place—feelings that his filial piety would prevent him from bringing to consciousness at that moment.

This reason for Reik's haunting melody is certainly more sophis-ticated than Freud's explanation would have been. For Freud, who did not take a very keen interest in music, could only conceive of the importance of musical associations by taking recourse to their *texts*—and thus by reducing the musical to the verbal. This, of course, only works if the musical piece in question *has* a text, such as a choral work or a song setting. Otherwise, Freud might look for other cues of a purely verbal nature, such as the title.

Thus on at least two different levels, Reik's explanation manifests Oedipal rivalry. On the level of thematic content, Reik has discovered the rivalry between himself and Abraham. But in addition, his explanation itself is an act of Oedipal rivalry in relation to Freud.

Yet, as Lacoue-Labarthe points out, the very same gesture of rivalry is also a gesture of imitation: to defeat Abraham is also to take his place, that is, to be like him, or to see oneself in him. Here both Lacoue-Labarthe and Reik are making reference to Freud's *Totem and Taboo,* in which Freud posits a myth to explain the origin of civilization—a scientific or true myth—in which the sons conspire to overthrow and murder their tyrannical father, but then feel the return of their repressed love for him in the form of guilt. Their love can ultimately be traced to a narcissistic identification with the father. In other words, the revalry with Abraham and Freud is also *specular:* it is a simultaneous destruction of the other and a reinforcement of the self as reflected in the other.

Not only is Reik's fantasy of being a great figure in psychoanalysis a specular relation with Abraham (and I use the word *figure* advisedly); all autobiography, Lacoue-Labarthe points out, is specular. Because autobiography is always the writing of the self as seen unconsciously in reflection in the other, Lacoue-Labarthe points out that self-writing is always really other-writing; that autobiography is always *allo-biography.* But the moment at which the other is simultaneously destroyed and incarnated in autobiography (allobiography) is also a moment at which the whole phenomenon of the specular self becomes unstable. This instability is particularly powerful because Reik is not only the subject of his self-writing but also the subject of theorizing about his self-writing, within the theoretical framework provided by Freud. So one can imagine, not only Reik looking into the mirror— or into Mahler or Abraham—who serve as mirrors, but Reik himself holding himself up as another mirror, with the result that there is an endless series of reflections back and forth, in which the self itself gets lost.[6] The subject is not quite itself (because it is always elsewhere,

---

6. In other words, we find Reik in the midst of a *mise en abîme. Mise en abîme* is, originally, a figure in heraldry, in which the figure in the center of the shield

in all the reflections), but not quite nowhere either. In Lacoue-Labarthe's parlance, it *desists*—that is, it "stands away" from itself (1979, 259–61).

> The "theoretical" consequence (though at the limit of the theorizable): the figure is never *one*. Not only is it the Other, but there is no unity of stability of the figural; the imago has no fixity or proper being. There is no "proper image" with which to identify totally, no essence of the imaginary. What Reik invites us to think, in other words, is that the subject "desists" because it must always confront *at least* two figures (or one figure that is *at least* double), and that its only chance of "grasping itself" lies in introducing itself and oscillating *between* figure and figure (between the artist and the scientist, between Mahler and Abraham, between Freud and Freud). . . .
>
> Everything seems to point to the fact that this destabilizing division of the figural (which muddles, certainly, the distinction between the imaginary and the symbolic, and broaches at the same time the negative or absolute alterity of the "real") is precisely what is involved in the "musical obsession," connecting it, as a result, with the autobiographical compusion itself. ([1979] 1989a, 175)

In other words, this moment at which the subject begins to lose itself is also the moment at which music comes in to fill the gap. Music is left when the subject falls away, but it also brings the subject back, reinitiates self-writing, in somewhat the same manner as the fear of madness (i.e., Dionysos) compelled Heidegger to impose thought in opposition to Nietzsche's philosophy. That is, the loss of the subject leads to the musical obsession, which is nonspecular and nonimaginary, but this musical obsession in turn triggers the compulsion to confess, to write oneself, to restore a subject.

The idea that music returns the listener to the state before subjectivity and thus to the death of the subject comes to Lacoue-Labarthe not from Reik, but rather, of course, from Nietzsche's *The Birth of*

(the "abyss" of the "escutcheon") reproduces the whole shield, and in the center of that is yet another, smaller representation of the whole, and so on. So we have an infinite repetition with infinite regress.

Tragedy. At one point, Lacoue-Labarthe compares Reik's comments on the composer's need to have his music go beyond the expressive power of the choral text to Nietzsche's theory:

> [This is a] Nietzchean, "melocentric" analysis, opening . . . onto nothing other than the phenomenon of *musical catharsis*—or, to paraphrase Nietzsche's words in the last chapters of *The Birth of Tragedy,* the discharge of an unbearable affect (of an originary pain or suffering) provoked by music. Music would provoke such an effect in that it is the first reproduction or repetition, the first *immediate* mimeme [representational image] of the originary One (in which case, its mode of action, the catharsis it causes, is of a strictly "homoeopathic" nature; in short, music heals—this is the theme of consolation, of the death it evokes). But [music] would also provoke such an effect [i.e., catharsis] . . . inasmuch as it engenders mimetic reduplication (the constitution, on the order of the visible and the figural, of the individuated, the Apollonian, theatricality, etc.); so that the subject can be engulfed in it through emotional discharge but without losing itself irretrievably. ([1979] 1989a, 187–88)

Note at this point that Lacoue-Labarthe's Nietzschean analysis of what music does to the subject—"engulf . . . it through emotional discharge, but without [the subject] losing itself irretrievably"—is very close to my conception of the effect poetry has on the reader, given its special relation between meaning and rhythm. He continues, "To put this in other terms, music's catharsis is such that it permits the subject to mime the return to the originary One, to the undifferentiated, to chaos (even while preserving itself . . . without risk)" ([1979] 1989a, 188).

What happens to the subject in musical catharsis is, in other words, its death—while it yet lives on to witness that death. This paradox accords with Freud's observation that no one can really conceive of his or her own death—one is always the spectator who lives on (Lacoue-Labarthe 1979, 204–7). But musical catharsis is not simply a fantasy of death; it is a real interruption of the subject's ordinary life, a "caesura" (1979, 277). In fact, this musical catharsis explains Reik's twenty-five-year interruption in his self-analysis of his original experience of the "haunting melody."

To this experience, which is a kind of "desistance," Lacoue-Labarthe also attaches the word *émoi*, which ordinarily means "emotion" or "excitement," but which he playfully etymologizes as *é-moi*, "outside-me" (1979, 285; think of *ecstasy*, "standing outside"). Yet, just as music draws one outside of oneself, it simultaneously brings back the image of the self, the register of the imaginary, as a kind of apotropaic act—a gesture to ward off the danger. Lacoue-Labarthe here draws upon Freud's analysis of the logic of the Medusa fantasy. Medusa's hair is composed of phallic snakes because the multiplication of phallic symbols wards off the castration anxiety she really represents. Thus, for the analyst as for the dreamer, the multiplication of images always betokens an original lack, an absence. In Reik's case, as in Heidegger's, the threat of the loss of subjectivity music portends provokes the compulsion to write autobiography and theory—but these latter simultaneously *confess* to the lurking threat of the original lack, which is, as in Lacan and in Nietzsche, the truth that always lies behind the specular illusions that provide us with our identities.[7]

Accordingly, Reik's analysis always falls short of fully recognizing that the experience of music goes beyond the phenomena of self, rivalry, rebellion, guilt—in short, all the phenomena of the *imaginary* register made so familiar by psychoanalytic theory and therefore easier to talk about than the real loss of self. But he frequently confesses to his failure fully to account for his experience. In two ways, then, as Lacoue-Labarthe says, Reik's "failure is his success." His failure to face up to the loss of the (psychoanalytic) subject is the sign of the success of his repressive, apotropaic compulsion to write himself. But his confession of his theory's failure is also his success in apprehending that there is something within his experience that goes beyond the province of theory itself.

The etymological history of the word *rhythm*, elaborated by Émile Benveniste, provides an interesting case of the phenomenon Lacoue-Labarthe is repeatedly pointing to: the hidden interdependence between subjectivity and images on the one side and death and music on the other. For rhythm originally did not mean what it does now, but

---

7. Neither Reik nor Lacoue-Labarthe—nor Lacan, for that matter—seems to mention that rhythm might also be pleasurable—that the temporary loss or disruption of subjectivity affords not only a liberating truth but a moment of pleasure. My own theory attempts to acknowledge this pleasure more directly.

rather something more visual, a pattern or form of organization. Plato's use of this word, coupled with *metron* (meter, or what we today mean by "rhythm") to describe the momentary physical *forms* held by dancers as they move from moment to moment, seems to have opened the way toward the word's present meaning.[8] The word thus went from meaning the pattern that stamped or formed the character, the social identity, the specular self, to meaning the very thing that interrupts that character, but that also provokes its reemergence. Rhythm is "the condition of possibility of the subject" (285).

Probably because rhythm thus compels the subject in two ways—first to disappear, and then to reemerge through self-writing—Lacoue-Labarthe refers throughout his essay to the experience of being haunted by a melody as the "catacoustic" phenomenon. *Catacoustic* is derived from the Greek verb *katakoúein*, which means both "to listen to" and "to obey." One must always hear and follow the behest of rhythm, the musical voice from beyond the self.

The power of musical rhythm (in the modern sense) to interrupt the subject, and yet its necessary role in bringing the subject into being—this conception of rhythm may seem very similar to Kristeva's concepts of the chora and the semiotic. Also like Kristeva, Lacoue-Labarthe links rhythm to the maternal body ([1975] 1989b, 127; 1979, 294–98). But unlike Kristeva, Lacoue-Labarthe shows no interest in analyzing the origin of rhythm itself. For him, the biological fact of the maternal body is sufficient. More importantly, for Lacoue-Labarthe, rhythm is necessarily the *untheorizable* physical experience that interrupts theory and then calls theory into being. Accordingly, Lacoue-Labarthe makes no effort to interpret rhythmic or sonic devices themselves, as we have seen Kristeva do with a Mallarmé poem.

Rather, theory is the effort to interpret rhythm into something within the orders of the imaginary and the symbolic, an effort that always fails, because what is represented or mimed in theory is entirely unrepresentable, a reserve that can never be brought entirely within the empire of theory. As we can readily see, then, the relation between theory and rhythm in Lacoue-Labarthe's recent thought is

---

8. Modern dance practice returns, in a sense, to this idea of rhythm, since in some high modern schools such as Graham and Cunningham, dance is conceived as a movement from shape to shape.

quite comparable to the relation between these two in poetry, according to the theory of poetry as telling rhythm. Hence it is no accident, but a happy choice, that Lacoue-Labarthe begins "L'Écho du sujet" by quoting two early modern poets, Hölderlin and Mallarmé, and he finishes the essay by quoting a poem by Franz Rückert, and, at the very end, one by Wallace Stevens. The two passages that serve as legends for the whole essay are: (Hölderlin) "everything is rhythm [*Rhythmus*], the whole destiny of man is a single heavenly rhythm, just as the work of art is a unique rhythm"; and (Mallarmé) "because every soul is a rhythmic knot" (1979, 220).

The form of the essay itself, "L'Écho du sujet," and of all the other of Lacoue-Labarthe's essays discussed here, shows a striking slipperiness in the relation between theory and rhythm. For the convenience of exposition, I have continually presented these two items as if they were binary opposites, detachable from each other. But as in Nietzsche's relation between the Dionysian and Apollinian (that is, when treated as allegories and not as moral types), neither one can exist without the other. Moreover, if one follows the one logically for long enough, one finds oneself in the midst of the other. Lacoue-Labarthe's essays thus have a thought structure comparable, not to a structuralist chart with two opposed columns, but rather a Möbius strip. This is, by the way, one of the features that makes Lacoue-Labarthe's writing difficult to read: whenever one expects to find a clear definition that will provide closure to a passage of argument, instead, one gets Lacoue-Labarthe hinting, suggesting coyly, and going on to something else. These moments are where we have found ourselves "outside" of philosophy—so, necessarily, they cannot appear clearly in Lacoue-Labarthe's words. For Lacoue-Labarthe, theory is always theatrical. Hence, the framing of "L'Écho du sujet" between prose words of poets and actual poems is another way of enacting— dramatically—the slippage from the otherness of rhythm to the comparative visual clarity of theory and representation, and then back again to rhythm.

This structure serves one of Lacoue-Labarthe's chief purposes, which is to respond, affirmatively, to a problem brought up by deconstruction in its by-now classic phase: If there is nothing outside the text, nothing that is not text, to which texts would refer as their truth, then is there any such thing as truth? Or, if we take up this same question as it was posed more politically at the beginning of this chapter, if there is nothing outside what people already think (philosophy), how can we have any freedom to change our society instead of endlessly repeating the same injustices, the same awful cycles of revolution and repression, of liberation and bureaucracy, without any possibility of something really new, and perhaps better? Lacoue-Labarthe's answer shows its links with the older poststructuralism: it is that the answer is already there. Self-writing always leads to its own failure, and the intimation that there is something beyond, which we are presently calling rhythm or music. Rhythm is the truth to which the text refers (and which it also represses), but, since rhythm is *nothing* from the point of view of meaningful language and texts, we can still hold both to the Derridian tenet that there is nothing outside the text and to the affirmative truth of rhythm.

But if self-writing leads to its own failure, and thus opens out to a recognition of the rhythm beyond it, we need not fear that we will fall into a Dionysian madness forever. For that very outside conducts us back into subjectivity. One has room to hope that this outside, this unutterable truth, provides a momentary space from which the reentry into subjectivity really can be somewhat different, while not necessarily repeating the false newness of revolution.

But while philosophy reinstates subjectivity by overtly *denying* the power of what is beyond it and by covering over its own failure, poetry, I would argue, draws attention to this very failure, for that is the source of its pleasure. The poem that assures us compellingly and convincingly that it can only barely hint at a truth that it knows and that will come to us without being spoken is the poem that lives on with us and that we love to repeat.

We are now ready to turn head-on to the theory of poetry as telling rhythm. I have traced the Nietzschean tradition through a variety of its versions in the twentieth century, including Freud and Lacan, Abraham, Kristeva, and Lacoue-Labarthe, and I have drawn connections between this tradition in theory and the observations of the formalists and structuralists, especially Jakobson. Throughout, we have found elements of a notion of poetry as an effort to represent in words, images, and ideas—in metaphors—the unrepresentable energy that its own rhythm is simultaneously realizing in sound and meter. Where this allegorical relationship has not been pursued, as in Kristeva and Lacoue-Labarthe, we have seen how it would be useful to bring it in. In Lacoue-Labarthe, moreover, all the ingredients are there for an allegorical theory of poetry, although these ingredients are separated out as the relation between rhythm and thought, which are brought together in poetry. But even in Lacoue-Labarthe, thought and self-writing, which repress the power of rhythm, simultaneously represent it and confess to their inadequacy in representing the unrepresentable. This dual work of repression and representation is analogous to that of the Freudian dreamwork, which can be read allegorically.

We have seen throughout the Nietzschean tradition how rhythm in music, poetry, and dance stands for the immediacy of physical reality itself, when it is beheld in all its wonder, and when it is allowed momentarily to challenge the complex structure of prejudices and values that make our reality perceptible and manageable. Repeatedly, poetry has offered a relief from these prejudices and values and yet at the same time a way back into social life, with the benefits of that momentary glimpse into freedom. I shall now pursue this theoretical structure and its implications for today's reader of poetry.

Part 3:
Telling Rhythm: Allegories of Its Sublime Power

13

Telling Rhythm: Solutions to Postmodern Problems

Poems are allegories of the sublime power of their rhythm. Their images and themes represent the power of rhythm, while the very words that convey to us these images and themes physically manifest that rhythm. Yet at the same time, the power of rhythm is not a meaning effect; it does not participate in the process of signification. It is a power without rational meaning—a sublime force. The images and themes of poetry are ways of telling rhythm and thus of representing the unrepresentable, and these elements of content also represent their *inability* to fulfill their mission. Yet the specific manner in which the language of a poem attempts and fails to represent the sublime power of its rhythm and in which it acknowledges the fact that rhythm is beyond its reach—*how* the poem's language tells this story—can be meaningfully situated in history and culture. Poetry is a moment of encounter between the specifically, historically engaged and the sublime, between the socially constructed body and the rhythmic body at free play among constructs. As such, poetry challenges socially prevalent concepts, dislodging them momentarily so that they can change as part of historical processes.

This is a very brief encapsulation of the theory of poetry presented here. It draws from the Nietzschean tradition traced in the foregoing chapters, from related structuralist thought, and from recent, postmodern trends in theory that inform culture studies.

Like structuralist Roman Jakobson and his formalist circle, I define poetry as language that intentionally draws attention to its physical features, without losing its capacity to mean. The reader's attention is divided and held in tension between the meaning of the words and their physical, sonic features. But as Jakobson observes, a common principle unites the opposing elements, sound and meaning: repetition, or rhythm—the expression of the principle of equivalence as it is played out across time, along the axis of combination. Poetry is composed of sequences of equivalent units of sound arranged in hierarchies of larger equivalent units, giving us the intricacies of metrical rhythm. The language of poetry is highly metaphorical, since metaphor is the rhetorical figure motivated by the principle of equivalence. And poetry tends to stack up one metaphor after another, all equivalent (or neatly opposed) to each other.[1]

But what do all these metaphors indicate? Insofar as there is a clear answer—the subject matter of the poem—then wouldn't the simple name of the thing be even a closer equivalent than a metaphor? Why the indirection, the riddling quality, of poetry? To this crucial question, which has direct bearing on a theory of reading poetry, an answer is to be found not in formalism or structuralism per se, but in the Nietzschean tradition to which these are related. In this tradition, the metaphors of poetry ultimately refer to the sublime power of a musical effect—the rhythm of the poem. They must go about it indirectly because they are attempting to bring the nonverbal and unrepresentable into the realm of the verbal and imaginary.

Like Nietzsche, I consider the musical element of poetry a force that draws the listener or reader away from the ordinary world of separate objects with their individual meanings and values, and toward a state of being not-oneself, free of social codes of value, without language. The words of poetry keep us protected from the mere insanity of such a state, even while they also lead us toward its freedom because they pose images of its power before us. But unlike Nietzsche, I would not speak of either a Dionysian or an Apollinian

---

1. Obviously, not all tropes in a poem are metaphors—there can be any sort of rhetorical trope in a poem. But even while these local rhetorical devices are not metaphors, the *images* that they form strike the reader as probably *meaning something that they resemble.* In other words, the interpretation of a poem almost always assumes a metaphorical application of its apparent thematic content. Roman Jakobson's work demonstrates how the prevalence of the principle of equivalence would contribute to the reader's assumption of metaphorical meaning. It seems to me that the assumption of metaphor is almost by definition what we mean by interpretation of poetry, and interpretation is one of the elements in the engagement in poetry that a good theory of poetry must preserve.

music, nor of either as a type of person. The theoretical structure informing the Nietzschean tradition makes sense only if these two gods are taken as purely allegorical figures representing principles and not moral types. The primal unity to which the allegorical figure of Dionysos refers is only meaningful to us insofar as it is a *negation* of the principle of individuation under whose control we normally live. But the principle of individuation is afforded by the veil of illusions or dream images, the province of Apollo, and these illusions can only exist insofar as they veil *something,* the primal unity that is their negation. The two, Apollo and Dionysos, are two sides of the same coin; it would be nonsense to conceive of the one in isolation from the other. The Apollinian dream image simultaneously represents the primal unity for consciousness and represses it from direct contact with us. It is how we know that the Dionysian is there, but it prevents us from dwelling within the Dionysian, which would be unimaginable without that dream image.

In a postmodern context, the opposition Apollo/Dionysos might be regarded as a suspect binary pair, the sort that appears in structuralism and that deconstruction would wish to undermine. This particular dyad, however, is always already deconstructed, insofar as neither category can be chosen as the grounding of the other, and there can be no hierarchy between them. Each one vanishes as soon as it is isolated, like electrical charges or magnetic poles. Each term is in a supplementary relation to the other, and both of them constitute a mutually elaborating play of *différance.*

The next major step in the Nietzschean tradition is Freud and psychoanalysis. Following the Freudian model, I consider the language of poetry to be a kind of dreamwork generated by the drive to rhythm, which the images simultaneously make accessible and repress through representation. Nietzsche's Dionysos becomes Freud's drive; Apollo becomes the dreamwork, which is accessible to consciousness. But Freud never conceived of poetry that way, nor did he consider rhythm's appeal to the body as anything like a drive. Rather, it is Nicolas Abraham who speaks of the fulfillment of rhythmic expectations in terms that resemble those appropriate to a psychic drive.

Like Freud, Lacan, and Abraham, I view this drive as unrepresentable, but unlike them, I insist on leaving it as a preserve of the unknowable. It would be nonsense to say that we can bring it to consciousness—that is, as words; for then the entire structure of drive/

representation would collapse into nothing. There would be nothing more to represent. We can only enable listeners or readers of poetry to experience the drive to rhythm by themselves (by training them to be sensitive to rhythms), while we interpret poetry's own interpretation of it into symbols, an interpretation that, in the poem, always falls short of its object, rhythm.

Like Lacan, I see a nothingness of sorts at the core of the subject's being, but unlike him, and somewhat more like Lacoue-Labarthe, I see this nothingness as full of something nonverbal, rhythm. Lacan tends to slide rapidly from this nothingness at the center to the unconscious, which is "structured like a language" and therefore an internal microcosm of the sociosymbolic order. Likewise, Abraham relegates rhythm under the general rubric of affect, which can then be further categorized and named. But this power remains a preserve of the unknown, a source of the sublime. It is not necessary to reduce it to the verbal in order to understand the verbal aspects of mental life as referring to it. The rhythm of poetry compels affect, which can then be put into words; rhythm does not represent affect.

The rhythm of poetry stimulates the poet and the audience to think of words and images to address it, and at the same time, because its power is beyond those words and images, it destabilizes language— and with it, prevailing codes and prejudices in society.[2] Like Kristeva, I consider rhythm to be a force that both propels and disrupts rational speech; but again, that force itself cannot and should not be replaced by speech on the part of the theorist. And finally, with Lacoue-Labarthe, I see a two-directional process, wherein rhythm leads to speech, and speech alludes to rhythm by means of its own inadequacy before it. But whereas Lacoue-Labarthe concentrates on philosophy's efforts to repress its relation to rhythm, I see poetry as inducing and celebrating this relation as an ongoing process.

----

2. One might well pose as a counterexample the requirement of Chinese aspirants to the civil service to demonstrate their ability to convert a message into verse— for here, how could poetry challenge the social structure? I would argue, however, that even though the government can intend to recruit poetry for its purposes, if the poetry is successful, the government will always get more than it bargained for. One could compare this effect to the problem of education in the United States and elsewhere: when students become too well educated, they challenge the despotic elements in the very governmental structure that had underwritten their education in the hopes of ensuring its own wealth in an information-based global economy.

Perhaps it will be convenient now to summarize the theory of poetry as telling rhythm in a series of numbered points. After the summary, I shall discuss some of the philosophical implications of the theory in the postmodern context. In the next chapter, I shall illustrate its practice in readings of some ballads. The theory offers attractive possibilities, I think, to help make poetry more readable today and to restore its place in culture after this place has been seriously eroded in this century. In addition, the method suggested by this theory has some implications in relation to larger social and political issues today, such as the possibility of real understanding in a world of difference, and the possibility of beneficial social change.

1. Poetry is an utterance that draws the mind simultaneously in two opposed directions because of its dual nature. On the one hand, poetry is a statement that makes sense. On the other hand, poetry is a sequence of sounds producing a rhythm and drawing attention to the physical properties of words. These two elements, sense and non-sense, transparency and opaqueness, are in tension with each other—the non-sense element of poetry cannot be subsumed into sense as one among various other rhetorical devices.

2. The principle of rhythm controls both elements of the poem, meaning and sound. Rhythm itself is repetition of discontinuous elements. Physical rhythm can be said to have meaning only in a very limited way, insofar as it alludes to well-known rhythms that are in turn attached to certain ideas, conventions, and moods, and therefore to words and images. But aside from this occasional allusion, rhythm has no meaning; it has only the effect of physically attracting the listener or reader to engage in the rhythm. Physical rhythm is quite different in kind from either words or images, which are fundamental to the economy, codes, and values of ordinary social life.

3. The mental process that corresponds to physical rhythm is that of comparing and contrasting. This process governs the making of metaphors, which characterize poetic language, and of some other rhetorical devices, such as puns, which are frequent in poetry. On the level of meaning, the poem is composed of metaphors that follow one another without intervening connections. On the level of meaning, then, a poem is a riddle. Interpreting a poem means solving the riddle, that is, understanding the relation between the literal terms of the poem and their solution. The principle that unites the metaphors across their discontinuity is the solution to the riddle and the meaning of the poem.

4. The metaphors are either direct or (more usually) indirect representations of the engaging power of the physical rhythm of the poem itself. This engaging power is nonverbal and not rational; a power beyond words, it is sublime. The words of the poem thus provide an *allegory of the sublime power of rhythm.* The effort to represent the unrepresentable is itself often symbolized in the metaphors of the poem. Poems tend to announce that they are telling about something that cannot be put into words, while at the same time, their sounds are attracting the reader into their rhythms, which are beyond the reader's socially and historically constructed individual identity.

In turn, rhythm itself can be thought of as a local manifestation of the infinitude of physical reality in general, as compared with the finitude and inadequacy of the words, images, and concepts used to understand that physical reality. Physical reality itself is ahistorical because it is not constructed in any meaningful way and thus not fully knowable.[3] The images and ideas of poetry are historical; they construct the immediate physical reality of the rhythm that their words simultaneously embody.

The hearer is never completely abandoned to the rhythm, for that would no longer be poetry, which always has linguistic and imaginary components. (Even the experience of listening to abstract, instrumental music includes the observation of ordering principles, allusions to other works and traditions, and the characters of individual instruments, which mediates the pure experience of the supraindividual power of music.) But hypothetically speaking, if one could imagine the state of being of the hearer dwelling in rhythm alone, this state undermines all distinctions ordinarily perceived in reality (as it is linguistically constructed), both spatially and temporally.[4]

For this reason, poetry brings the present together with the past and tends toward a sense of tradition, even when it is innovative. This is an important, somewhat paradoxical effect in poetry that has been rather obscured by the modernist trend toward making poetry resemble prose. Poetry tends to undermine prevalent social codes and

---

3. This is essentially an epistemological point. For a further elaboration in the context of the history of science, see Fleck [1935] 1981.

4. On this process and my use of the term *sublime,* see my discussion of Nietzsche's Dionysian primal unity with its negation of the principle of individuation in chapter 8.

values and thus to call traditions and prejudices into question. But at the same time, it evokes a powerful sense of its own traditionality, its link with the past and the future. Thus in more traditional cultures, there is almost always a close link between poetry and prophecy: for example, the biblical prophetic books, the verses attributed to the oracle at Delphi, the hexametrical Sybilline books at Roman Cumae, and the verses interpreting the throw patterns of the I Ching. These two contradictory principles—destabilization and tradition—come together if one thinks of poetry as undermining the *provinciality* of the day's values by encouraging a larger, more timeless view of them. The broad sweep and distant historicity of ancient epic would fit into this picture of poetry, as would the contemplative lyric, the choral ode, and folk ballads and rhymes.

In recommending this allegorical reading of poetry, one might well ask whether I am taking as allegorical something that is not truly an allegory. I might be said to be propounding *allegoresis*—that is, the reading as allegory of texts not overtly, generically, necessarily allegorical, the way that, say, John Bunyan's *Pilgrim's Progress* and Spenser's *The Faerie Queene* are overtly, generically, and necessarily allegories. Nevertheless, I have been using the term *allegory* throughout this book because my concept is not far from the notion that the text itself really is allegorical and gives generic signals of it. After all, poems are almost always apprehended as in some way metaphorical for something. We assume that they tell us something because it has a point to it, usually a point beyond the obvious one. Perhaps advertisement jingles and propaganda would be an exception, but even there, their being clearly *poetry* urges one to bracket off their obvious propagandistic message as less than the whole meaning effect.

I find most useful Maureen Quilligan's suggestion that allegory signals itself through the use of puns (1979); for in poetry, if one looks for it, one finds everywhere possible double references secondarily referring to rhythm or its effects. But because one has to look for these puns, I acknowledge that my theory is somewhere between the *allegorizing* of the text and the recognition of the text as already intentionally allegorical.[5] But both Quilligan and Northrop Frye (1974)

---

5. For the distinction between allegoresis or allegorizing reading and allegory proper, see also Frye 1974.

proceed for the most part on the assumption that allegory must be *narrative*. By contrast, I assume simply that the signs on the surface of the text must have some connection, some principle of coherence, which is not necessarily temporal. It may be, for example, descriptive. The connection may itself, directly, be the reference to the sublime power of rhythm, or it may be something else that itself can stand as a metaphor for the effect of rhythm. The latter is more often the case. Walter Benjamin presents a brilliant historicizing view of allegory that foregrounds nonnarrative allegories such as baroque emblems and imitations of hieroglyphs (1977). What I am suggesting here, however, is that allegory's use of visual images to allude to something powerful and invisible, and allegory's tension between sound and meaning, are to be seen in poetry of many periods and provenances. The historical changes can be seen more in the particular methods of allegorical representation. The generic allegories of which Quilligan and Benjamin speak do indeed have another level of reference, between, as it were, the concrete images and the effect of rhythm, a level of reference to abstract ideas that, themselves, may be seen as metaphors for the sublime power of rhythm.[6]

5. *How* the poem attempts to make sense out of this nonverbal, nonsocial process has historical, social, and individual significance. Reading the poem means understanding the socially and historically specific ways in which the nonsocial and ahistoric process of rhythm is being addressed in words and symbols. At the same time, and in a complementary way, reading a poem means witnessing the undermining of social and historically specific meaning, which can only occur if one understands precisely what meanings are being undermined.

The theory of poetry as allegory of the sublime power of rhythm, or *telling rhythm,* is not a way of getting rid of history. Far from it.

---

6. Quilligan also points out that both allegory proper and allegorizing reading come and go together in and out of fashion—even though they are somewhat at odds with each other, because allegoresis wants to treat as allegory texts that do not announce themselves as allegorical. She suggests that the periods when allegory and allegoresis are popular, such as the Renaissance, are times "when language is felt to be a numinous object in its own right" (1979, 281). While perhaps bracketing the word "numinous," I would argue that such a period is our own, the postmodern, in which we feel the effects of the linguistic turn in the human sciences and even in the physical sciences such as biochemistry and physics.

The specific figures used in any particular poem to interpret the drive of rhythm, and simultaneously to admit the impossibility of ever fully representing its sublime reality, are historically and culturally specific and must be read in appropriate historical and cultural contexts in order to make sense. Yet there is also something outside of history, going on at the same time. Without this something, the power of rhythm, history itself is impossible. For history is always a history *of*. The changes of history would be imperceptible and meaningless unless we can grant that there is something that endures, as a backdrop, so to speak, against which the scenes of history play themselves out.[7] Now if we try to name this thing—family, society, sexuality, or whatever—we can see that each of these terms itself has a history and is itself a theoretical construct. But it is probably a mistake to say, as a result, that everything is a historically specific construct. Rather, something makes history possible, but that something is itself, necessarily, inexpressible. In the terms I have been using throughout, it is *sublime*. In poetry, that sublime something can be experienced as physical rhythm.

The history of poetry is, then, a history of how the sublime, nonverbal power of rhythm gets figured in the various allegories that come out of specific cultural and historical frameworks and, of course, out of specific individuals with all their happenstances. And yet that history must also acknowledge that none of those allegories exists whole and complete, without a figure for its own undoing, the place where it is disrupted, where it falls short before the power of rhythm to which it responds. Typically, the end of any poem is the moment at which the allegory surrenders before the excessive demand placed upon it—a death, an end, the cessation of the voice. But that, too, brings the rhythm of the poem to the closure of a momentary silence as well.

At this point, my reader may protest: "After reading all this, I can admit the possibility that particular poems *may* function as

---

7. Here is where I disagree with Tzvetan Todorov's conclusion that "*poetry* [*la poésie*] doesn't exist, but there exist conceptions of poetry that vary, not only from one era or country to another, but also from one text to another" (1987, 84). Yes, conceptions of poetry *do* vary, but there must be something constant in order for us even to be able to compare one to another. To say that poetry is whatever anyone happens to think it is is not, after all, a very helpful or edifying theory.

allegories of the sublime power of rhythm insofar as looking at them
that way will result in interesting interpretations of them. But why
should *all* poems be such allegories? Why *must* they be?"

I have presented at two earlier points ways in which a justification
of why poems might be conceived as *by nature* allegories of the
sublime power of rhythm could be derived from an extension of the
concepts already set forth by, respectively, Jakobson and Nietzsche.
In Jakobson's case, this involves recognizing a relation of equivalence
not only among elements within a given stratum of language in the
poem—phonological, syntactic, semantic, or thematic—but also
between strata. Thus the thematic material, which the reader already
tends to read as primarily metaphoric, is similar to the phonological
parallelism, which is rhythm. But rhythm does not mean, while
metaphors do. So the metaphors on the thematic surface mean the
rhythm—the prevalence of parallelism itself—as the nonmeaning.
This extension brings out the reader-oriented, or phenomenological,
tendency of Jakobson's theory. Nietzsche's theory is writer oriented,
or genetic. The poem emerges out of the efforts of Apollo to clothe—
both to hide and to represent—the rhythmic energy of Dionysos,
which itself is characterized by the undoing of the individuation
Apollo makes possible. Thus reading or interpreting the poem should
reverse the process of veiling—it should reveal the relation between
the veil and the imageless spirit of music behind it. The images of
the poem, then, would be an allegory for their rhythmic origin.

Both of these arguments attempt to justify the reading of poetry
as telling rhythm by extending theories answering the question, What
is poetry? But the question of poetry's nature is inseparable from the
question of theory itself—What makes a good theory of poetry? For
to some degree, the object of the theory will be constructed by the
theory, insofar as the theory makes a particular perception of the
object possible. And theories of poetry, in turn, must thus be evaluated
not so much for how accurately they reflect the true nature of poetry
(we don't know what that is before we have a theory), but prag-
matically, for what they enable us to do.

Now, given the two distinct and heterogeneous aspects of poetry,
rhythm and meaning, there are only three possible ways of placing
them both within a single, coherent theory of poetry that would
allow for the interpretation of poetry as well as the appreciation of
(or participation in) its rhythm. First, rhythm can be subordinated

to meaning as a rhetorical device. We have seen in chapter 4 how this inevitably leads to the undermining of poetry itself—rhythm becomes more or less translatable, and poetry becomes prose. Second, rhythm and meaning may have no relation whatsoever—they may be only accidentally found in the same utterance, or, as in Jakobson (without the extension developed earlier), they may both be guided by the same principle, which is in fact rhythmic, but they may otherwise have no interpretable relation. This solution is dissatisfying because we expect a strong theory of poetry to discover the elegance and unity among the various elements in the poem rather than to view them as accidentally thrown together. As a result, we may witness a slide from this view to the first (rhetorical), as I attempted to point out in Jakobson's case in chapter 7. Finally, we may reverse the relation between rhythm and meaning from the first, rhetorical, approach: rather than rhythm contributing to meaning, meaning refers to rhythm. This approach has the advantage of preserving *both* the importance of rhythm *and* the possibility of satisfying interpretation. Interpretation does not reduce poetry to prose, and yet we need not fall into unintellectual impressionism in order to preserve the importance of rhythm and thus the difference between poetry and prose. It is inevitable that, in practical application, the theory will come up against poems in which it is, not so much simply false, but rather not highly productive. There are poems in which the thought that the thematic surface of the poem serves as an allegory for the power of the poem's rhythm does not lead us to anything interesting beyond what we would have had without that thought. But that is the worst case. I believe that there are many other poems, such as those discussed throughout this book and in chapter 14, that bear interesting results in the context of this theory. And meanwhile, even the poems for which the theory does not add much at least have the benefit of preserving their status as poems even after interpretation.

Meanwhile, the theoretical approach I am suggesting opens up some potentially beneficial avenues for theory in a social context as well as for the reading of poetry.

Poetry, because of its special relation between rhythm and meaning, reveals the limits of language in its efforts to make sense of the world, so that, as a result, we are more aware that language *is* specific and limited and can change over time. Language may be thought of as an infinite, inexhaustible resource, but each individual utterance struggles to address reality (including a pragmatic reality, a need or desire) in a way that is necessarily limited. By contrast, reality itself is at every moment beyond the limitedness of any particular utterance.[8] We are made aware of the infinitude of physical reality relative to this momentary finitude of language and social structure, and we are therefore capable of questioning and changing language and social structure, without attempting to abandon them altogether. For while physical rhythm undermines the distinctions and definitions of reality as we ordinary live them, it also brings self and other, present and past, together, and thus insures the continuity of tradition. The way out of language and into rhythm is also the way out of rhythm and back into language and sense—with a difference. That difference is the effect of a momentary glimpse of freedom from the specificities of identity, history, and society that, for better or worse, constrain us in our ordinary interactions that use language. Poetry helps us to keep our social constructs changing and therefore helps to ensure the survival of social life itself.

In teaching, the theory of poetry as telling rhythm addresses a problem posed by current methods, including cultural studies. For although the placing of poetic meaning within its historical context alone may be useful for us to understand the message of a particular poem for a particular audience, there is the danger of poetry becoming of interest exclusively to students of an historical period and not to potential lovers of poetry. We can imagine an extreme situation— surely things are not this bad—in which, say, only Renaissance scholars read Shakespeare's sonnets in order to understand more about the Renaissance mind-set. But why are these scholars interested in the Renaissance to begin with? At worst, because they are simply in love with another time and place. I say at worst, because, in the classroom, it will be difficult to bring Renaissance poetry into the worlds of our students if we require that they all fall in love with the Renaissance in order to do so. Rather, or in addition, the reading of poetry is assumed to be a skill in itself, and it would seem desirable that this skill should, on its own, provide the student a means toward some appreciable pleasure. The theory of telling rhythm makes it possible

---

8. Language also cuts the infinite continuum of reality into provisional "cultural units" of perception and meaning. See Eco 1979, 66–68 and 76–81.

to bring history into the picture, and yet at the same time to preserve the unique pleasure that the reading of poetry has to offer.

There are other, more general ways in which the theory of poetry as telling rhythm can contribute to the teaching of poetry and to the appreciation of poetry, both inside and outside the classroom. Both the New Criticism and poststructuralism have tended to emphasize the meaning effects of poetry, to the exclusion of poetry's physical effects as rhythm. (That is, the New Criticism, when it would take any notice of formal features at all, would subordinate them to meaning by considering them to be rhetorical devices contributing to the effectiveness of the presentation of meaning.) As we have seen in chapters 2 and 3, this trend has had the effect of effacing any difference between poetry and prose, while allowing poetry to appear as an elaborate, bothersome, and roundabout way of saying what one could much more easily say in prose. Modern poets have in their practice contributed to poetry's loss of a "market niche" by abandoning rhythm altogether and by encouraging the view of poetry as nothing more than individual, verbal self-expression. In recent times, avant-gardists such as the $L = A = N = G = U = A = G = E$ poets have resisted this view of poetry as a patent meaning effect, but only by making poetry simultaneously arrhythmical *and* meaningless—so that hardly any audience is left for it. Meanwhile, these modes of analysis of poetry have not had much to say about the poetry that survives most vigorously in this very unpoetical age, that is, the oral poetry of rap music, protest chants, traditional rhymes, and lullabies.

On the opposite side of the New Criticism, so to speak, is the formalist-structuralist approach to poetry exemplified by Jakobson and Lévi-Strauss's collaborative formal analysis of Baudelaire's "Les Chats" (1972). This method foregrounds rhythm and sound effects, but it has little or nothing to say about meaning.

The theory of poetry as telling rhythm provides a way of bringing together the two extremes of the analysis of poetry, sound and meaning. But unlike the New Criticism, the present theory preserves the importance of sound without subordinating it to meaning and thus reducing it to one of any number of rhetorical vehicles whose purpose is effectively to convey the tenor. The relation between sound (or form) and meaning is analogous to Nietzsche's relation between the Dionysian and the Apollinian: the two elements are mutually dependent, but the process of reading treats the Apollinian, or meaning, as an interpretation, a representation (and a repression) of the Dionysian rhythm.

No longer must teachers of poetry present meter as a trivial but necessary irrelevancy—or, much worse but also much more common—ignore meter altogether. Meter is, in fact, to be learned as an artificial, nonmeaningful system for understanding the organization of sounds into rhythms in poetry, but the emphasis can be on the *pleasure* of rhythm itself—beginning a syllabus, perhaps, with nursery rhymes, folk ballads, folksongs, lullabies, and rap music, introducing the methods of allegorical interpretation there, and then moving on to the more individualistic, less conventional works of the literary tradition. The present theory thus enables teachers and students to experience a continuum between their own nonliterary experience of popular poetry and the study of canonical poetry.

In the society at large, poetry conceived as allegory of the sublime power of rhythm may help to restore a sense of the uniqueness of poetry—its special relation to its rhythmic appeal to the body. But the *sublime* aspect of the theory, the idea that poetry is a structure in which meaningful words are attempting to make sense of a nonmeaningful, physical power, has some possible social implications as well. Because rhythm is always beyond the limits of what can be expressed meaningfully, poetry always enables us to recognize the limitedness, the falling short, of our familiar symbols and constructs, face-to-face with the excess of physical reality. In this way, poetry has an appreciable and enduring value for society, enabling it to recognize its own limitations and to avoid a rigidity that would stifle necessary change.

The foregoing sounds more limited than Shelley's claim that "poets are the unacknowledged legislators of the world." Poetry does not have any more force than any other discourse, and arguably has less, to propose concrete ideas to be put into practice in society. To be fair, Shelley's definition of poetry extended to the imaginative work forming social structures and was thus much broader than my definition—since his purpose was not, as is mine, to rediscover the specificity of poetry in relation to other practices. For the present purposes, aside from any explicit political content in poetry—which could also be expressed in prose or in images—poetry's social and political value is probably much better approximated by the formalistic notion of defamiliarization—a notion anticipated by none other than Shelley (1977, 487 and 505).

Defamiliarization is a common trait in all kinds of art, verbal and nonverbal alike, but in poetry, language itself is defamiliarized. The relation between rhythm and meaning causes words in their ordinary, transparent meanings to seem odd and inadequate relative to the awesome, sublime infinitude of reality itself, both the reality around us and our own reality as human beings. Defamiliarization has a great deal of political significance. If words or images or social constructs become too familiar, then they are no longer seen at all, and people accept them without question. People usually take action for social change only if they believe that the social reality they currently experience is not the only one possible—that is, if they see it as limited and temporary, as worthy of comment, not as a simple fact of nature. In other words, defamiliarization encourages individual, creative thinking. Perhaps this close tie between defamiliarization and individual political action may have been one reason why Stalin found the formalists threatening enough to banish them.[9]

The concept of telling rhythm in poetry could be thought of as a more detailed, post-Nietzschean elaboration of the notion of defamiliarization. But defamiliarization as a general principle is not the only point that makes telling rhythm an attractive theory relative to today's real and theoretical problems. I should like to point out a few ways in which the theory of telling rhythm responds to current problems being expressed in poststructuralist theory that correspond to serious concerns in the practical world.

Our contemporary world is characterized by instability. Cherished ideas suddenly become irrelevant or untrue and fall away. The promises of politics, economics, and technology are betrayed. Politicians deceive us, whole systems of government collapse, and long-held social

---

9. Another reason could have been the formalists' insistence on conceiving literature, whether poetry or fictional prose, as language focused upon itself. This concept would defeat the purpose of social realism and other sorts of art specifically intended to serve propagandistic aims. Neither of these reasons is given by Erlich (1981); he and others generally seem to assume that Stalin found objectionable the bourgeois and déclassé aristocratic provenance of the formalists themselves, suspecting them of retaining their class perspectives. But the reasons I suggest here show how their theory itself could be associated in the Stalinist perspective with bourgeois or reactionary, counterrevolutionary thinking, if placed within the context of a revolution that is highly centralized and totalitarian and that emphasizes thought control.

prejudices are shattered by the rising voices of those who have long suffered as their victims. Injustice seems to prevail, even in societies that were constitutionally framed so as to ensure justice. Technology, which had promised to make human life easier, gives us less leisure, more boring work, and more unemployment—with the additional cost of irrevocable harm to the natural environment. The very means we have used to make our lives more comfortable and to safeguard the survival of our children are polluting the world, overpopulating it, and threatening all with extinction. Even medicine, the most intimate of applied sciences, cannot always fulfill people's expectations of its ability to cure serious illnesses such as AIDS and breast cancer or even the common cold. Under these circumstances, it is only natural that we wonder how we can ever know what is true and how we can trust anyone. How can we be certain about anything? How do we know what reality is? In its own modest way, the present theory of poetry suggests a direction to find answers to these questions. But poetry itself does not solve the world's problems. Poetry is not a better law, a better medicine, or a better economy. Poetry is an *experience* that may, in turn, contribute to people's practical work of survival.

In the midst of our uncertainty, we may consider many ways to view reality. These ways may be characterized as positions between two extreme poles. At one extreme, reality is described in very careful words. Laws, political principles, philosophies, theories, psychologies, and proverbial wisdom purport to be able, if drawn up carefully enough, to address reality accurately. At the other extreme, we recognize that all of these laws, political principles, theories, and so on are ways of rationally constructing reality, of calling things by their names in order to understand them and find order in them. Outside of any such constructs—if we could conceive of such an outside, which we cannot do so long as we are trying to say it in words—there is a kind of nothingness. But this nothingness is only empty from the point of view of rational construction and language. It is the manifestation of reality denuded of preconceptions and verbal formulas. This is the experience of reality that people hope to approach through meditation and mystical practices, in which they attempt to banish all verbal thoughts and simply to see, to hear, to feel, without knowing what they are sensing in any verbally mediated way. Many of these mystical practices are rhythmic and musical, such as the dancing of the Sufis, the chanting of Tibetan monks, and the rhythmic chanting and dancing of many Native American nations. The reality which they aim to disclose is reality as the sublime.[10]

The rhythms of poetry and music are instances of the manifestation of sublime reality, but unlike the mystical sublime available through meditation, rhythms are shared communally as they engage the bodies of their common audiences. Meanwhile, the words of poetry (which, of course, are the material that realizes the rhythm) describe images and express ideas that interpret sublime reality in terms of what Lacan calls the imaginary and symbolic registers—that is, in the terms in which we usually conduct our social life and in which we construct our identities. Rhythm in poetry is to the body and to physical reality as images and ideas in poetry are to social, language-mediated constructs. These constructs are necessary for us to live at all, just as the words of a poem must make sense in order for us to be engaged in the poem and thus to follow its rhythm.[11] But constructs

----

10. The mystical reality I am describing here is not transcendental in the usual sense of the term within the Western philosophical tradition. This reality transcends the individual in that it is before and beyond the limitations of individual consciousness (in Lacanian terms, it exceeds the imaginary and symbolic registers); but it does not transcend the world of the physical senses. On the contrary, it *is* the world of physical sensation, unmediated by imaginary and symbolic constructs. There is no coherent self or other in this condition of being.

Interestingly, interdisciplinary work in anthropology and brain science from the late 1970s and since provides a quasi-scientific analogue for my theory of poetry. Barbara Lex (1979) explores the function of rhythm and the trance it induces in ritual as a vital support of the connection between higher brain functions and the body, while Eugene D'Aquili and Charles Laughlin, Jr. (1979) suggests that myths are generated in the context of rituals in order to match left-brain with right-brain activity and to provide answers to the unanswerable questions that rhythm-induced ritual trance provokes. Thus the relation between D'Aquili and Laughlin's and Lex's essays corresponds to the relation between meaning and rhythm in poetry in the theory developed here. Nevertheless, from a philosophical point of view, the scientific project represented by Lex and Laughlin begs questions as to which comes first, the socially produced theory of rhythm or the factual observation of the brain. These questions are, of course, beyond my present scope.

11. Even "nonsense rhymes" such as Lewis Carroll's "The Jabberwocky" or the poems of Edward Lear must make *syntactic* sense and must therefore *resemble* language

are never adequate to the reality they construct, for that reality is itself, in relation to any particular utterance in language or any unit of culture or social value, inexhaustible. How many different descriptions can there be, for example, for the same sunset? How many for the same person? The number of these descriptions is limited only by the resources of language itself—in other words, virtually infinite.

Social constructs are historically, culturally, and otherwise specific. They necessarily change because they are never quite adequate to begin with. Likewise, laws, political systems, philosophies, and scientific explanations necessarily change because they necessarily fall short of the infinitude of human reality. Their inadequacies become evident over time, as the problems they create come to increasing awareness, and they are eventually replaced, altered, or enriched. What endures through all this is not any particular construct or theory, but physical reality, itself ultimately untheorizable, which provides an inexhaustible occasion for new theories and new constructs.

Wallace Stevens dramatizes the discovery of the limitations of social constructs in "Sunday Morning." This is a particularly interesting instance for us, because, as he often does in his poetry, Stevens makes the poetry's process of challenge particularly clear on the thematic level. The theory construct becoming exhausted in "Sunday Morning" is Christianity, with its emphasis on salvation after death and on the transcendence of the body. The woman, who is the only character in the poem besides the speaker, stays at home to have a late, relaxed breakfast on Sunday morning, instead of going to church—so we know that she is no longer absolutely held by Christianity. Yet she cannot quite abandon the "need of some imperishable bliss" that goes beyond the almost paradiselike world around her. The speaker engages in a kind of debate with her through free indirect discourse.

> There is not any haunt of prophecy,
> Nor any old chimera of the grave,

---

that makes sense. This type of poetry is a special case, where its humorous appeal is in part a kind of parody of real sense. Some of these poems are in other ways clearly parodic. "The Jabberwocky" may parody the traditional ballads collected by Francis James Child and Jakob Grimm, and its opaque words with transparent syntactic values may thus imitate the archaic words from the medieval English, Scottish, and German ballads.

Neither the golden underground, nor isle
Melodious where spirits gat them home,
Nor visionary south, nor cloudy palm
Remote on heaven's hill, that has endured
As April's green endures; or will endure
Like her remembrance of awakened birds
Or her desire for June and evening, tipped
By the consummation of the swallow's wings.

                                          (1971, 6)

Spring, here, is the figure for the inexhaustible, sublime reality
that the speaker recommends in place of the belief system from which
the woman already finds herself drifting away. The terms deliberately
invoke a situational irony: every one of the outmoded images of the
afterlife that the speaker lists—whose obsolescence he points up with
the archaism of "gat them home"—was at one time or another
promulgated as the antidote to the variousness and ephemerality of
earthly comforts such as spring. Spring, proverbially, is the most
ephemeral season: "Where are the songs of spring?" laments Keats's
speaker. But "April's green endures" because it is a moment in a
natural cycle that continues to return long after civilizations have
vanished from the face of the earth, along with their myths of the
eternal afterlife. In other words, spring is a metonymy for the year's
natural *rhythm,* which is there before and beyond the imaginary con-
structions of the afterlife, which are always nothing more than pale
imitations of the spring. Meanwhile, the poem's own rhythms, its
iambic pentameter, its stanzas, and the alternation of the woman's
and the speaker's voices—these make real and palpable, audible and
(in the meter's case) physically felt, the rhythm that remains when
images of heaven are revealed to be mere passing constructs.
    Later in the poem, the figure for sublime reality echoes the figure
serving this purpose in Whitman: death itself. This may be an echo
of Whitman in the first instance, but it is also used in much other
poetry through the ages in the West. But just as rhythm, as Lacoue-
Labarthe shows, brings forth the subject and philosophy, so death
propels all the social rituals that sustain us even as they continue to
change and to be imperfect:

Death is the mother of beauty. Hence from her
Alone shall come fulfillment of our dreams

And our desires. Although she strews the leaves
Of sure obliteration on our paths,
The path sick sorrow took, the many paths
Where triumph rang its brassy phrase, and love
Whispers a little out of tenderness,
She makes the willow shiver in the sun
For maidens who were wont to sit and gaze
Upon the grass, relinquished to their feet.
She causes boys to pile new plumbs and pears
On disregarded plate. The maidens taste
And stray impassioned in the littering leaves.

(7)

What makes *us* stray impassioned among the leaves of mortality is, of course, the rhythm of Stevens's poem, making its irresistible call to us. The Dionysian imagery of the maidens' straying is unmistakable and recalls the entire Nietzschean tradition. Rhythm pulls the maidens and boys out of whatever they had been doing, but it also sets their love, and their history, into motion.

Because the allegory of the sublime power of rhythm brings together the historical with the nonhistorical, the specifically represented with the unrepresentable, it also addresses a problem left within de Man's deconstructive approach to poetry. De Man's method of reading is important, for one thing, because he is one rigorous poststructuralist who has tended to concentrate heavily on the reading of poetry. In addition, although de Man conceives of poetry *exclusively* in terms of rhetoric (i.e., as metaphors), de Man's theory shares certain important elements with my own. For de Man—to put it very briefly and reductively—poetry always attempts to bridge the gap between language and things in themselves. But by the very nature of language, this gap cannot be bridged. That is, for something to mean anything, it cannot simply *be* the thing that it means. Poetry issues out of a longing for reconciliation between meaning and being, so that we might escape all of the uncertainty and inadequacy involved in communication through language. But poetry also always reveals its own failure to bridge this gap—indeed, as poetry (i.e., literature), it can only *widen* the gap. This is because—and here de Man follows the formalists—poetry or literature is what it is precisely because it turns *away* from the business of communication in order to be itself, a work

of art. Poetry is language turned in on itself. But in order for us to
engage in poetry at all, we must temporarily forget this fact and
pretend that poetry really is presenting the real world, as it is, with
no separation either between poetry and fact or between language
and reality. Then, as we read along, poetry will remind us, by means
of its own failure, that it cannot really tell a message plain and simple,
let alone be the world about which it claims to speak, except insofar
as it tells about itself, as poetry, and about its own failure to do or
to be any more. This is why, in "The Resistance to Theory" (1984),
de Man says that reading is the resistance to reading. Reading is only
possible because we temporarily forget that we are just reading.

This summary is drawn primarily from "The Resistance to The-
ory," which I take to be a kind of summa of de Man's career of
thinking about poetry and literature. But it also holds, more or less,
for de Man's essays on poetry throughout his career, including, espe-
cially, those in *The Rhetoric of Romanticism* (1984). Indeed, de Man's
readings of philosophers including Nietzsche in *Blindness and Insight*
(1983) follow the same basic pattern. It is as if de Man must insist,
over and over again, that literature (even philosophy) is nothing but
literature. The reason for this repetitive insistence is revealed in "The
Resistance to Theory," where de Man defines ideology as a mistake
whereby the reader takes literature to be life. As an example, we
might consider, say, the Nazis' implementation of a mere theory—
mere literature—about the natural superiority of their "race" over
the Jews and others—in such a way that they tried to *make* reality
to conform to their literature. This is the danger of forgetting that
one is reading literature, and, de Man tries to show, it results from
a blindness to literature's own insistence on its own failure.

All, or most of this, makes very good sense and constitutes a
very powerful insight. The chief problem with it is that it succeeds
only too well in making reading, if not impossible, then at least
unattractive. For if every literary text, whether poetic or philosophical
or otherwise in appearance, always ultimately says and does the same
thing, no matter how salutary, then there's no real point in reading
one more text just to rediscover the same message. In fact, this
problem may characterize what happens when one reads an essay of
de Man in which he reads a poem—such as "Shelley Disfigured"
(1984). The reading seems to be very close and very revealing, but
one doesn't quite know what the point of it all is, until the very

end, at which point, it all seems rather empty and not worth all the trouble it took to get there—since the point is the stern lesson of the failure of language and the fact that the literary text is no more than a mere illusion. There is also the specific problem posed in the beginning portions of this book: how can this theory explain what poetry might specifically have to offer, as opposed to any other kind of literary text?

The advantage of the theory of telling rhythm over de Man's deconstruction is that the specific joys and pleasures of poetry are preserved, as are the distinctions among poems. For if we think of poems from the outset as riddles whose solution is ineffable—the unrepresentable power of the rhythm which the poem itself is meanwhile realizing—then the interpreter can focus on the process, or rather, the relation between the process (representation) and the outcome—the affirmative, sublime experience of the rhythm that lies beyond the efforts of representation.

The historical particularity that makes each period and each poem different is preserved in the interpretive process, as are the individual features that make each poem different from all others. The interpreter can focus on questions such as: What does *this* poem make of its rhythm? To what uses does *this* poem place the recognition of the failure of its own allegory relative to its own rhythm? How does *this* poem reveal the limits of the constructions made available by language, and what particular freedom does it draw us into, relative to those constructs? Freedom from what ideas, prejudices, or conceptions? And in this way, a vast and limitless array of possibilities for social and individual meaning opens up before us, without, in the meantime, abandoning the features that poems have in common with each other and that make poetry attractive *as poetry,* rather than as mere message.

This combination of the specific or individual with the supra-individual also, finally, makes poetry a model to help us think about the problem of humanism, a problem that faces us in our thinking about politics, anthropology, and even education today. Humanism in its traditional form, inherited, more or less, from Enlightenment thinkers such as Locke, has become a problem in the postmodern world because it seems too continuous with imperialism. Postmodern theory has elaborated on the critical insight that when someone says that everyone feels something, it only too often means that only the group in power feels it and expects everyone else to feel the same and to act accordingly. Too often, everyman has been male, white, Euro-North-American, middle to upper middle class, Christian, heterosexual, and socially empowered. Institutions made for "the average man" are made for this powerful minority, while everyone else is disenfranchised and alienated.

We have responded to this problem by launching endless critiques of humanism and by championing difference as against sameness. But this, too, has its limits. How does a community have any cohesion at all, if all we have is difference? How, in the classroom, does one compose a syllabus, if any particular syllabus already institutionalizes a canon and therefore, despite itself, imposes a kind of sameness? How even draw up any theory about anything or anyone, if everything and everyone is so fundamentally different? In poetry, if every utterance is utterly different through and through, then how can we hope to understand anything at all?

But poetry as telling rhythm contains both sameness and difference. The locus of difference is in the words as they attempt in their particular way to construct into images and ideas the power of rhythm. But they also allude to their own insufficiency with regard to that power, and this is where the cohesion and unity lie. Terms such as *power of rhythm, sublime,* and so forth are necessary but inadequate terms for use in this theoretical discussion, but their inadequacy does not mean that there is nothing there to which they are, however inadequately, referring. What human beings have in common is their infinitude, their tendency to exceed the limits of any construct or formula, and that infinitude is experienced through the body in rhythm. This is no simple answer to the problem of humanism today, but perhaps it can start us thinking in a fresh direction, since we have tended to be bogged down by debates between sameness and difference, literacy and multiculturalism, universality and individualism, debates that have locked us into their own terms and have kept out the flights of our imagination.

The foregoing discussion has been deliberately abstract, so that I might present some ways in which the present model of poetry might imply fruitful possibilities even in areas beyond the reading of poetry itself. I have assumed a continuity between the practice of reading poetry and many other important activities in life—the reading of other utterances, the understanding of other human beings, and the conception of a just society. But my chief purpose is to try to make poetry itself readable in fresh ways, so as to breathe some new life into the reading of poetry, in a day when few people are reading poetry and fewer seem to enjoy it. The next chapter will exemplify this theoretical model with some practical readings. I have chosen a particular problem that is connected to the larger questions of history, but at the local level of an individual poem: If, as Jakobson demonstrates, poetry is controlled by the principle of equivalence, then why do poems begin and end as they do? What accounts for the diachrony of a poem? To explore this question further, I shall explore a few poems of different historical provenances within a tradition that necessarily implies a difference between the beginning and the end, and some process through time in between: the ballad.

14

Cases for Interpretation: Ballads Old and New, High and Low

The theory of poetry as telling rhythm helps us to see the uniqueness of poetry in relation to other discursive modes, such as prose fiction. But it is not clear yet that it helps us to understand the uniqueness of each moment within a poem. If all the images in a poem follow the principle of equivalence, if they are all as equivalent to each other as the repeated stanzaic or other metrical forms are, and if they all stand as figures for the sublime, unrepresentable power of the rhythm that they simultaneously embody on the level of pure sound, then why do we have any particular figure before any other one? What principles arrange a poem in an internal sequence?

The best test case of the theory would be a type of poem whose internal order seems quite necessary to its general effect and sense, such as a poem that tells a story—a ballad or an epic. If a ballad can be shown to be an allegory of the sublime power of its own rhythm, and yet can make sense as a narrative sequence, all within the same theoretical structure, then we have a real advantage over now-prevalent approaches to narrative poetry. Usually, one finds in criticism of such works the same problem noted earlier in criticism of poetry generally: critics discuss the content, which in this case is easy, because it is a story; they occasionally mention the verse form as an ornament, a genre indicator, or an unanalyzable feature of the entertainment value of the work; but the two cannot be pulled together meaningfully. Exclusive focus on the story is the commonest procedure, and here, one can see no difference between the appreciation of ballads or epics and the appreciation of prose narratives. Scholars may point out the usefulness of the respective verse forms of epics or ballads in memorization, and verse structure has been considered within the theory of oral formulaic composition, but these have nothing to do with meaning—in fact, they *decrease* the possibility of meaning by explaining away both verse structure and narrative elements in such a way as to minimize individual artistic intention. Again, one wonders why people, even illiterate people, couldn't just transmit these stories in prose—especially since so many stories *are* in fact passed along orally in prose. Fortunately, modern readers sometimes still do respond to the evocative power of ballads and still listen to both old and new ballads. But that experience is assumed to be entertainment. The learned game of interpretation is reserved for the serious poetry, where it can afford, or at least where it pretends that it can afford, to ignore rhythm. Ballads are assumed to be emotionally stirring and fun but not very deep or interesting on the level of meaning.

There is another reason for my choosing ballads as examples for the application of my theory to reading, which is typified by the other side of the coin of mainstream scholarship on ballads. A few scholars, like Bronson, who do not catalog the literary themes of ballads or look for real historical events commemorated in traditional ballads, catalog and describe the formal features of ballad rhythms and melodies—their music. For even spoken ballads and literary ballads, composed with no intention to be sung, are inseparable from the idea of music, since they refer back to a form that is traditionally sung and that is very easily set to music. The ballad is intrinsically musical because it is built on a four-beat, four-line rhythmic paradigm, which, as both Attridge and Abraham variously demonstrate, is the rhythmic paradigm that most easily engages natural expectations and fulfills them. The rhythmic side of poetry is very strong and unavoidable, then, in the case of ballads.

Ballads are typically defined as narrative folksongs (see Bronson 1959–72, ix–xiii; Richmond 1988). The theory of poetry as telling rhythm should be able to take the two most obvious features of ballads, narrative and music, and account meaningfully for their relationship.

If the theory of poetry as telling rhythm can be shown to work for both folk ballads and the ingenious ballads of known, literate poets, then it will help us to discover both the principles that motivate the diachronic development of a ballad and the deeper meaning of a ballad as a whole, when considered synchronically. This is what I hope to do by discussing four sample ballads as representative cases.

It may well be that my approach will not work for all ballads, or that another theory would come along to help make even more ballads interesting and meaningful. But if the present theory can go further than the mere cataloging and historical speculation that has prevailed in ballad scholarship, then it is of some value.

I shall consider four ballads: the traditional "Lord Randal," Emily Dickinson's "Because I could not stop for Death—" Gwendolyn Brooks's "the ballad of chocolate Mabbie," and the American popular song of the late sixties, "The House of the Rising Sun." These are intentionally diverse; I choose them in the hope that diversity will reveal more about the diachrony of ballads and about how ballads in general, however various the subject matter, might work as allegories of the sublime power of rhythm, without any one of them losing its uniqueness.

My procedure will be to consider the content of the poem first, using the poem's larger units of structural organization as guides. After I have considered the thematic meaning of the ballad, I shall place it in the context of the present theory by showing how it can be thought of as allegorizing its own rhythmic form. Thus in each case, the first part of my reading will resemble somewhat traditional thematic discussion—benefiting, however, from structuralism, post-structuralism, cultural studies, and feminism; but each such reading will lead into an awareness of poetry as telling rhythm, while retaining a sense of the principles guiding the diachrony of narration.

1. "Lord Randal": The Rhythm of the Maternal Body

"O where ha you been, Lord Randal, my son?
And where ha you been, my handsome young man?"
"I ha been at the greenwood; mother, mak my bed soon,
For I'm wearied wi hunting, and fain wad lie down."

"An wha met ye there, Lord Randal, my son?
An wha met you there, my handsome young man?"
"O I met wi my true-love; mother, mak my bed soon,
For I'm wearied wi huntin, an fain wad lie down."

"And what did she give you, Lord Randal, my son?
And what did she give you, my handsome young man?"

"Eels fried in a pan; mother, mak my bed soon,
For I'm wearied wi huntin, and fain wad lie down."

"And wha gat your leavins, Lord Randal, my son?
And wha gat your leavins, my handsom young man?"
"My hawks and my hounds; mother, mak my bed soon,
For I'm wearied wi hunting, and fain wad lie down."

"And what becam of them, Lord Randal, my son?
And what becam of them, my handsome young man?"
"They stretched their legs out an died; mother, mak my bed soon,
For I'm wearied wi huntin, and fain wad lie down."

"O I fear you are poisoned, Lord Randal, my son!
I fear you are poisoned, my handsome young man!"
"O yes, I am poisoned; mother, mak my bed soon,
For I'm sick at the heart, and I fain wad lie down."

"What d'ye leave to your mother, Lord Randal, my son?
What d'ye leave to your mother, my handsome young man?"
"Four and twenty milk kye; mother, mak my bed soon,
For I'm sick at the heart, an I fain wad lie down."

"What d'ye leave to your sister, Lord Randal, my son?
What d'ye leave to your sister, my handsome young man?"
"My gold and my silver; mother, mak my bed soon,
For I'm sick at the heart, an I fain wad lie down."

"What d'ye leave to your brother, Lord Randal, my son?
What d'ye leave to your brother, my handsome young man?"
"My houses and my lands; mother, mak my bed soon,
For I'm sick at the heart, and I fain wad lie down."

"What d'ye leave to your true-love, Lord Randal, my son?
What d'ye leave to your true-love, my handsome young man?"
"I leave her hell and fire; mother, mak my bed soon,
For I'm sick at the heart, and I fain wad lie down."

(Child version A [1882–98] 1965, 1:157–58)

Although the distinction between folk ballads and minstrel or professional ballads is always open to question (see Richmond 1988), I believe that the scholar who made this ballad available to us in print, Francis James Child, was probably right in considering this ballad an item of folk tradition. I shall follow the more recent scholar in considering a folk ballad a creation of an individual poet or singer whose name has been lost, and who may well have been a woman, as Virginia Woolf suggested with regard to all traditional ballads.[1] Assuming that this ballad was probably of the sort passed down from generation to generation orally, I agree with Linda L. Maik (1989) that a thematic discussion of the ballad's meaning should focus on its apparently "universal" concerns, and that psychoanalysis furnishes us with some useful concepts in discussing such concerns, although I shall also bring in a few somewhat more specific features of culture in medieval Europe (however vague even that category is) and surrounding the ballads in order to negotiate a path between the universalizing pronouncements of psychoanalysis and the local historicity of cultural studies. The "universal" qualities of this and other traditional ballads may also usefully be placed in the context of popular myths, which can be analyzed structurally. All of these tools will be of service in examining the thematic content of the ballad. Ultimately, however, this examination will lead us to the ballad's rhythm, and thus to the idea that the ballad works as telling rhythm.

But before I explore the thematic content of the ballad, it will be useful to point out several facts about the rhythm and some probabilities about the production of such an oral ballad during the long period of its active practice. "Lord Randal" has the clear four-beat rhythmic structure that characterizes ballads, with a generally triple movement (two offbeat syllables between the beats), but sometimes with fewer and sometimes with many more offbeat syllables, creating a roughness characteristic of poetry that can be sung to a traditional tune that reinforces the beat and thus prevents unstressed syllables from confusing the listener. Typical of the simple line is the first (B designates beat, o offbeat):

O where ha you been, Lord Randal, my son?
o   B   o   o   B   o   B   o   o B

---

1. See Bold 1979, 39–43; Woolf 1929, 51. Woolf's use of the names Mary Beton, Mary Seton, and Mary Carmichael draws on the traditional ballad "Mary Hamilton."

But sometimes we have more than two offbeat syllables in a row:

They stretched their legs out an died; mother mak my bed soon.
o   o   o   B   o   o   B   o   o   B   o   o   B

Of course, the musical accompaniment could treat the triple offbeat at the beginning of this line by means of the subdivision of musical beats into subordinate beat units, and the listener will still apprehend the whole as quite metrical:

They stretched their legs out an died; mother mak my bed soon.
o   B   o   B   o   o   B   o   o   B   o   o   B

—where *b* represents a subordinate unit of the subdivided beat, and where, probably, the *o* (offbeat) syllables are usually given half the amount of musical time given the syllables on the beat (*B*). If this were meant to be strictly written and spoken poetry, the triple offbeat at the beginning of this line would make the meter less convincing. But as trained readers, we already find other signs in the written text, such as the use of nonstandard dialect, leading us to expect a poem either from or alluding to the oral tradition, which would either have a real musical accompaniment or resemble other poems that do. In music, as in contemporary rap, the complex subdivisions of the beat into subordinate patterns actually contributes to the effect of rhythm rather than detracting from it as it would do in a purely written and spoken medium.

Who would sing this ballad? As I have mentioned, women were frequently the singers of ballads, especially in private settings, and they may well have been the composers of many, if not all, of the noncommercial, traditional oral ballads (Bold, 39–43). More specifically, mothers and nursemaids would commonly sing such ballads to children as lullabies, even if they did not specifically thematize going to sleep, and even if, as they often did, they represented troubling or violent events. It will be useful for the present reading if we keep this probable cultural context in mind. Indeed, we may right away associate the death of Lord Randal with the desired effect of the child's sleep. The child, boy or girl, would be placed in the position of the boy in the narrative, Lord Randal.

Now to move on to the meaning of this ballad, it will be

convenient first to explore how it is structured—to outline the syntax of the poem, as it were. "Lord Randal" divides up quite neatly into two near-halves, signaled at the sixth quatrain by the change of the first portion of the last line of each quatrain (the refrain) from "For I'm wearied wi huntin" to "For I'm sick at the heart." This change occurs at the first climax of the poem, right after the mother has suggested and Lord Randal has accepted the fact that he has been poisoned. In fact, version D of the ballad in Francis James Child's collection ends after the first five quatrains. The four quatrains making up the rest of the ballad are a "nuncupative testament," proceeding sequentially through mother, sister, brother, and truelove.[2] There is a second climax on the last quatrain, pointed up by the sharp contrast between its curse and the preceding bequests, and the ironic use of the phrase, "I leave her." Finally, upon rereading, one must note another, subtler climax on the third line of the third quatrain, where Lord Randal reveals that he has dined on "Eels fried in a pan."

This climax suggests itself *in retrospect* because we are left wondering, naturally, *why* the truelove has poisoned Lord Randal. This is not the first question in the reader's mind; it comes to him or her afterward. From the outset, the poem proceeds as if Lord Randal enters with a secret, a riddle whose solution his mother must elicit. This riddle is solved: Lord Randal is dying, and it is because he has been poisoned. But these solutions only leave us with a now more pressing question, the reason it is all happening. And the solution to this riddle neither the mother nor Lord Randal gives away to us; that is our first task as interpreters, and it is pressing, because it is natural when we read of an instance of tragic malice to have some explanation for it—otherwise it could happen to any one of us at any time!

The solution will have to lie in the *method* of poisoning: eels fried in a pan. Why that? The mystery is heightened by the fact that this meal is not necessarily poisonous by nature. The details cannot be gratuitous; they must be symbolic. Almost all other versions have, if not eels, then fish, which are, if not fried, then served in a broth ("broo") or in butter; many of the versions have eels.

---

2. A nuncupative testament is a ceremonial oral recitation of bequests that a character makes before death ("To *x* I leave *y*," etc.). The figure is very old indeed. See, for example, Theocritus's *Idyll* 1:128–29.

Lord Randal dines upon eels fried in a pan when he meets his truelove in the greenwood (or "wild wood"); he insistently refers to his trip as a hunting trip. The clues are sufficient to put us in mind of the tradition, extremely popular in the Middle Ages, of comparing the pursuit of a beloved—especially a man's pursuit of a woman—to the aristocratic sport of hunting. Familiar examples in English are the evident puns on "venery" in Chaucer's portrait of the Monk in the prologue to the *Canterbury Tales*; Wyatt's sonnet "Whoso List to Hunt"; Spenser's *Amoretti* 67 ("Lyke as a huntsman after weary chace"); and much of Shakespeare's *Love's Labor's Lost.* The tryst with the beloved in the woods not only fits in with this convention (although it deallegorizes it), it also may make logical sense in the cultural environment of medieval Europe, where both men and women generally lived in the communal quarters of the manor house to which they were attached, and where privacy for erotic escapades was scarce.

The meal of eels fried in a pan would then occupy the position in our minds reserved for the consummation of the lover's/hunter's desire with his beloved. This is an easy step: eels are manifestly phallic, as are fish to a less obvious extent, insofar as they swim in water, and in view of the almost universal association between swimming and sexual intercourse and between the sea and the female body or the vagina. The heat of frying the eels and the mention of the pan (container, that is, vagina) further support this idea. The reading of the meal as a figure for sexual consummation is also assisted by the fact that eels are traditionally regarded as an aphrodisiac, although the dating of this folk belief is necessarily imprecise.

So why should sexual consummation lead to death on the allegorical level? The association between sex and death, underscored by the commonplace use of the words *die* and *death* in Renaissance English poetry to mean sex or orgasm, is mentioned so frequently in modern theory that it has become an overfamiliar cliché. It may be worthwhile to mention a few of the possible reasons for the association that are germane to "Lord Randal," lest the overfamiliar become invisible. First—and this seems to be the principle of association most commonly cited today—there is the idea that in both orgasm and death, there is a loss of the subjective self, momentary in orgasm and (presumably) permanent in death. (Whether this is any more true of the orgasm than of many other activities in life, I do not know, but it seems to be a commonplace enough assumption today.)

The second and third reasons are more specific to Lord Randal. Lord Randal's tryst with the truelove and his poisonous meal are not part of his habitual life; rather, they symbolize the sexual *initiation* of an adolescent, pointed up by the mother's repeated address to her "handsom young man" and by the mere closeness of his relationship to his mother. But sexual initiation for the young man means, precisely, his death as his mother's boy, her handsome young man (or "croodlin dow," crooning dove, in other versions). In real life, of course, no passage is so neat; as we become adults gradually, we still remain children at moments and in part, and we never lose traces of our childhood selves. But in the logic of myth, which is the logic of ballads, passages and transformations are sharp and tend to rest upon binary oppositions.

Sex is associated with death because sexual initiation introduces one into the larger stream of mortality and into the knowledge of one's own place in that stream. John Freccero's comments are specific to literature of roughly the period under discussion:

> According to our [i.e., European Christian] mythology, it was after the fall in the garden of Eden, that sexuality first entered the world and with it entered death. According to the Church Fathers, the act whereby a man asserted his manhood was the same act whereby he entered the cycle of generation and corruption that indicated, unmistakably, how transient his life would be, how soon he would have to make way on the generational line for his own children and those of others. (1971, 124)

The young man's sexual initiation, figured allegorically here by Lord Randal's poisonous meal, is not only a momentary loss of self and a permanent loss of his boyhood self, especially in relation to his mother. It is also an initiation into the full life cycle itself. Sex, the boy knows, can lead to procreation. When one has a child, one is now in the *older* generation, and the next major passage will be death. Before sexual initiation, adulthood is a remote time, and death an unreal possibility for oneself. When one joins the world of adults, parents, heads of household, one's death becomes a much more real inevitability. The logic of myth will tend to take these two ideas, sexual initiation and real mortality, and combine them together into a single, polysemous moment. The logical operation here is akin to Freud's process of "condensation" in the dreamwork. The hunting hounds, then, can easily work as representations, via the equivalent of dream distortion (displacement), of Lord Randal's specifically sexual self—his "animal" nature. Naturally, however, if they die, then he will soon die, too—the dogs and he are, after all, really the same being.

Several of the same elements—hunting in the woods, sexual encounter (with emphasis on *visual awareness*), and death are prominent in the ancient myth of Actaeon, who, while hunting in the woods, accidentally glimpses the naked goddess Diana (the virgin goddess) bathing with her attendant maidens and is punished by turning into a stag and having his own hounds prey upon him. (The story is told in Ovid's *Metamorphoses* 3:138–252.) Likewise, Polixenes in Shakepeare's *The Winter's Tale* recalls nostalgically to his friend Leontes's wife Hermione his condition before the onset of adulthood:

> We were, fair Queen,
> Two lads that thought there was no more behind [i.e., to come]
> But such a day tomorrow as today,
> And to be boy eternal.
>
> (1.2.62–65)

In the following exchange (75–84), both Polixenes and Hermione make clear that the end of boyhood and the onset of guilt (and hence death in a Christian context) results from the temptation of women and marriage.

So much for the first portion of "Lord Randal," through the fifth quatrain. But what of the following portion, the nuncupative testament? Within the logic suggested thus far, this portion follows, since one of the basic attributes of adulthood is responsibility to one's family and community, which, in a feudal aristocratic context, would be typified well by the responsibility of the management and transfer of property—since one of the essential features of aristocracy is the passage of hereditary estates and social status.

The specific bequests within Lord Randal's testament have a peculiar symbolic appropriateness. They are as follows:

Mother: 24 milk-cows.
Sister: Gold and silver.
Brother: Houses and lands.
True-love: Hell and fire.

Milk cows are an obvious maternal image. Perhaps the number twenty-four can even be associated with Lord Randal's age, although it seems a bit advanced if he is to be imagined as an adolescent.[3] Lord Randal then seems to be giving back, as it were, the maternal objects to the mother. Gold and silver, on the practical level, are appropriate to give a sister as her future dowry. But on a mythic, psychoanalytic level, it has been suggested that the gold coins that boys give girls in the fairy tales collected by the Grimm brothers figure the gift of sperm. Here, of course, the sister would be a figure for women of the young man's generation, not his literal sister. Whereas maternal objects must be returned to the mother, Lord Randal must give something valuable of himself to his sister. Here, the sister may well be contrasted with the truelove. The sister represents the chaste, virginal aspect of young womanhood, and the gold and silver figure the procreative aspect of sexual relations. They may also figure, in a way closer to their literal value, the fact that the desired aristocratic marriage was one that brought in money (dowry and family alliances), and even that aristocratic marriages tended to be endogamous (see Duby 1978) in order to keep lands and wealth as closely concentrated within the family as possible.

To the brother, Lord Randal bequeaths his houses and lands, the fundamental property that makes him an aristocrat. He is then leaving to another young man, his substitute, the equivalent of his place in society. It is interesting to note here that the *father* is not mentioned. The disappearance of the father would go well, on a psychoanalytic level, with the idea that "Lord Randal" is about the moment of the young man's sexual initiation. There is no father, because Lord Randal has taken his father's place. This idea is supported by the fact that Lord Randal himself possesses the houses and lands that are to be passed on to his brother—in the absence of a son. Other versions explore other interesting aspects of the social and psychological complex of male sexual initiation, including the role of the father. In version B, Lord Donald got his "dish of sma fishes" from his "father's black ditches." As Maik has suggested, the father's black ditches are

---

3. The presence of "four-and-twenty blackbirds baked in a pie" in the well-known nursery rhyme suggests that this number may have traditional, magical, or otherwise mythic significance, perhaps associated with the twelve months of the year; but further speculation on this point is beyond my scope.

the female body that belongs to him—the body of the mother, viewed in genital-sexual terms.[4] This makes sense if we consider the B version of the ballad as condensing the truelove and the mother when it considers the *sexual* aspect of the women; in other roles, the women are kept separate. Lord Donald leaves his houses and land to his father. This version emphasizes the power of the father within the son's sexual initiation: Lord Donald's property is, after all, ancestral property, and his own death can be figured as the return of the all-powerful father.[5]

In the version which I have been reading, Lord Randal leaves for his truelove "hell and fire." This bequest is strikingly similar to the cause of death. Hell and fire, too, can be and are frequently in Renaissance English poetry taken to be figures for sex, especially for the female sexual body or sexual intercourse with a woman. Other versions of the ballad leave a noose or rope upon which the truelove should be hanged, but that, too, is a punishment very rich in sexual associations—as could be seen just a few years ago, when there was a rash of accidental deaths caused by young people experimenting with asphyxiation as a sexual or masturbatory device. So there is a covert tautological principle drawing this second climax together with the first, wherein Lord Randal's poison meal is revealed: both connote sex.

All of the important figures seem to be women, and they surround Lord Randal in a way reminiscent of how Odysseus is surrounded by women and goddesses: his universe is controlled by feminine principles. His mother gave Lord Randal birth, but knowledge of his oncoming death is elicited by his mother as well. Lord Randal bequeaths his gold and silver, figures for the procreative (and economically enriching) aspect of sexual relations, to his sister, the "virginal" aspect of the female coeval. To his truelove, the erotic aspect of the female coeval, Lord Randal bequeaths hell and fire, figures for sexual excitement, passion, and lust.

---

4. Maik 1989 argues that "Lord Randal" and several other ballads rest upon the Freudian castration complex and place the blame for castration on women. Although I find some fine insights in her discussion, I believe that the psychoanalytic framework can be used more subtly to provide a contrastingly feminist reading, which I sketch here.

5. This reading works well with Freud's theory as developed in *Totem and Taboo* (1950).

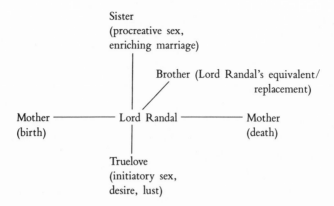

As the diagram shows, in the "deep structure" of "Lord Randal," the events begin and end with the mother. The pivotal central event, sexual initiation, is both a turning away from the mother, because it is an initiation into adulthood, and a turning back toward the mother, because it initiates Lord Randal into his mortality, where he would be reunited with the mother. For the mother, as birth giver, is the locus of the boundary between life and death. As such, she already knows the territory of mortality, as is revealed by the uncanny rightness of her questions and her correct solution to the opening riddle. We now have an important clue in answering our initial theoretical question: what is the principle of diachrony of the ballad, as typified in "Lord Randal"? How does Lord Randal proceed from beginning to end? If all the images in the poem, all the stanzas, are equivalent to each other, as metaphors, ultimately, for the sublime, unnameable power of rhythm, then why does one follow another in an apparently narrative order? We can at least say that this narrative *begins and ends with the mother*. This fact will have to be integrated with our other observations of the structure of "Lord Randal" for us to have a coherent reading within the framework of the present theory.

What else have we seen about the diachronic organization of "Lord Randal"? None of the poem is precisely a telling of events in chronological order. To use the terms of Russian formalist narratology, the *fable* ("original" events) is quite different from the *subject* (narration as it occurs). The first portion of the poem has the structure of a riddle with its solution. The mother, as if playing twenty questions, guesses the correct questions to ask, and then gives the correct solution. Although the events whose report the mother elicits from

Lord Randal are recalled in the same order as their original occurrence, the motive for recollection is the *revelation* of the mystery hidden in the past events. The climax to this retelling is, simultaneously, (*a*) the solution to the mystery—for the reader, it explains why the mother has even been asking any questions; (*b*) the climax of the original events in the fable—the poisoning of Lord Randal; and (*c*) the etiological explanation of why things are the way they are now—why Lord Randal is weary, is asking for his bed, and is (apparently) dying—as we may infer he appears to be, retrospectively, now that we have this knowledge. The solution to this riddle explains to us what has given rise to all of the utterances we have just heard or read within the fictive world of the ballad.

The method of this first portion resembles a catechism or a confession. The mother asks questions within a set formulaic structure, and the son answers only as much as he must for each question. The uncanny rightness of the mother's questions has led Maik to compare her to a modern psychotherapist. My own students are more suspicious: they wonder whether the mother knows the answer all along, because she has conspired with the truelove to poison her son in order to get his property. (Why else, they ask, would she leap from her surmise of his being poisoned straight into the question of his bequests?) Although this latter theory may take too literally the impression created by repeated formulaic structures, it points up the control that the mother exerts over the entire narrative, corresponding to her crucial (literally—a cross) role within Lord Randal's life: she begins and ends his life; she begins and ends the narrative. She is the force that sustains Lord Randal, and she is the force that elicits the confession and propels the untelling of the ballad onward to its close.

But women, and mothers or mother figures in particular, are not only important *within* the thematic content of "Lord Randal." They also surround its telling in the real world. According to scholars of the traditional ballads, there is a great deal of evidence for the fact that traditional, popular ballads were the province of women. Nursemaids sang them to their charges, mothers to their children. Most of the ballads recited or sung to Child ([1882–98] 1965) and Bronson (1959–72) were recited or sung by women, and most of these women reported that they had learned them from their mothers or from other older women. Ballads were, apparently, passed down as a tradition from mother to daughter.

As we have seen, what the binary structure of "Lord Randal" (confession, testament) reveals to us, but not to Lord Randal, is that women form a closed circle around Lord Randal. The two climaxes, poisoning and curse, may be taken as figures for sexual union with the truelove. Birth, sex, and death are under woman's control, just as the telling of the ballad is under a woman's control.

But as readers, we *desire* to put ourselves under that control. The ballad, as soon as it begins, elicits our desire, simultaneously, for the pleasure of its rhythm and for the knowledge of its secret. But as we proceed in our reading, our desire to know Lord Randal's secret falls away before the much more immense question of *the mother's secret*. What does the mother know? What is the secret of her power? And this is the question that the poem refuses to answer in words, because it cannot answer. The circle of knowledge is closed—we cannot get beyond the figure of the mother, through whom we have access to the world of the ballad, and from whom Lord Randal obtains both his life and his death. The secret of the ballad is *the same* as the secret of its rhythm, which is the secret of the mother. The maternal body is the figure for the rhythm of the life cycle: birth, sex, death. Hence the uncanny inevitability of her questions: she always already knows the rhythm that must follow, which has the same inevitability of fulfillment as does the markedly formulaic structure of each stanza. Within this allegory, Lord Randal is a figure for the reader: his consummation with the truelove figures our consummation with the rhythm of the poem, which is our momentary loss of ourselves *as constructed subjects*—our temporary death.

When the circle of this revelation of the unknowable is completed twice, the poem comes to an end. But why twice? Why end there? Two of the versions recorded by Child, D and E, do not go through two cycles: finishing with Lord Randal's acknowledgment that he has been poisoned, they omit the nuncupative testament and therefore the curse. But the nuncupative testament adds much to the overall effect. The first three items, cows to the mother, money to the sister, and real property to the brother, tend momentarily to restore Lord Randal's control within his world: these are his possessions, and he will bestow them as he chooses. But his control over the last item is betrayed by the words themselves, insofar as they name an (ambiguously) erotic figure when he intends a curse. It is when the words and images of the poem have done their task of revelation only too well—and thus can no longer pretend to keep separate the lover from the killer, the mother from the truelove—that the work of meaning must cease. As Flatto says in the context of an astute New Critical reading of the D version of this ballad:

> From the very first stanza, the poem provides us a glimpse of Lord Randal's hurt.... But ... [t]he theme must be more fully developed, elaborated, objectified, before it can be grasped, giving rise to that catechismal incantation of question and answer which the poet recites with almost ritualistic precision. But as Lord Randal's cry "I'm weary wi' hunting" is unfailingly repeated at the end of every stanza and is finally transmuted to the "I'm sick at the heart" at the poem's conclusion, the leitmotif has become a dominant theme that can no longer be ignored or misunderstood. Further elaboration and qualification are no longer necessary, as words give way to music and that, in turn, to the primeval silence from which all art originates and derives its inspirational force. (1970, 334)

How much more is this last sentence true, if the underlying secret is not "Lord Randal's hurt" but the loss of self in rhythm itself, and if, as in the A version, a nuncupative testament struggles to recover control and to forestall that loss of self, only to fail again before the sublime power of the circle of maternal rhythm that contains it.

If "Lord Randal" is to stand as our example, then the diachrony of the ballad proceeds from mystery to revelation; but when it reaches the point of revealing the unspeakable principle of its own rhythmic process, its life cycle, which is its birth and its death, the ballad must come to an end. Lord Randal's weariness is the same as his desire (death/sex). This is only one instance of the process whereby the binary opposites that structure thematic meaning in "Lord Randal" also collapse together in the diachronic course of the poem. Likewise, the poem draws together the father and the son, the truelove and the sister, the mother and the truelove, curse and lust, childhood and death. The opposites collapse together because they are unstable structures, the illusions that make the apparent progress of narrative possible. They are instances of the principle of individuation, which generates figures that simultaneously represent and hide the primal unity that underlies them, the primal unity manifested by the poem's enchanting rhythm.

2. Emily Dickinson's "Because I could not stop for Death—": Irony and Sublimity in Theme and Rhythm

Because I could not stop for Death—
He kindly stopped for me—
The Carriage held but just Ourselves—
And Immortality.

We slowly drove—He knew no haste
And I had put away
My labor and my leisure too,
For His Civility—

We passed the School, where Children strove
At Recess—in the Ring—
We passed the Fields of Gazing Grain—
We passed the Setting Sun—

Or rather—He passed Us—
The Dews drew quivering and chill—
For only Gossamer, my Gown—
My Tippet—only Tulle—

We paused before a House that seemed
A Swelling of the Ground—
The Roof was scarcely visible—
The Cornice—in the Ground—

Since then—'tis Centuries—and yet
Feels shorter than the Day
I first surmised the Horses' Heads
Were toward Eternity—

(Dickinson 1960, 712)[6]

Unlike "Lord Randal," "Because I could not stop for Death—"
is written in what is usually called ballad measure in its neat, pure

---

6. All quotations of Dickinson are taken from this edition and designated by poem number or first line.

form—an obvious sign of its being a literary rather than an oral
product. In the ballad measure, there are four beats per line, and four
lines per stanza, as in "Lord Randal"; but here, the second and
fourth lines leave the fourth beat in silence, as a musical rest. Words
realize a pattern of four beats, then three, then four beats, then three.
The silent beat at the end of the even-numbered lines adds a sense
of cadential completion to the pattern, a completion supported by the
rhymes between the second and fourth lines. One might think of
them as elongations of the third beat to cover the fourth, giving
those lines a sense of finality and closure because of the double-long
unit at the end. The ballad measure is also called the *common measure*
because it is used for hymns in the early versions of the *Book of
Common Prayer*; it is often used for other Christian hymns as well
(such as, for example, the American hymn "Amazing Grace"). If we
consider the meter of the poem in semiotic terms, as a sign of the
poem's genre, then its ambiguity between the hymn and the ballad,
the sacred and the profane, will be important in our reading of the
poem's thematic content. Necessarily, in order to read that content,
it will also be useful to glance at some other Dickinson poems for
context. All of the ones to be cited will be in the ballad or common
measure.

"Because I could not stop for Death—" functions clearly as an
allegory.[7] On the literal level, a woman recounts how she eloped with

---

7. Sharon Cameron argues that it is not quite allegory (1979, 128), but she seems
to prefer what I would consider too narrow a definition of allegory, and I think
that most readers would allow that we have a coherent set of items on a concrete
level (visitor named Death, carriage trip, "House") that have an immediate other
level of reference that is independently coherent (death, funeral, grave). Both Came-
ron's and E. Miller Budick's readings (Cameron 1979, 122–28; Budick 1985, 223–
28) emphasize the theme of eternity or immortality and its contrast with the earthly
and verbal process of time. In strictly thematic readings, however, neither connects
either eternity or time to the process of poetic rhythm, which is, in a sense, both
at once—temporal because it marks off time, but static because it removes the
listener, slightly, from the normal subjectivity by which units of time are measured
and compared.

Dwight Eddins places Dickinson's work in the context of Nietzsche and what
he calls "a nineteenth-century *Zeitgeist*" that includes Schopenhauer and Emerson
(1981, 96). His readings of the Dionysian primal unity and primal pain as thematized
in Dickinson's poems are compelling and square well with my own. He does not,
however, draw any connection between these thematic concerns and the effect of
the actual rhythm of Dickinson's poems.

(or was carried off, abducted, or seduced by) a genteel gentlemen named Death. She is naive to the otherworldly qualities of Death, unaware that she must leave this world behind to go with him, that his "House" is a grave, and that she must remain in that "House" forever, until, at some later moment in the day recollected in retrospect, she "surmised the Horses' Heads / Were toward Eternity." Upon leaving to go with Death, the speaker must put away both her labor and her leisure: she must give up her life in her household (or her parents' household) in order to labor for her new husband; as the mistress of his house, she will not have much of the leisure of her girlhood. On the way to Death's house, which is driven by Immortality (the coachman?), the bride and groom pass schoolchildren fighting or wrestling in the center of a circle of onlookers, and then fields of grain, which seem to gaze at them as they go by as if they were townspeople. The next stanza is the first clue, not for us (we already know) but for the speaker, that she is leaving, not her world, but *the* world behind: passing the setting sun is impossible before the age of jet airplanes, and the correction ("Or rather—He passed Us") renders the speaker appropriately passive, as would be a dead body. She recognizes her unpreparedness, wearing thin clothes that ambiguously connote a bridal gown or burial clothes, and the elements encroach upon her through them.

On the allegorical level, we know that the speaker is actually recounting *her death*. The children striving suggest the business of life, which becomes small and childlike from the distant perspective of the passage into death. The grain becomes one's townspeople as one becomes a thing of nature rather than an agent to farm or to eat the grain—and so forth. The disparity between the somewhat belabored allegory and the obvious meaning creates a sense of intense dramatic irony.

But there is another kind of irony as well: a situational irony. If this ballad recounts a marriage, then it should end either (a) tragically, as most ballads do, with the death of *one* of the marital partners— but since it cannot be the speaker, it would have to be the beloved husband; or (b) happily as a celebration of the married state. If the poem should be taken as a hymn, then it should end happily, with the speaker's joy in her eternal union with God after death. These two expected patterns—marital bliss for ballads and beatific bliss for hymns—are closely related to each other, since Christianity perennially uses marriage as an allegorical figure for the relationship between the blessed soul and its maker in the afterlife, and since, in the Protestant (and especially the Puritan) tradition, earthly marriage is a *typological figure* for the union between the soul and God that will, for the elect, be realized in the world to come. This view of marriage would be central to the Christianity that characterizes the social milieu of Dickinson's poetry—more specifically, the Congregationalist church in New England, which was the heir of New England Puritan ideology.[8] Thus on both counts, in both genres, ballad and hymn, in both the secular and sacred spheres, and in both the marriage and death strands of the allegory, the ending is a shock, a surprising anticlimax.

It is not that the poem ends with the *opposite* of our expectations—at least, not exactly. Rather, instead of heavenly jubilation or earthly satisfaction, we have—nothing at all: "Since then—'tis Centuries—and yet / Feels shorter than the Day" recounted, which is the last day the speaker lived, the day of her death. This is because her dying day was the last day in which *anything happened.* Centuries feel shorter than a day because there is no event to fill them up, just the recollection of the day before they began. So, to her surprise (in terms of marriage) and ours (in terms of death and the afterlife), despite everything everyone has told her and us, it turns out that the state being described is one of utter emptiness. It is negative when we expected something positive. But the very idea of centuries of such emptiness is, itself, *sublime.* The thought boggles the imagination, and is a suitable place for the poem to end—that is, on the word "Eternity," with all its irony, because it is not the eternity we expected, but with all its deep truth, because it is much more sublime, since it is truly without image, unimaginable. By comparison, Christian mythology crowds its sublime moments with images that reflect earthly realities—God as King, the Son at his right hand, the choruses of the blessed singing their praise, and so forth.

Dickinson calls to mind the Christian paradigm of life's meaning, which is found in the salvation of the soul *in the afterlife* and not in this world, in order to reveal its failure and to propose in that very

---

8. For more on Dickinson's cultural-historical context, see St. Armand 1984. He does not, however, read Dickinson as consistently as a rebel from Christianity as I do. I would argue, however, that he and other critics have tended to read many items in Dickinson poems as sincere that seem to me to give very clear signals of irony. In this case, the irony can be seen in the surprise ending.

revelation an alternative source for the experience of mystical sublimity. This procedure summarizes Dickinson's project in a great many of her poems. Again and again, she explicitly defeats Christian expectations of what comes after death or of the nature of God. Again and again, she puts forth *poetry itself* as an alternative religious experience because of its ability to reveal the sublime within the world of the senses and within the very logic that negates Christianity. In poem no. 1545 ("The Bible is an antique Volume"), Dickinson views the Bible through an ironic lens by considering it an oppressively didactic and less than engaging romance or ballad, and then contrasts it with lyrical poetry:

> Boys that "believe" are very lonesome—
> Other Boys are "lost"—
> Had but the Tale a warbling Teller—
> All the Boys would come—
> Orpheus' Sermon captivated—
> It did not condemn—

What matters is the "warbling." The speaker here does not so much recommend that the behests of Christianity be clothed in the seductive garments of musical verse, but rather that *verse itself—rhythm itself,* is a "sermon" or a spiritual experience that affords enlightenment without the condemnation and exclusion so central to institutional religion, which is, in this case, Christianity. "I like a look of Agony," Dickinson writes elsewhere (241), "Because I know it's true— / Men do not sham Convulsion," as they do, one may infer, sham *conversion* within those Christian sects, such as the Congregationalist and Holiness churches, that demand of their members a conversion experience to demonstrate their status within the elect.

That poetry itself is Dickinson's religious alternative to Christianity is clear from the conclusion of no. 657:

> I dwell in Possibility—
> A fairer House than Prose—
> More numerous of Windows—
> Superior—for Doors—
>
> Of Chambers as the Cedars—
> Impregnable of Eye—

And for an Everlasting Roof
The Gambrels of the Sky—

Of Visitors—the fairest—
For Occupation—This—
The spreading wide my narrow Hands
To gather Paradise—

The house of poetry, which is the house of "Possibility," is sublime
in the infinitude of the reading experience. It defamiliarizes the world
that we think we know too well—"numerous of Windows"—and
it offers an infinite variety of possible ways of thinking or imagining.
Its visitors are the readers, eager to explore its many mansions. But
the speaker busies herself within the house, not doing mundane
housework, but gathering "Paradise" with her "narrow Hands"—
that is, with the sparseness and brevity of her lines. One need not
wait for the afterlife to gain paradise—in fact, it would not come
that way. Paradise is available "to Him of adequate desire" (370)
through poetry—and, in other poems, through the keen observation
of the world of the senses, as it is made possible and celebrated
in poetry.

In "Because I could not stop for Death—" the relationship
between poetry and the sublime is not made explicit. This is because
the speaker in this case is naive, the vehicle of dramatic irony, so that
she can witness the failure of the mythological dogma which she and
the audience expect. In contriving such a situation, Dickinson makes
possible a critique that cuts both ways, against both marriage and
the afterlife as they would be understood in conventional Christian
terms. Insofar as marriage should be like the afterlife, it turns out
to be surprisingly empty and anticlimactic: the woman puts away her
labor and her leisure in order to get, quite literally, nothing. The
emphasis is not on the *state* of this nothingness, about which nothing
really can be said, but on the process of getting there—so the act of
getting married is really rather like death, and the state of marriage
is a living death. Insofar as the afterlife should be like an earthly
marriage, that promise, from the point of view of a woman within
the framework of post-Puritan Protestant Christianity, is no great
bargain. In retrospect, giving up both her own labor and her own
leisure for the sake of a state of nothingness in someone else's house

would not exactly be her idea of heaven. But this emptiness *must* be the result of both marriage and death because they are, for the speaker, the permanent loss of her own proper sphere, her own joys, her own pain, and her own voice. The moment at which she recalls the recognition of this loss is the moment at which her voice, in the present, ceases once more.

And yet at the same time, this nothingness has a positive side to it, not for the speaker, but for the reader. In clearing away the baggage of imagery that makes of religion a stick with which to beat women over the head and cause them to fall in line beneath the authority of their earthly husbands, Dickinson's poem demonstrates that these images and their earthly, political practices (such as hierarchical marriage) *come in the way* of the sublime experience. The poem puts away the labor and leisure of dogma and convention in order for us to experience the sublime space where they fail.

This final moment is carefully prepared by earlier images and moments within the poem. Each of them involves, simultaneously, a renunciation ("I had put away ... We passed ... We passed") and a defamiliarization. To begin with, the appearance of Death as a suitor with his carriage literalizes the overfamiliar metaphor of death being a passage to the afterlife where the innocent soul becomes a bride of Christ. Here, the suitor is not called Christ, but Death, as if to call a spade a spade. (He is called "Savior" in another, somewhat similar, poem: "A Wife—at Daybreak I shall be—" [no. 461].) The strangeness of the situation, eloping with Death, reflects back upon the original myth to reveal its grotesqueness. At the same time, the moment brackets off, puts at a distance, and questions the supreme importance of the speaker's daily activities; her labor is, itself, her conventional service to her household.

The strife of the children at recess provides a marked contrast with the peaceful but indescribably empty nothingness of the end. This is the only glimpse of human activity we have in the poem's passage from the speaker's house to that of Death, and it is one of leisure ("Recess"), learning ("School"), and struggle ("strove"). What are they fighting over? Our passing by, and renouncing, this strife as we go on toward eternal nothingness challenges the necessity and importance of the small tasks and causes that, in their overfamiliarity, fill up our minds in everyday life. Since the poem was probably composed near or at the close of the Civil War, it is possible that this passage and renunciation defamiliarizes the passions and parochialisms that wrought so much destruction. They are among the social codes that the forward rhythm of the poem undermines.

The fields of gazing grain are what preoccupy people when they are adults: the labor that sustains them. These, too, seem small as they stand gazing while the speaker and her escorts pass on. Thus not only the smaller struggles of people—their strife in the ring— but the larger, more fundamental labor of survival also seems less urgent and more distant. Next, even the cosmic movement of the sun, the passage of earthly days, seems small and limited: "We passed the Setting Sun."

At the next moment, the last of the renunciation-passages, the speaker is compelled to challenge the last item of her that pertains to the social code: her own identity. In correcting herself from "We passed the Setting Sun" to "Or rather—He passed Us—" the speaker draws attention to her own having become a mute object of nature. This aspect of death, of course, makes the speech we are witnessing quite impossible—but that is the paradox inherent in the poem and in many of Dickinson's poems in which a speaker speaks from a state after death. It is also the paradox of poetry, where speech and images are attempting to address the experience of rhythm, which is, precisely, the state of being in which there is neither imagery nor speech. Likewise, the fragility of the speaker's dress comes to her attention because of the greater power of earthly elements: "The Dews drew quivering and chill— / For only Gossamer, my Gown— / My Tippet—only Tulle—." The speaker's clothing here provides a neat allegorical symbol for the imagery of the poem itself—a veil of illusion that simultaneously protects and fails to protect the elemental power of the bodily rhythm which it renders socially visible.

The ambiguity between the social (labor, strife, farming, gown, house) and the elemental (dews, ground) is emphasized in the next quatrain: is the grave a "House" or a "Swelling of the Ground"? The terms *house* and *cornice,* because of their ironic application to the grave, stress the inadequacy of the conventional, sentimental, and mythic metaphors we cherish and live by as compared to the elemental infinitude of earth, death, and rhythm.

In "Because I could not stop for Death—" as in most of Dickinson's poems, the principle of diachrony is to proceed from the familiar to the bizarre, from the expected to the sublime. In many poems, this process is even reflected in the syntax, which becomes increasingly tortuous and difficult to follow toward the end. But along with this movement toward the surprising and sublime—that is, toward the point at which words fail, there is a movement analogous to the one we found in the traditional ballad, "Lord Randal": a movement of *revelation,* from the hidden to the patent. When the secret is hidden from the speaker, she can generate stanza after stanza, figure after figure, allegorizing the process of death without knowing it. But when the secret is revealed to her as well as to us, there is nothing left to allegorize; we are left with the eternal emptiness itself. One's own nonbeing is utterly unimaginable (Freud [1900] 1965, 287–89; [1923] 1962, 47–48; [1915] 1963b, 122), so the speaker must be driven on by the figure of Immortality; but what fills up this immortal eternity is nothing. When the sublime nothingness is revealed to her—to borrow words from poem no. 7—her "figures fail" her, and the poem must come to an end.

This movement from narrative to revelation and the end of narrative and of images altogether coincides with the movement of the carriage—"We slowly drove ... We paused ... " And both of these coincide with the movement of the meter itself, with its built-in pause, which is a silent beat, on every second and fourth line. It is as if the thematic content of the poem, its images, reproduce on large scale what the meter is doing on the smaller scale at every half quatrain. The emptiness at the end of the poem stands as an image for the rhythm of the whole, in which, at every eighth beat, one feels the rhythm go on even when there are no words. Every eighth beat reminds us that, behind and before the words, there is the demand of rhythm. This demand is not metaphysical, it is not in the afterlife; it functions within the world of the senses, although it takes us beyond the limits of the construction of the self. And this is just what Death does with the speaker—he takes her beyond her "labor and her leisure too" to the point where she has no more words to speak her own existence. The words of the poem can only exist *in retrospect,* as she retraces her path to the present. But her present condition is a nonself, in which she has no words. Yet this condition is not a mere negative; it is the vastness of eternity, a powerful, sublime moment.

3. "Hush in the Heart": Gwendolyn Brooks's "the ballad of chocolate Mabbie"[9]

Like Emily Dickinson's "Because I could not stop for Death—" this fairly early poem (published 1945) of Gwendolyn Brooks is in a neat, literary version of the ballad measure. The rhythm follows a four-beat, four-line paradigm, with words realizing all four beats in the first and third lines and three out of the four in the second and fourth. Unlike the Dickinson poem, however, the meter is triple rather than duple: in much of the poem, there are two offbeat syllables between each beat, creating a jiglike subdivision of the major beats. This is the same rhythm as is found in many nursery rhymes ("To market, to market, to buy a fat pig ... "), and it is closer to the tendency in traditional, oral folk ballads. Generally, we find duple meters (only one offbeat syllable between each beat) in hymns and triple meters in ballads, so the meter of this poem does not call up the hymn tradition, whereas it does call to mind both folk ballads and children's rhymes. There are many exceptions to this rule, including "Jack and Jill"—but even this rhyme is sung to a triple meter— and the rule is still generally valid. These preliminary comments approach the meter in semiotic terms, as a sign of genre; how the poem relates to its rhythm as an allegory of its sublime power can be seen only after an examination of the thematic content.

The ballad tells a story whose structure resembles that of the myth of the fall in the Garden of Eden. In the beginning, little seven-year-old Mabbie is yet unschooled in the social barriers of race and the attendant alienation felt by people of the oppressed race. For her, her color is an emblem of her sweetness—she is "cut from a chocolate bar"—and life is heaven. Life is particularly heavenly because of the love of, and proximity to, Willie Boone. The fact that it "Was only her eyes" that "were cool" can be taken in several ways. The rest of her body may have been warm with the thrill of sitting next to Willie Boone, while her eyes carefully and coyly hid her feelings. Just as likely, it was only *her* eyes that were cool—the surrounding girls had eyes hot with furious envy. In this case, sitting next to

---

9. Unfortunately, Gwendolyn Brooks withheld permission to reproduce the full text of this poem. The text can be found in *Selected Poems* (1963, 7).

Willie Boone is a special and exclusive privilege, and its bestowal represents her special status as Willie's chosen.

But if so, Mabbie does not remain the chosen for long. She awaits her beau in vain, as, emerging late, he bears in attendance a "lemon-hued lynx / With sand-waves loving her brow." That is, Willie has preferred a lighter-colored (although still African-American) mate over the chocolate Mabbie.[10] Mabbie has thus acquired two lessons at once: first, that she is not the only possible object of her beloved's affections and thus is not the center of her world; second, that the principle whereby she would be excluded from her heaven is, quite simply, a matter of color. To be lighter is to be preferable to the eyes that count, those of Willie Boone. These recognitions simultaneously leave Mabbie alone, because without Willie Boone, and in company, because her very exclusion has now placed her in the somewhat anonymous category of all little girls who are equally excluded because they are dark: "chocolate companions had she: / Mabbie on Mabbie." Whereas, in her joy waiting for Willie Boone, Mabbie's lips had borne a song, her "bubble of song" has now burst, and she bears, among like companions, a "hush in the heart." The transformation of her world from a heaven with herself and Willie Boone at the center to a state in which she is a common Mabbie among the multitude of chocolate companions is permanent: "Mabbie on Mabbie *to be.*" Mabbie begins the course of events having been "cut from a chocolate bar"; at the end, she is, in a sense, reunited with the chocolate bar. But whereas in the beginning the sweetness of the chocolate bar from which she was cut is a sign of her desirability, her sweetness, at the end, the chocolate is a sign of rejection. What all the Mabbies share together is their isolation: each of them is a "Mabbie alone." The return to chocolatehood is an ironic transformation.

The ballad is thus an instance of a thematic genre, or recurring theme, to be found in many works of African-American writers: the discovery of one's blackness within a racist social context, the revelation of one's social position as tied to one's perceived race, generally figured as a kind of fall from grace, a simultaneous education as to social

---

10. For a brief conventional reading of this poem as an instance of "what Arthur P. Davis calls the black-and-tan motif . . . , i.e., the white culture-inspired valuing of lightness among blacks themselves," see Melhem 1987, 27.

realities (thus the fruit of knowledge) and an expulsion from the
heaven of self-confidence and nonalienation. The young Janie in Zora
Neale Hurston's *Their Eyes Were Watching God,* for example, discovers
that she is racially different from the white children with whom she
plays when she sees her image in a group photograph for the first
time: "Aw, aw! Ah'm colored!" ([1937] 1978, 21). Likewise, the
schoolgirl Audre's sisters correct her when, not quite knowing the
difference between "white" and "Colored," she claims that she is
white like her mother (who is Afro-Caribbean but light; Lorde 1983,
58–59).

As an instance of the racializing fall, "the ballad of chocolate
Mabbie" moves diachronically from a positive value attributed to the
character's body, because she is not drawn into a racist social code,
to a negative value, because she is indoctrinated into that code. This
movement would seem to be the very opposite of the effect I have
been claiming for poetry—that is, that the sublimity of the power
of rhythm should undermine the limited social codes that inform
prejudice. If the poem allegorizes this effect of rhythm, then we
should begin with Mabbie already racialized, and finish with her being
set free of prejudicial values applied to her. We cannot conclude yet
that this ballad is an exception or a refutation to the theory, however,
for we have not yet completed our examination of the thematic content.
There is an important element thereof which should not be neglected:
tone. For here we see a prime example of the delicately cutting irony
that so informs the mysterious brilliance of Brooks's work.

The tone of the narration of "the ballad of chocolate Mabbie" is
complex and crucial to our understanding of the poem's thematic
content. When, in the fourth line, the narrator informs us that
"Mabbie thought life was heaven," the tone is fraught with irony: if
she thought that, we know she must have been wrong; indeed, the
line rhymes with her being "all of seven," so her naïveté is clear. We
are prepared to witness her lose some of her naïveté in the course of
the poem, which is just what we do. The next two quatrains are
written in free indirect discourse, with the narrator speaking for
Mabbie—"He would surely be coming soon." Free indirect discourse
in general puts a distance between the narrator and the character being
imitated, ironizing the character's thoughts or words precisely by imi-
tating them without actually being the character or sharing the char-
acter's experience. It can have a delicately mocking effect, as it does

here. In the next quatrain, however, the mockery seems to be turned from Mabbie to the readers: "Oh, warm is the waiting for joys, *my dears!*" We have been put in the position of waiting with Mabbie for the arrival of Willie Boone, only to have the narrator patronize us from a position of knowing better. Thus the narrator knows not only that Mabbie—and we—are wrong to await the "heavenly" arrival of Willie Boone, but that we are wrong to be empathizing with Mabbie's anticipation; we would be naive to share with her the "warm ... waiting for joys." Thus if, in the next quatrain, "It was woe for our Mabbie now," that "woe" is not worthy of any deep compassion. Here, as in "life was heaven," the mere hyperbole of "woe" is a signal of the narrator's ironic distance in relation to the character, as if urging us at once to know her suffering and to disdain it.

Yet in the second half of this fifth quatrain, the irony of "like a jewel" is directed against Willie Boone's new companion and thus sympathizes with Mabbie's experience. But it is still more complicated. That the rival's hair is "sand-waves *loving* her brow" suggests that, from Mabbie's perspective, as imitated by the narrator in free indirect discourse, this rival *deserves* Willie Boone's attention more than does Mabbie—her superiority is *visible* and patent, since, at one and the same time, Mabbie learns that she is not preferred and why. In other words, Mabbie has no frame of reference, no discourse, and no social structure to oppose the values implicit in Willie Boone's selection of a lighter girl as preferable. Rather than noting, say, Willie Boone's stupidity or obtuseness—why would anyone find light skin and light, lank hair preferable to the chocolate-brown?—Mabbie seems to acquiesce, and thus, in the absence of a remonstrance, we assume that she at least to some degree internalizes the racist values he enacts. Likewise, the narrator characterizes Mabbie's companions as her peers because they are all equally alone and equally excluded from preference. They all have in common a "hush in the heart"—they do not speak together of their pain, so they do not create an alternative discourse or system of values to the one manifested by Willie Boone's choice. Here again, the narrator's subtly disparaging characterization of the many Mabbies is in free indirect discourse and suggests that Mabbie herself has acquired a kind of alienation or self-loathing from the experience. Life is no longer heaven, and she is no longer "cut from a chocolate bar"; she is now merely one of the many rejected chocolate Mabbies. The finality of this verdict seems to keep us from ironizing Mabbie's experience as the narrator had done earlier for us: it is as if the narrator presents this self-loathing as a more realistic vision of Mabbie's place in the world. There is only the slightest pathos in the "hush in the heart" to enable us to question the narrator's cruel distance and to wonder whether that, too, is ironic—whether the narrator is testing us to see whether we would fall for the temptation to write off Mabbie's suffering as silly, childish, and a necessary part of her education in the real facts of life.

The ironic cruelty of the narrator's distance can be compared with the narrator's matter-of-fact ending of "Sadie and Maud," also in *A Street in Bronzeville*:

> Maud, who went to college,
> Is a thin brown mouse.
> She is living all alone
> In this old house.

(G. Brooks 1963, 9)

Here, again, there is only the subtlest hint that the condemnation of the studious Maud, as opposed to the adventurous Sadie, is less than unequivocal. In this instance, it is in the "this" of "this old house": are we, too, in that house? Which of the two does the voice of poetry most resemble? Is there not at least some studiousness involved in its creation? Could not "this old house" be compared to Emily Dickinson's house of poetry, however old, still "a fairer house than Prose"?[11]

In "the ballad of chocolate Mabbie," Mabbie's ordeal is painful, and enough of the facts are presented us so that we must empathize with her. The narrator's irony is marked and thorough, enough to draw us away from Mabbie. We are left in a middle ground, a gap between the world of Mabbie and the world of the narrator, not quite knowing which one to call our own. What we *do* know is that, in some sense, the narrator is right: the facts are as the narrator has told them, even if we wish to remonstrate.

---

11. A full discussion of "Sadie and Maud" is, unfortunately, beyond my present scope. For another interesting analogue to this poem, however, that follows the reading I am hinting, see Sylvia Plath's "Two Sisters of Persephone" (1981, 31–32).

The situation is similar to that we experience in tragedy—and, indeed, in traditional ballads. The voice of the narrator is the voice of fate, and fate is unfair. But the voice of fate in tragedy is usually cruel only because of its coolness, its impartiality; here, the voice is not impartial, it is engaged in patronizing its subject, Mabbie. One would be tempted to identify the narrator's voice with the inevitability with which the rhythm of the poem proceeds; and the old traditionality of the ballad measure is reflected in the sense that the narrator is recounting the racializing fall of a typical African-American child, a scene that has been repeated for generations. Yet we cannot but remonstrate against this fate, as would Mabbie, if she could. She has been silenced: she and her many chocolate companions bear a "hush in the heart." The narrator's voice is too loud. It drowns out the voice of its own subject; it protests its knowledge too much.

So the narrative voice of "the ballad of chocolate Mabbie" is in fact a figure for the ballad rhythm of the poem, a traditional fate, wrought by and fraught with prejudice—internalized prejudice, for the narrator's very familiarity with Mabbie's world shows that the narrator comes from that world and has learned to master its pain only by alienating itself artificially from the suffering, through condescension and fatalism. But the subtle twinge at the end, the "hush in the heart," lets us know, if we have had any doubt, that the narrator's representation of the sublime force of rhythm is inadequate; it is shaped by prejudice; it does not have to be this way. The fullness of Mabbie's being, which is as sublime as the power of her life's rhythm, cannot be wrapped up neatly in the little package of mockery the narrator provides. Even the narrator's figure for that larger Mabbie, before even the individuation that predates the recounted fall, is inadequate: Mabbie "was cut from a chocolate bar." For even that chocolate bar, however sweet, is not all that Mabbie is to begin with, only what the narrator can construct for her.

We shall never hear Mabbie's own "bubble of song." The very fact that the narrator *calls* Mabbie's joy a "bubble of song" is tantamount to the narrator popping it in the act of recounting the events. The irony of this figure lies in the fact that the narrator's own construction of the rhythm of Mabbie's life is in its own way limited— limited by the narrator's condescension—and is itself a bubble that pops underneath our compassion for Mabbie and our sense that even a seven-year-old's life and feelings are much larger than these words can say, more than any words can say. In this sense, a "hush in the heart" is a more adequate expression of Mabbie's experience or of the power of the rhythm being identified with her life story.

But the narrator's patronizing distance is sadly humorous, and humor is how people survive pain. The rhythm through which the narrator has revealed Mabbie's defeat is also the rhythm that sustains both the narrator and Mabbie. The more life is like a ballad, however tragic, the more its pains can be appreciated as beautiful or even funny. This sustaining side of the ballad's rhythm is perhaps figured in Mabbie's many companions, who are repetitions of Mabbie, one rhythmic Mabbie upon another sustaining their rhythm forward, "Mabbie on Mabbie to be."

"the ballad of chocolate Mabbie" then simultaneously reveals to us the manner in which Mabbie's being is constructed—in contrast to the infinitude of her real being, which can only be rendered with a "hush in the heart"—and the way in which the construction of life's rhythms can be sustaining even as they are at the same time repressive. This double message, the revelation of a dream of freedom and simultaneously the suggestion that its normal repression is part of survival—this message forms a theme in *A Street in Bronzeville* (reprinted as a section of *Selected Poems* [1963, 3–29]). In the first poem of the book, for example, the oft-anthologized "kitchenette building," there is only "a minute" for the speaker to "wonder" about whether "a dream [could] send up through onion fumes / Its white and violet." The dream must be mentioned, but one must also rush to put it aside and get into the lukewarm bathwater before it gets any colder. In this poem, the rhythm being constructed is the traditional form of the sonnet, which is allowed to "flutter its aria" briefly, without pulling the speaker into its world of dreams forever.

In "the ballad of chocolate Mabbie," the rhythm of the ballad, with its repeated quatrain pattern, is constructed in two ways that work against each other. On the one hand, the narrator takes the opportunity of a ballad to put a distance between herself (and us) and Mabbie, since ballads are traditional and thus can evoke thoughts of clichés and the mock-heroic. On the other hand, the narrator betrays her own inability to speak the whole truth of Mabbie, leaving us to feel its enormity in the "hush of the heart." In the first instance, the ballad works semiotically by recalling the tradition of ballads and thus being a sign of "balladness," of the quaintly or tritely sentimental.

In the second instance, the ballad works as a rhythmic structure to remind us that any such construction is as limited as are the prejudices that racialize Mabbie and that cause her to feel alone and isolated among the multitude of her companions. Furthermore, on the semiotic level, the meter of this particular ballad, with its tendency toward triple movement, recalls children's rhymes, creating an impression of "cuteness" that supports the narrator's ironic distance. At the same time, however, the meter gives us a kind of bodily pleasure that goes beyond any hierarchical relation between Mabbie and the narrator: we are engaged despite the narrator's distance.

The principle of diachrony in the poem follows the structure of the fall into racialization. As in the other ballads that we have looked at, this movement is also one from mystery to revelation, for we discover the reason for the narrator's irony at the opening—what exactly was so naive about thinking that life was heaven. Each stanza, in its own way, bursts another bubble of song, by recalling Mabbie's naïveté, until the last two, when we discover just what disillusionment the narrator's tone has been anticipating and what the resulting transformation is. At the same time, the stanzas are revealing one after another, with subtly increasing intensity, the degree to which the narrator's complicity with Mabbie's fate silences the depth of feeling that may be there but that remains hushed in the heart. When the hush itself is named, the ballad is ready to come to an end. The hush figures that aspect of the ballad's rhythm that comes prior to any assignable meaning. This aspect of rhythm simply fills us with its vitality, the vitality in Mabbie which can no longer be expressed in words, if it ever could. Compared to this power to which the hush in the heart alludes, even the fickle Willie Boone falls away as an inadequate image. For no image, neither the desired Willie Boone, nor the lemon-hued lynx, nor the narrator's irony, nor even the chocolate bar from which Mabbie was cut, is adequate to the immensity of Mabbie's being, which is the same as the rhythm that gives her life.

4. "The House of the Rising Sun": "Tell my sister"

There is a house in New Orleans
They call "The Risin' Sun,"

And it's been the ruin of many a poor boy,
And Lord I know, I'm one.

My mother was a tailor,
Sewed my new blue jeans.
My father was a gamblin' man
Down in New Orleans.

Now the only thing to gamblin'
Is a suitcase and a trunk.
And the only time he's satisfied
Is when he's on a drunk.

Go tell my baby sister
Not to do what I have done;
To shun that house in New Orleans
They call "The Risin' Sun."

One foot on the platform,
the other's on the train;
I'm goin' back to New Orleans,
to wear that ball and chain.

(Shipton 1989, 17)[12]

This ballad, made famous in a rock and roll version by the Animals in the late sixties, is dubbed traditional in songbooks. Like "Lord Randal," then, it issues from an anonymous source and, presumably, has many oral variants. It is certainly more recent than "Lord Randal," however. New Orleans and trains both place it in a modern context. The centrality of gambling and the general tragic pessimism of the ballad may place it in the era of the Great Depression, although, as often with folk ballads, the specific details of history seem to have been worn away to a minimum, like a polished stone in a riverbed, leaving only the bare essentials of feeling and experience. Still, gambling, prostitution, poverty, and punishment—issues that come up in the poem—are specific social phenomena, even if they are found in many cultures. They are the stuff of which this ballad constructs the sublime energy of its rhythm into imagery and a message.

------

12. I have altered some of the punctuation and capitalization and have set the lines in quatrains rather than in couplets.

As in the other ballads, we begin "The House of the Rising Sun" in mystery, and we expect that the ballad's narration will answer our questions. In what way has the house been the speaker's ruin, and that of others? That the speaker mentions the other poor boys first and himself only as one of them suggests a sense of shame about his having fallen into the trap. What is this source of shame? Right away, we can string together these first clues to form a pattern: "house" with a name, in a city legendary (notorious) for decadence; ruin; and shame. One would think of a "house of ill repute"—a haven for prostitution and gambling (and drinking—could this traditional modern American ballad date to the period of prohibition?). Will the rest of the poem bear this out? Why has the speaker turned to prostitution or gambling?

The speaker, as if to answer our questions, reverts back to his mother and father, giving an emblematic role in two lines to each. These lines emphasize occupation—the mother a tailor, the father a gambler. That the father is a gambler "Way down in New Orleans" suggests that the speaker was not with the father when the mother sewed him new blue jeans—indeed, that she sewed them for him to prepare him for the journey to New Orleans to go to work with his father, where the House of the Risin' Sun is. Whereas the mother's occupation is what provides the speaker with new blue jeans, it is not stated what the father's occupation enables the father to give the speaker. This further supports the idea that the answer is also the answer to the opening mystery: the speaker has been ruined as an eventual result of his having left his mother's home to go work for or with his father, a gambler in a house of ill repute in New Orleans. This departure also involves an archetypal choice: the son leaves the sphere of his mother to join that of his father; he declines an occupation, tailoring, that brings modest but reliable rewards, in favor of one, gambling, that promises plentiful rewards but at a high risk. The speaker makes a choice to go where his sun may rise, so that he may be the rising son; hence he joins his father at the House of the Rising Sun.[13]

---

13. One may even recall here, as an archetypal analogue, the myth of Phaeton, the mortal son of Apollo, the sun-god, who persuades his father to let him drive the chariot of the sun one day: not holding the reigns fast enough, Phaeton rises

But the narration is told in such an order that we know of the son's fall (ruin) before his rise, and thus the name of the house, which is the name of the ballad, is immediately ironic. The relation between rise and fall is further explained in the third quatrain, which takes a critical look back at the father's gambling life, from the vantage point of the painful lessons of experience. Gambling may bring in some money, but it is as quickly lost again: one lives out of a suitcase and a trunk, one never accumulates earthly goods. The money disappears in part because losses are inevitable in gambling, and one falls into a vicious circle of debt; this destitution is aggravated by drinking, to which one resorts in order to forget the tenuousness of existence under the curse of gambling debts.

One element of our initial hypothesis has not so far been supported: that the House of the Rising Sun is also a house of prostitution. But this suggestion does make sense in the context of the fourth quatrain: the speaker warns the sister not to do what he has done—that is, not to go to the House of the Rising Sun—where, in her case, presumably the temptation would be to make some quick money through prostitution. That the recipient of this warning should be a sister and that she should be the younger, "baby" sister makes sense: these physical differences from the speaker may offer some hope that she will not repeat the cycle of repetitions wherein the speaker has followed his father into ruin.

We are left with one more question: we still do not know exactly wherein the speaker's ruin consists, although we can gather something of it from his description of his father. In the last quatrain, we know that the speaker is being led off on a train to New Orleans, where he will wear a ball and chain. That is, he is being taken off to jail; he must have committed some serious crime within the context of his life in gambling, and its exact nature is not necessary for us to know. What we do know is that he has tried to escape the scene of the crime, his punishment, and his ruin, since, if the train is taking him *back* to New Orleans, he must not be there now. He is to be imagined issuing a moralizing summary of his life story, and his ruin, at the last moment he has to be free and to issue such warnings—

---

too fast and falls as precipitously to his death. The story is told in Ovid's *Metamorphoses* 1:31–328.

with one foot in our world and the other, in effect, in the silence of prison.

Here, as in Brooks's "the ballad of chocolate Mabbie" (and in the other ballads as well), there is a strong sense of tragic fatedness about the events in the tale, strengthened by irony—in Brooks's case, by the ironic distance of the speaker, and in the present case, by the retrospective irony in the name of the House of the Rising Sun. There is an additional twist to the effect of fatedness in this poem. The last phrase, "*that* ball and chain," refers in the first instance concretely to the speaker's future in prison—as a metonymy; but in the second instance, it can work metaphorically for the life of gambling itself, in which one is beset by debt, never gets anywhere, and only finds solace in a drunkenness that ultimately tightens the grip of one's penury and hopelessness. So the speaker has simply gone from one prison to another, the first metaphorical and seductive, the second physical and without illusions. And it is at this moment of the loss of illusions, as the train door is about to close, that the speaker must fall silent. Here, as in Dickinson's poem (and in the others), it is the falling away of illusions that brings about the disclosure of the poem's mystery and, at the same time, the end of the poem's speech.

As in "the ballad of chocolate Mabbie," the speaker's voice constructs the rhythm of the ballad as a voice of fate: an inescapable cycle of poverty and ruin, where growing up male—"rising"—means coming to a fall—"ruin." But if this fate were so inescapable, then why would the speaker think to warn his sister to avoid it? The possibility suggested by the sister demonstrates that the speaker's fate is only his *construction* of the rhythms of life as pursuing a certain line defined by his culture and his class. That his younger sister is called his "baby" sister recalls to us how we might associate that aspect of humanity that is all possibility and no construction with the image of the newborn baby. The baby is as yet all rhythm and no words.

And that is the condition to which the speaker returns at the closing moment of the poem: he has told his tale and issued his warning, and he must now take the train—another metaphor for the rhythm of the poem, the rhythm of his life—to prison, the place of silence. The speaker takes this last moment to have his baby sister warned—he is not in the same world as she, so he must tell some bystander to tell her—because, at the same time that he reveals how his own fate has been constructed out of the rhythm of life, he recognizes that *he* has so constructed it. Here, as in tragedy, the character's actions and his fulfillment of his fate coincide; and here, as in tragedy, there is a freedom, not within his experience, but from our vantage point, figured by the sister, as we witness how his life has been constructed with the narrowness of a pair of iron rails.

So far I have allegorized the poem's thematic surface using the literal terms of family relations and experience it supplies; but beyond this, we may read the poem along a secondary level of allegory, which will still contribute to the same fundamental relation between images and rhythm. The poem is called traditional, but it must have been composed since the advent of industrialism, and more likely at a time when New Orleans would represent the decadent last hope of the poor, that is, in the early twentieth century. If so, then the practice of traditional oral balladry is fast fading; popular songs are almost exclusively *commercial* rather than folk products. The imagery of gambling and prostitution both work as allegories for commercial song making—the metaphor of prostitution for commercial artistic production has become a cliché in this century, and the investment of time and money in producing a new popular song is always a gamble. The mother's handcraftsmanship—she *sewed* the speaker's blue jeans, by hand—would associate her with the older craft of oral folk ballads; while the father is already a part of the new, commercial and industrial mode of production. Hence it makes good sense that the speaker's warning should be issued to his *sister*: he may hope that she will follow in her mother's path, remaining within the folk sphere within which ballads were primarily women's contribution to cultural life.[14] "The House of the Rising Sun" in this case voices a longing to return to the preindustrial mode of musical and poetic production. And the remaining vestige of this earlier mode of being, its enduring afterlife, is none other than the ballad rhythm itself.

Either way, whether we stay within the literal level of the narrative or accept the foregoing secondary allegory, the speaker's life seems always already determined. His mother has sewn together its pattern,

---

14. The respective association of women with folk ballads and men with commercial broadside ballads goes back a few centuries: see Bold 1979, 39–43, on women and popular ballads, and 66–82, on broadside ballads—wherein all the known authors mentioned are men.

and his father has gambled it away. The cycle of winnings ("killings") and debts that keeps the speaker's father poor also draws the speaker into a cycle of generations, and both of these are representations of the cycle of ballad quatrains. But the speaker's construction of these representations in words coincides with a moment of vision in which he can issue his warning to his baby sister. The rhythm as it is represented has the rigid inevitability of iron, but the rhythm pure and simple has nothing but freedom. Of course, it also has no speech. The moment of the speaker's falling into silence is the moment at which we witness the failure of his cultural life pattern in attempting to encompass the sublime infinitude of rhythm—that is, of life's infinite possibilities.

In the foregoing four readings, the same basic structure was applied: the supposition that the images in the ballad were socially contextualized constructions of the sublime power of rhythm, and that they at the same time in some way betrayed their inadequacy before that sublimity, so that they allowed the reader a sense of freedom from the narrowness of life as it is determined in a given society, perspective, or way of life. Although the fundamental approach was the same, the theory is not a cookie cutter: the results differed substantially, and each poem could retain its uniqueness. The procedure always began with a close reading, as would the New Criticism (and as would deconstruction, in another way). But the readings could grow beyond the limitations of the irony, ambiguity, and paradox that so often seems to summarize and conclude a New Critical reading.

Clearly, none of the foregoing readings is a thoroughgoing instance of cultural studies. That would have required much more space, and then the theoretical framework proposed as the chief aim of this book would have been lost. I have hoped instead to show how room can be made for the insights of cultural studies, while preserving the transindividual and transhistorical power of rhythm. As a result, the reading of poetry could be at once a matter of understanding its place in a historically and culturally specific context, and of engaging in its rhythmic energies as a reader today. I see no reason we cannot have both the historical and the transhistorical in the reading of poetry, why the one cannot enrich the other; and it is my hope that the foregoing readings have supplied hints as to how this inclusivity in reading might be achieved.

In each case, the allegorical relation between images and rhythm has expanded, I hope, the possibilities of reading that were made possible by New Criticism or deconstruction or cultural studies alone. On the one side, as it were, the reading is expanded to touch upon the specificities of society—gender, race, class, and so forth. On the other side, the readings work as a relation between these issues and the sublime power of the rhythm upon which the poem's images are constructed and to which they allude.

Because of these features, these readings make sense out of the diachrony of ballads without forgetting that they are poems and without eclipsing the importance of their rhythms. The diachronic development of the narratives differs in interesting ways: for example, both of the written ballads have the surface narrative (subject, in Russian formalist terms) coincide with the sequence of events narrated (fable), while both of the oral ballads have the fable more or less inverted in relation to the subject, as the previous events must be reconstructed to explain the present state of crisis. But in all of the ballads, the general principle of diachrony is not cause and effect so much as mystery and revelation. Each of the stanzas contributes to the solution to the mystery, and each takes away something of the state of illusion in which the central character is found to begin with: Lord Randal's love, Dickinson's speaker's marriage, Mabbie's Willie Boone, and the final speaker's ambitions. As in Nietzsche's theory, the self of the speaker would be revealed to be a web of illusions; but when this web is stripped away in the process of narration, what is left is an unutterable rhythm—and the narration must cease. This cessation itself might be figured as death, as eternity, as "hush," or as the prison. At the same time, the way to that point has been prepared, very *variously* prepared, for us to see how other constructions might be possible, and how our construction is limited and inadequate to the sublime infinitude of life manifested by rhythm itself, an infinitude toward which the only unlimited response is silence.

But, as in keeping with Lacoue-Labarthe's discussion of rhythm, that silence cannot last forever; for its very mystery has compelled me to spin out complex webs of interpretation to make sense out of them. Yet, insofar as these interpretations, too, are limited and do not cover the whole truth of any of the poems, they are mere constructions—second order constructions in prose—and my recognition of their limits can best be felt in the silence that follows them.

Works Cited

Abraham, Nicholas. 1985. *Rythmes: De l'oeuvre, de la traduction et de la psychanalyse.* Ed. Nicholas T. Rand and Maria Torok. Paris: Flammarion.

Aronowitz, Stanley. 1988. "Postmodernism and Politics." In *Universal Abandon,* 42–46. *See* Ross 1988.

Assoun, Paul-Laurent. 1980. *Freud et Nietzsche.* Paris: Presses Universitaires de France.

Attridge, Derek. 1982. *The Rhythms of English Poetry.* London and New York: Longman.

Aviram, Amittai F. 1990. "The Unreadable Black Body: 'Conventional' Poetic Form in the Harlem Renaissance." *Genders* 7:32–46.

Bakan, David. 1975. *Sigmund Freud and the Jewish Mystical Tradition.* Boston: Beacon.

Bannet, Eve Tavor. 1989. *Structuralism and the Logic of Dissent: Barthes, Derrida, Foucault, Lacan.* Urbana: University of Illinois Press.

Barthes, Roland. 1957. *Mythologies.* Paris: Seuil.

——. [1953] 1972A. *Le Degré zéro de l'écriture: suivi de nouveaux essais critiques.* Paris: Seuil.

——. *Mythologies.* 1972b. Trans. Annette Lavers. New York: Hill and Wang.

——. 1973. *Le Plaisir du texte.* Paris: Seuil. 1973.

Barzilai, Shuli. 1991. "Borders of Language: Kristeva's Critique of Lacan." *PMLA* 106:294–305.

Beaucourt, Michèle. 1974. "Mallarmé (Stéphane)." In *La Grande Encyclopédie,* 12:7534–36. Paris: Librairie Larousse.

Bedient, Calvin. 1990. "Kristeva and Poetry as Shattered Signification." *Critical Inquiry* 16:807–29.

——. 1991. "How I Slugged It Out with Toril Moi and Stayed Awake." *Critical Inquiry* 17:644–49.

Benjamin, Walter. 1977. *The Origin of German Tragic Drama.* Trans. John Osborne. London: NLB.

Benveniste, Émile. [1951] 1966. "La Notion de 'rythme' dans son expression linguistique." In *Problèmes de linguistique générale,* 1:327–35. Paris: Gallimard.

Blount, Marcellus. 1990. "Caged Birds: Race and Gender in the Sonnet." In

Engendering Men, ed. Joseph Boone and Michael Cadden, 225–38. New York and London: Routledge.

Bold, Alan. 1979. *The Ballad.* London: Methuen.

Boutot, Alain. 1989. *Heidegger.* Que sais-je? no. 2480. Paris: Presses Universitaires de France.

Brandt, Joan. 1984. "The Theory and Practice of a 'Revolutionary' Text: Dennis Roche's 'Le Mécrit.'" *Yale French Studies* 67:203–21.

Bronson, Bertrand Harris. 1959–72. *The Traditional Tunes of the Child Ballads.* 4 vols. Princeton, N.J.: Princeton University Press.

Brooks, Cleanth. 1947. *The Well-Wrought Urn.* New York: Harcourt, Brace and World.

———. [1951] 1989. "Irony as a Principle of Structure." In *The Critical Tradition,* ed. David H. Richter, 799–807. New York: St. Martin's Press.

Brooks, Gwendolyn. 1963. *Selected Poems.* New York: Harper and Row.

Budick, E. Miller. 1985. *Emily Dickinson and the Life of Language: A Study in Symbolic Poetics.* Baton Rouge: Louisiana State University Press.

Burke, Edmund. [1758] 1958. *A Philosophical Enquiry into the Origin of our Ideas of the Sublime and Beautiful,* ed. J. T. Boulton. New York: Columbia University Press.

Burke, Kenneth. [1931] 1964. "The Nature of Form." In *Discussions of Poetry,* ed. Francis Murphy, 1–11. Boston: DC Heath.

Butler, Judith. 1990. *Gender Trouble: Feminism and the Subversion of Identity.* New York: Routledge.

Cameron, Sharon. 1979. *Lyric Time: Dickinson and the Limits of Genre.* Baltimore: Johns Hopkins University Press.

Campbell, David A. 1967. *Greek Lyric Poetry: A Selection of Early Greek Lyric, Elegiac and Iambic Poetry.* New York: Macmillan and St. Martin's.

———. 1982. *Greek Lyric: With an English Translation by David Campbell.* Vol. 1: *Sappho and Alcaeus.* Cambridge, Mass.: Harvard University Press.

Child, Francis James, ed. [1882–98] 1965. *The English and Scottish Popular Ballads.* 5 vols. New York: Dover.

Cohn, Robert Greer. 1965. *Toward the Poems of Mallarmé.* Berkeley and Los Angeles: University of California Press.

Corngold, Stanley. 1983. "Error in Paul de Man." In *The Yale Critics: Deconstruction in America,* ed. Jonathan Arac, Wlad Godzich, and Wallace Martin, 90–109. Minneapolis: University of Minnesota Press.

Coward, Rosalind, and John Ellis. 1977. *Language and Materialism: Developments in Semiology and the Theory of the Subject.* Boston: Routledge and Kegan Paul.

Culler, Jonathan. 1981. "Literary Competence." In *Essays in Modern Stylistics,* 24–41. See Freeman 1981.

D'Aquili, Eugene G., and Charles D. Laughlin, Jr. 1979. "The Neurobiology of Myth and Ritual." In *The Spectrum of Ritual,* 152–82. See D'Aquili, Laughlin, and McManus 1979.

D'Aquili, Eugene G., Charles D. Laughlin, Jr., and John McManus. 1979. *The Spectrum of Ritual: A Biogenetic Structural Analysis*. New York: Columbia University Press.

Deloffre, Frédéric. 1984. *Le Vers français*. 4th ed. Paris: Société d'édition d'enseignement supérieur.

de Man, Paul. 1979. "Genesis and Genealogy (Nietzsche)." In *Allegories of Reading*, 79–102. New Haven, Conn.: Yale University Press.

———. 1983. "Form and Intent in the American New Criticism." In *Blindness and Insight: Essays in the Rhetoric of Contemporary Criticism*, 20–35. 2d ed. Minneapolis: University of Minnesota Press.

———. 1984. *The Rhetoric of Romanticism*. New York: Columbia University Press.

Derrida, Jacques. 1982. "White Mythology: Metaphor in the Text of Philosophy." In *Margins of Philosophy*, trans. Alan Bass, 207–71. Chicago: University of Chicago Press.

———. 1990. *Was ist Dichtung? / Qu'est-ce que la poésie? / Che cos'é la poesia? / What is Poetry?* Berlin: Brinkmann und Bose.

Dickinson, Emily. 1960. *Complete Poems of Emily Dickinson*. Ed. Thomas H. Johnson. Boston: Little, Brown.

du Bellay, Joachim. 1910. *Oeuvres poétiques*. Ed. Henri Chamard. Tome II. Paris: Société Nouvelle de Librairie et d'Édition.

duBois, Page. 1988. *Sowing the Body: Psychoanalysis and Ancient Representations of Women*. Chicago: University of Chicago Press.

Duby, Georges. 1978. *Medieval Marriage: Two Models from Twelfth-Century France*. Baltimore: Johns Hopkins University Press.

Ducrot, Oswald, and Tzvetan Todorov. 1979. *Encyclopedic Dictionary of the Sciences of Language*. Trans. Catherine Porter. Baltimore: Johns Hopkins University Press.

Eagleton, Terry. 1983. *Literary Theory: An Introduction*. Minneapolis: University of Minnesota Press.

Easthope, Antony. 1983. *Poetry as Discourse*. London: Methuen.

———. 1989. *Poetry and Phantasy*. Cambridge: Cambridge University Press.

Eco, Umberto. 1979. *A Theory of Semiotics*. Bloomington: Indiana University Press.

Eddins, Dwight. 1981. "Emily Dickinson and Nietzsche: The Rites of Dionysus." *ESQ* 27:96–107.

Eliot, T. S. 1970. *Collected Poems 1909–1962*. San Diego: Harcourt Brace Jovanovich.

Elwert, Theodor W. 1965. *Traité de versification française des origines à nos jours*. Paris: Klincksieck.

Enterline, Lynn. 1987. "The Mirror and the Snake: The Case of Marvell's 'Unfortunate Lover.'" *Critical Quarterly* 29 (4): 98–112.

Erlich, Victor. 1981. *Russian Formalism: History—Doctrine*. 3d ed. New Haven, Conn.: Yale University Press.

Feyerabend, Paul K. 1988. *A Farewell to Reason*. New York: Routledge, Chapman and Hall.

Finch, Annie. 1993. *The Ghost of Meter: Culture and Prosody in American Free Verse.* Ann Arbor: University of Michigan Press.

Flatto, E. 1970. "Lord Randal." *Southern Folklore Quarterly* 34:331–36.

Fleck, Ludvik. [1935] 1981. *The Genesis and Development of a Scientific Fact.* Chicago: University of Chicago Press.

Fowlie, Wallace. 1962. *Mallarmé.* Chicago: University of Chicago Press.

Freccero, John. 1971. "BLOW-UP: From the Word to the Image." In *Focus on "Blow-Up,"* ed. Roy Huss, 116–30. New York: Prentice Hall.

———. 1983. "The Significance of Terza Rima." In *Dante, Petrarch, Boccaccio: Studies in the Italian Trecento in Honor of Charles S. Singleton,* ed. Aldo S. Bernardo and Anthony L. Pellegrini, 3–17. Binghamton: SUNY-Binghamton Press.

Freeman, Donald C., ed. 1981. *Essays in Modern Stylistics.* London: Methuen.

Frege, Gottlob. [1892] 1980. "On Sense and Meaning." Trans. Max Black. In *Philosophical Writings of Gottlob Frege,* ed. Peter Geach and Max Black, 56–78. Oxford: Basil Blackwell.

Freud, Sigmund. 1950. *Totem and Taboo.* Trans. James Strachey. New York: Norton.

———. [1920] 1961. *Beyond the Pleasure Principle.* Trans. James Strachey. New York: Norton.

———. [1923] 1962. *The Ego and the Id.* Trans. Joan Riviere. Ed. James Strachey. New York: Norton.

———. [1912] 1963a. "Instincts and Their Vicissitudes." Trans. Cecil M. Baines. In *General Psychological Theory,* ed. Philip Rieff, 83–103. New York: Macmillan-Collier.

———. [1915] 1963b. "Reflections upon War and Death." Trans. E. Colburn Mayne. In *Character and Culture,* ed. Philip Rieff, 107–33. New York: Macmillan-Collier.

———. [1908] 1963c. "The Relation of the Poet to Day-Dreaming." Trans. I. F. Grant Duff. In *Character and Culture,* ed. Philip Rieff, 34–43. New York: Macmillan-Collier.

———. [1915] 1963d. "Repression." Trans. Cecil M. Baines. In *General Psychological Theory,* ed. Philip Rieff, 104–15. New York: Macmillan-Collier.

———. [1915] 1963e. "The Unconscious." Trans. Cecil M. Baines. In *General Psychological Theory,* ed. Philip Rieff, 116–50. New York: Macmillan-Collier.

———. [1925] 1963f. "Negation." Trans. Joan Riviere. In *General Psychological Theory,* ed. Philip Rieff, 213–17. New York: Macmillan-Collier.

———. [1900] 1965. *The Interpretation of Dreams.* Trans. James Strachey. New York: Discus-Avon-Basic Books.

———. [1940] 1969. *An Outline of Psychoanalysis.* Trans. and ed. James Strachey. New York: Norton.

———. [1905] 1975. *Three Essays on the Theory of Sexuality.* Trans. and ed. James Strachey. New York: Basic Books.

———. [1905] 1989. *Jokes and Their Relation to the Unconscious.* Trans. and ed. James Strachey. New York: Norton.

Frye, Northrop. 1974. "Allegory." In *Princeton Encyclopedia of Poetry and Poetics,* ed. Alex Preminger, 12–15. Princeton: Princeton University Press.

Fuss, Diana. 1989. *Essentially Speaking.* New York: Routledge.

Fussell, Paul. 1965. *Poetic Meter and Poetic Form.* New York: Random House.

Gioia, Dana. 1991. "Can Poetry Matter?" *Atlantic,* May, 94–106.

Goodman, Paul. 1971. *Speaking and Language: Defence of Poetry.* New York: Random House.

Halle, Morris, and Samuel J. Keyser. 1979. "The Iambic Pentameter." In *The Structure of Verse,* ed. Harvey Gross, rev. ed., 173–93. New York: Ecco.

Hayes, Nancy Karl. 1989. "Negativizing Narcissus: Heinrich von Morungen at Julia Kristeva's Court." *Journal of the Midwest Modern Language Association* 22:43–60.

Heidegger, Martin. 1971a. "Language." In *Poetry, Language, Thought,* 187–210. *See* Heidegger 1971c.

———. 1971b. "Language and the Poem." In *On the Way to Language,* 159–98. Trans. Peter D. Hertz. New York: Harper and Row.

———. 1971c. *Poetry, Language, Thought.* Trans. Albert Hofstadter. New York: Harper and Row.

———. [1951] 1971d. "The Thing." In *Poetry, Language, Thought,* 163–86. *See* Heidegger 1971c.

———. 1971e. "What Are Poets For?" In *Poetry, Language, Thought,* 89–142. *See* Heidegger 1971c.

Hollis, C. Carroll. 1983. *Language and Syle in* Leaves of Grass. Baton Rouge: Louisiana State University Press.

Hošek, Chaviva, and Patricia A. Parker, eds. 1985. *Lyric Poetry: Beyond New Criticism.* Ithaca: Cornell University Press.

Hough, Graham. 1960. *Image and Experience.* Lincoln: University of Nebraska Press.

Hurston, Zora Neale. [1937] 1978. *Their Eyes Were Watching God.* Urbana: University of Illinois Press.

Jakobson, Roman. 1960. "Concluding Statement: Linguistics and Poetics." In *Style in Language,* ed. Thomas A. Sebeok, 350–77. Cambridge, Mass.: MIT Press.

———. 1968. "Poetry of Grammar and Grammar of Poetry." *Lingua* 21:604.

———. 1971a. "Two Aspects of Language and Two Types of Aphasic Disturbances." In *Fundamentals of Language,* by Jakobson and Morris Halle, 53–82. 2d ed. The Hague: Mouton.

———. [1960] 1971b. "Why 'Mama' and 'Papa'?" In *Roman Jakobson: Selected Writings,* vol. 1 (Phonological Studies), 538–45. The Hague: Mouton.

———. [1923] 1973. "Principes de versification." Excerpted by Tzvetan Todorov. Trans. Leon Robel. In *Questions de poétique,* ed. Tzvetan Todorov, 40–55. Paris: Seuil.

Jakobson, Roman, and Claude Lévi-Strauss. 1972. "Baudelaire's *Les Chats.*" Trans. Fernande DeGeorge. In *The Structuralists: From Marx to Lévi-Strauss,* ed. Richard and Fernande DeGeorge, 124–46. Garden City, N.Y.: Doubleday-Anchor, 1972.

Jameson, Fredric. 1979. "Reification and Utopia in Mass Culture." *Social Text* 1:130–48.

———. 1988a. "Imaginary and Symbolic in Lacan." In *The Ideologies of Theory: Essays 1971–1986,* 1:75–115. Minneapolis: University of Minnesota Press.

———. 1988b. "The Politics of Theory: Ideological Positions in the Postmodernism Debate." In *The Ideologies of Theory: Essays 1971–1986,* 2:103–13. *See* Jameson 1988a.

Kant, Immanuel. [1790] 1987. *Critique of Judgment.* Trans. Werner S. Pluhar. Indianapolis: Hackett Publishing.

Kaufmann, Walter. 1967. "Friedrich Nietzsche." In *The Encyclopedia of Philosophy,* ed. Paul Edwards, 504–14. New York: Macmillan and the Free Press.

Kristeva, Julia. 1984. *Revolution in Poetic Language.* Trans. Margaret Waller. New York: Columbia University Press. Originally published as *La Révolution du langage poétique.* Paris: Seuil.

Lacan, Jacques. 1966a. *Ecrits.* 2 vols. Paris: Seuil.

———. [1957] 1966b. "L'Instance de la lettre dans l'inconscient ou la raison depuis Freud." In *Ecrits,* 1:249–89. *See* Lacan 1966a.

———. [1949] 1966c. "Le Stade du miroir comme formateur de la fonction du Je." In *Ecrits,* 1:89–97. *See* Lacan 1966a.

———. [1964] 1973. *Le Séminaire de Jacques Lacan. Livre XI. Les Quatre concepts fondamentaux de la psychanalyse.* Ed. Jacques-Alain Miller. Paris: Seuil.

Lacoue-Labarthe, Philippe. 1979. *Le Sujet de la philosophie.* Vol 1 of *Typographies.* Paris: Aubier-Flammarion.

———. [1979] 1989a. "The Echo of the Subject." Trans. Barbara Harlow. In *Typography: Mimesis, Philosophy, Politics,* ed. Christopher Fynsk, 139–207. Cambridge, Mass.: Harvard University Press.

———. [1975] 1989b. "Typography." Trans. Eduardo Cadava. In *Typography: Mimesis, Philosophy, Politics,* 43–138. *See* Lacoue-Labarthe 1989a.

Lakoff, George, and Mark Johnson. 1980. *Metaphors We Live By.* Chicago: University of Chicago Press.

Lakoff, George, and Mark Turner. 1989. *More Than Cool Reason: A Field Guide to Poetic Metaphor.* Chicago: University of Chicago Press.

Langer, Susanne K. 1951. "On Significance in Music." In *Philosophy in a New Key. A Study in the Symbolism of Reason, Rite, and Art,* 204–45. Cambridge, Mass.: Harvard University Press.

Laplanche, J., and J.-B. Pontalis. 1973. *The Language of Psychoanalysis.* Trans. Donald Nicholson-Smith. London: Hogarth Press and Institute of Psycho-Analysis.

Lechte, John. 1990. *Julia Kristeva.* London: Routledge.

Leech, Geoffrey. 1973. *A Linguistic Guide to English Poetry.* Harlow: Longman.

Lemaire, Anika. 1977. *Jacques Lacan.* Trans. David Macey. London: Routledge and Kegan Paul.

Levine, Lawrence W. 1977. *Black Culture and Black Consciousness.* New York: Oxford University Press.

Lex, Barbara. 1979. "The Neurobiology of Ritual Trance." In *The Spectrum of Ritual*, 117–51. *See* D'Aquili, Laughlin, and McManus 1979.

Lorde, Audre. 1983. *Zami: A New Spelling of My Name*. Trumansburg, N.Y.: Crossing Press.

Lyotard, Jean François. 1984a. *The Postmodern Condition: A Report on Knowledge*. Trans. Geoff Bennington and Brian Massumi. Foreword by Fredric Jameson. Minneapolis: University of Minnesota Press.

———. 1984b. "Answering the Question: What Postmodernism?" Trans. Régis Durand. In *The Postmodern Condition*, 71–82. *See* Lyotard 1984a.

———. 1986. "Rules and Paradoxes and a Svelte Appendix." Trans. Brian Massumi. *Cultural Critique* 5:209–19.

———. *The Differend*. 1988. Trans. Georges Van Den Abbeele. Minneapolis: University of Minnesota Press.

———. 1991a. *The Lyotard Reader*. Ed. Andrew Benjamin. Cambridge, Mass.: Basil Blackwell.

———. 1991b. "The Dream-Work Does Not Think." Trans. Mary Lydon. In *Lyotard Reader*, 19–55. *See* Lyotard 1991a.

———. 1991c. "The Sublime and the Avant-Garde." In *The Lyotard Reader*, 196–211. *See* Lyotard 1991a.

McGann, Jerome. 1987. "Contemporary Poetry, Alternate Routes." In *Politics and Poetic Value*, ed. Robert von Hallberg, 253–76. Chicago: University of Chicago Press.

Maik, Linda L. 1989. "Mothers in Ballads: Freud's Maternal Paradigm." *Southern Folklore* 46:117–32.

Mallarmé, Stéphane. 1966. *Poésies*. Paris: Gallimard.

Melhem, D. H. 1987. *Gwendolyn Brooks: Poetry and the Heroic Voice*. Lexington: University of Kentucky Press.

Meschonnic, Henri. 1985. *Les États de la poétique*. Paris: Presses Universitaires de France.

———. 1988. "Rhyme and Life." Trans. Gabriella Bedetti. *Critical Inquiry* 15:90–107.

Meyer, Leonard B. 1983. "Innovation, Choice, and the History of Music." *Critical Inquiry* 9:517–44.

Mitchell, Juliett, and Jacqueline Rose. 1982. *Feminine Sexuality: Jacques Lacan and the École freudienne*. New York: Norton.

Moi, Toril. 1985. *Sexual/Textual Politics: Feminist Literary Theory*. London: Methuen.

———. 1991. "Reading Kristeva: A Response to Calvin Bedient." *Critical Inquiry* 17:639–43.

Mouffe, Chantal. 1988. "Radical Democracy: Modern or Postmodern?" In *Universal Abandon?* 31–45. *See* Ross 1988.

Nietzsche, Friedrich. 1966. *Beyond Good and Evil*. Trans. Walter Kaufmann. New York: Vintage.

———. [1874] 1967. *The Birth of Tragedy and The Case of Wagner*. Ed. and trans. Walter Kaufmann. New York: Random House–Vintage.

Noland, Carrie Jaurès. 1991. "Yves Bonnefoy and Julia Kristeva: The Poetics of Motherhood." *French Literary Series* 18:134–44.

Paz, Octavio. 1972. *El arco y la lira*. 3d ed. Mexico City: Fondo de Cultura Económica.

Peirce, Charles S. 1955. *Philosophical Writings of Peirce*. Ed. Justus Buchler. New York: Dover.

Plath, Sylvia. 1981. *The Collected Poems*. Ed. Ted Hughes. New York: Harper and Row.

Poe, Edgar Allen. [1850] 1986. "The Poetic Principle." In *Criticism: The Major Statements*, ed. Charles Kaplan, 336–56. 2d ed. New York: St. Martin's Press.

Pope, Alexander. 1965. *The Poems of Alexander Pope*. Ed. John Butt. London: Methuen.

Quilligan, Maureen. 1979. *The Language of Allegory: Defining the Genre*. Ithaca, N.Y.: Cornell University Press.

Richmond, W. Edson. 1988. "And Thereby Hangs a Tale." *Fabula* 29:383–89.

Ross, Andrew, ed. 1988. *Universal Abandon? The Politics of Postmodernism*. Minneapolis: University of Minnesota Press.

Rubin, Gayle. 1975. "The Traffic in Women: Notes on the 'Political Economy' of Sex." In *Toward an Anthropology of Women*, 157–210. New York: Monthly Review Press.

St. Armand, Barton Levi. 1984. *Emily Dickinson and Her Culture: The Soul's Society*. Cambridge: Cambridge University Press.

Saussure, Ferdinand de. 1916. *Cours de linguistique général*. Paris: Payot.

Scholes, Robert, Nancy R. Comley, Carl H. Klaus, and Michael Silverman, eds. 1986. *Elements of Literature: Essay, Fiction, Poetry, Drama, Film*. 3d ed. New York: Oxford University Press.

Schopenhauer, Arthur. 1966. *The World as Will and Representation*. Trans. E. F. J. Payne. 2 vols. New York: Dover.

Seth, Vikram. 1987. *The Golden Gate*. New York: Random House–Vintage.

Shelley, Percy Bysshe. 1977. "A Defence of Poetry." In *Shelley's Poetry and Prose*, ed. Donald H. Reiman and Sharon B. Powers, 480–508. New York: Norton.

Soll, Ivan. 1988. "Pessimism and the Tragic View of Life: Reconsiderations of Nietzsche's *Birth of Tragedy*." In *Reading Nietzsche*, ed. Robert C. Solomon and Kathleen Marie Higgins, 104–31. New York: Oxford University Press.

Sperber, Dan, and Deirdre Wilson. 1986. *Relevance: Communication and Cognition*. Cambridge, Mass.: Harvard University Press.

Spitzer, Leo. 1948. *Linguistics and Literary History*. Princeton: Princeton University Press.

Steele, Timothy. 1990. *Missing Measures: Modern Poetry and the Revolt against Meter*. Fayetteville: Arkansas University Press.

Stevens, Wallace. 1971. *The Palm at the End of the Mind: Selected Poems and a Play.* Ed. Holly Stevens. New York: Random House–Vintage.

Stockton, Kathryn Bond. N.d. "Bodies and God: Poststructuralist Feminists Return to the Fold of Spiritual Materialism." *Boundary 2.* Forthcoming.

———. N.D. "'God' between Their Lips: Desire between Women in Irigaray and Eliot." *Novel.* Forthcoming.

Thompson, Robert Farris. 1979. *African Art in Motion: Icon and Act.* Berkeley and Los Angeles: University of California Press.

Todorov, Tzvetan. 1973. *Poétique: Qu'est-ce que le structuralisme?* Vol. 2. Paris: Seuil.

———. 1977. *The Poetics of Prose.* Trans. Richard Howard. Ithaca, N.Y.: Cornell University Press.

———. 1987. "La poésie sans le vers." In *La Notion de la littérature, et autres essais,* 66–84. Paris: Éditions du Seuil-Points.

Tone-Lōc. 1989. "Funky Cold Medina." *Loc'ed after Dark.* Audio cassette. Delicious Vinyl ZDV3000.

Winkler, John J. 1990. *The Constraints of Desire: The Anthropology of Sex and Gender in Ancient Greece.* New York: Routledge.

Woolf, Virginia. 1929. *A Room of One's Own.* New York: Harcourt Brace Jovanovich.

Index

298 *Index*